The Fourteenth Juror

One Woman's Story of Survival, Silence, and Systemic Injustice

by Amy L. Sortino

© 2025

Copyright © 2025 by Amy L. Sortino
All rights reserved. No part of this publication may be reproduced, distributed, or transmitted in any form or by any means, including photocopying, recording, or other electronic or mechanical methods, without the prior written permission of the publisher, except in the case of brief quotations used in reviews or scholarly works.

Library of Congress Control Number: 2025908123
This is a work of nonfiction. All events are true and based on the author's lived experience...

Printed in the United States of America
First Edition

Published by: Justice Unmuted | Powered by Reentry Ready
www.reentry-ready.org

ISBN-13: 979-8-218-71222-88
Page count: 331

"I've walked through hell, not just for myself, but for every person who was buried by a system that never asked who they are today."

-ALS

Disclaimer

This is a true story—my story. The events are real. The pain was real. The lessons were earned, not imagined.

Names marked with an asterisk (*) are aliases used to protect privacy. All others are real. Some identifying details may be blurred—not to distort truth, but because some people simply don't deserve the spotlight. If you think you recognize yourself in these pages, congratulations. That's your conscience talking.

This isn't an invitation to sue. It's an invitation to grow.

Some conversations have been reconstructed from memory. (This is over 30 years of memories.)

All statements of opinion in this book are based on the author's honest recollections, perceptions, and interpretations of real events. Any criticism of officials is made in good faith and based on information available at the time of writing. This work is intended to foster transparency, truth, and growth, not to harm or defame.

The feelings are untouched, the experiences are unfiltered, and the truth stands as lived.

This book is not a dramatization. It is not a "based on" version of events. It is a firsthand account of survival, harm, love, loss, addiction, motherhood, and justice.

Any resemblance to specific people is either coincidental, intentionally altered, or karmically inevitable.

If the shoe fits, don't blame the shoemaker.

To those looking for themselves in these pages: This book isn't about you.

It's about what I survived. And I have every right to tell it.

All rights reserved. No regrets.

Trigger Warning / Content Advisory

This book contains candid descriptions of traumatic experiences, including abuse, sexual violence, substance use, incarceration, grief, suicidal ideation, and systemic injustice. Some content may be distressing to survivors or readers sensitive to these themes.

Please take care while reading. If you need to pause, skip, or step away—do so. Your well-being comes first.

This story is shared to shine a light on what too many endure in silence, not to retraumatize—but to offer truth, understanding, and hope.

Praise for the Fourteenth Juror

"*Amy Louise Sortino was arrested and charged with murder on the same day the O.J. Simpson trial started—January 24, 1995. Unlike Simpson, her case did not receive national attention. She was just another of the more than 1,000,000 people incarcerated in the USA that year. Eighteen years old and pregnant, she was up against the all-powerful government seeking to put her in prison for life for a crime she did not commit.*

The Fourteenth Juror: One Woman's Story of Survival, Silence, and Systemic Injustice is an important story, as are all stories of wrongful arrest and incarceration. Each one teaches us about the system, its flaws, and the need to do better. Amy's story is no exception. It pulls no punches as it takes you on a traumatic journey. It is also a call for reform. As she says, 'Justice isn't a headline. It's a responsibility. And it belongs to all of us."
— **Justin Brooks**, Author of *You Might Go to Prison, Even Though You're Innocent*

Amy Sortino takes us on a very important journey in The Fourteenth Juror. *This is a journey that she took through pain, trauma, abuse, incarceration, and restoration.*

Many people who have had experiences like Amy would run away from the system because they were acquitted and set free, but this drew Amy into the fight. She saw and felt the injustices that were done. She couldn't sit by and allow people to be run over by the legal system. She has been fighting for loved ones and even those who have caused trauma and hurt to her family. That is what a true advocate does—not just fight for your loved ones, but fight for everyone.

Reading this book will give you a picture of a system that needs to be recreated and focus on actual rehabilitation and restoration. This type of vulnerability allows the reader to experience the pain, hurt, and heartache. This book is not for the faint of heart and why there are trigger warnings; but it will make you want to get out and make changes when you finish reading it.
— **David Garlock**, National Justice Reform Advocate, Speaker, and Survivor

Dedication

For my parents— Your love was my landing place.
You stepped in when I couldn't stand, loved my children like your own, and gave us the kind of stability that made survival possible. I am here because of you.

For Claudio—The man who saw me before the world did. This story wouldn't exist without your love, truth, and belief in redemption.

For my children—You are the reason I kept going.
May you always know the power of your roots and the beauty of becoming.

For every person who has been railroaded by the system,
every family enduring the broken commutation process,
and every advocate fighting to stop the madness of a vindictive carceral system—This book is for you.

To those who battle mental health or addiction,
who carry invisible wounds and fight to stay standing— You are not forgotten. You are not alone.

To those who were wrongfully convicted or acquitted but never truly freed, still screaming the truth in silence, still wearing labels they didn't deserve—
Your story matters. You are not the worst thing you were accused of.

To every mother who fought with nothing but instinct and love,
who stood guard over her children in a world that didn't always see her—
Your strength lives on in the next generation.

To those within the system—the corrections officers who refuse to join the "good ol' boys" when they see injustice, the public servants who lead instead of follow, and the policymakers brave enough to believe in second chances, even when it may cost them politically—
Your courage matters. You are proof that change is possible from the inside out.

And to you, the reader:
If this story stirs something inside you, don't ignore it.
That's where change begins. That's where we begin.

Table of Contents

Introduction: The Sentence Without Bars 1

Prologue: The Trial That Never Ended 3

Chapter 1: Claudio – The Love That Saved Me 5

Chapter 2: In the Palm of My Hand 30

Chapter 3: The Dream: A Sign Before the Test 34

Chapter 4: Thanksgiving and a Painful Lesson 42

Chapter 5: Three Damned Words 48

Chapter 6: The End of Innocence 53

Chapter 7: Arrested Twice 62

Chapter 8: Jail, Pregnancy and Prison Golds 67

Understanding Trauma: A Reflection Before the Next Chapter 80

Chapter 9: The Hollow Peace 82

Interlude One: The Vision 86

Interlude 2: Meanwhile, in the Papers 88

Chapter 10: Born into Chaos 89

Chapter 11: Thirteen Jurors and a Lie 101

Chapter 12: Acquitted, Not Innocent – Part One 116

Interlude: The Shifting Ground - Spiraling Forward 132

Chapter 12 – Part Two: The Wrong Kind of Attention 134

Chapter 13: The Fourteenth Juror 194

Chapter 14: Growth 214

Afterword: Writing Through the Wreckage 266

Epilogue: The Reality of Justice 267

Appendix 289

Introduction: The Sentence Without Bars

Freedom isn't always the moment the courtroom doors swing open.

For some, the weight of a trial lingers long after the verdict is read. I was acquitted, but my battle was far from over. The world still saw me through the lens of a case I wanted to forget. In many ways, I remained a prisoner. Just one without a cell.

This is not just a story about survival. It is a story about resilience, about breaking cycles, about redefining who you are when the world refuses to let go of the past. But it is also a call to action. This book isn't just a memoir—it's a challenge to lawmakers, reform advocates, and anyone who believes our system works the way it should.

Too often, people are defined by the worst thing they've ever done, or worse, by the version of guilt shaped by the media and courts. Newspapers craft headlines to fit compelling narratives. Prosecutors build cases that sometimes lean on assumptions rather than truth. And the result? Lives are shattered. Families left in limbo. And victims' loved ones often go without real answers.

For years, shame controlled my narrative. Today, I own every chapter because silence changes nothing.

Justice should be about truth, not speculation. It should hold people accountable, not condemn them to endless punishment that heals no one. Whether someone is guilty or innocent, there must be a path forward. Redemption must be possible.

I wrote it because truth matters—even when it's complicated, even when it's uncomfortable.

I've lived through a courtroom trial where—twelve jurors with one or two alternates. Twelve people tasked with deciding someone's fate. But the real trial didn't end there. It followed me into motherhood, addiction, advocacy, and healing.

That's why I titled this book The Fourteenth Juror.

Justice doesn't end in a courtroom, sometimes—too often—it doesn't happen there at all.

The Fourteenth Juror is the person who comes after. The one who sees what the system missed and how it really is. The one who asks the harder questions, who listens differently, sees things through a new lens and dares to demand better. Maybe it's an advocate. Maybe it's a neighbor. Maybe it's a lawmaker. Maybe—it's you.

This book is for the people who never had a seat in the jury box but know, deep down, they've got something to say. It's also for the ones still inside. The ones still waiting. The ones this system forgot—or ignored on purpose.

If you're here, if you're interested in making a change, consider yourself the fourteenth juror. Not to revisit a case, not to form a verdict that will incarcerate to death, but to explore reality, to consider real opportunities for people to rebuild and to ask the deeper question:

When is enough, enough?

When has a person paid enough, grown enough, suffered enough?

This isn't about deciding guilt or innocence. It's about facing the uncomfortable truths about justice, redemption, and the weight of labels that refuse to fade.

***

Prologue: The Trial That Never Ended

The trial was a blur—one day bleeding into the next, arguments made about me as though I weren't even in the room. The prosecution wove a story, and the defense tried to unravel it, but through it all, I felt powerless. The system was speaking for me, not to me.

I remember how the air felt in that room—stale, suffocating. The way the prosecutors looked at me like I was disposable. Like I was a mistake that needed to be erased. I was eighteen years old, postpartum, and barely surviving. I sat there, exhausted, while strangers debated the worth of my life.

And then came the verdict. Acquitted.

But it didn't bring peace. It didn't bring clarity. It brought more silence. More doubt. More distance between me and the rest of the world.

The judge said I could go home, but home didn't feel safe anymore. Delaware County had already made up its mind, and I wasn't part of the "good ones." I wasn't in prison, but I wasn't truly free either. I carried an invisible sentence—one that followed me into every room, every conversation, every opportunity that slipped through my fingers because my name was still attached to something I could never erase.

Freedom didn't feel like freedom when everywhere I turned, I was still that girl from the trial. The courtroom let me walk out, but the world never really did.

And then, there was Claudio.

He didn't get the chance to walk away. He didn't get to rebuild. The same courtroom that set me free condemned him to life without parole. The weight of that truth crushed me. Why him? Why not me?

We had the same trial, the same evidence—or lack thereof. Yet he was paying the price alone.

That's the cruelty of mandatory sentencing—it doesn't weigh fairness. It doesn't allow mercy. It hands out life like it's routine and calls it justice.

The unfairness of it burned deep inside me, but the world didn't care. It had already decided who we were. I was the one who walked free. He was the one who didn't. And the guilt of that truth would never leave me.

But before the courtroom, before the headlines, before the world judged him, there was Claudio Sergio Manzanet—the man who saved me.

***

Chapter 1: Claudio – The Love That Saved Me

I met Claudio by chance. It was random—almost didn't happen. I was deep in the chaos of my own life, but I wasn't a bad kid. At the time, I was using cocaine regularly—not to party, but to numb everything. For me, it wasn't an upper. It calmed me. Grounded me.

Or at least, that's what I believed back then. The night I met him at the party, I didn't use in front of him, but he knew damn well why I kept slipping off to the bathroom. I remember the last time I came back, after hours of us talking, he gave me a look. I knew exactly what it meant, but I wasn't having it.

I hadn't even planned to go out. I showed up just as I was, jeans, Timberlands, no makeup, no act. I wasn't trying to be anything I wasn't. That, I think, is what Claudio liked. I wasn't overly girlie. I wasn't flirtatious. We were both there with people we didn't know that well, and neither of us expected much from the night.

I was quiet. If I didn't know you, I didn't talk. Even when I did, I mostly observed. So, when I did speak, people noticed—probably because I didn't waste words.

That night, something about Claudio made me talk. He was just chill. Not flirting, not trying too hard, but he had this way of talking—comfortable, steady. No pressure. No game. Just calm. Grounded. Present.

And somehow, I felt safe in that. I don't even remember what we talked about, but I remember how it felt. Natural. Unforced. Real.

Now, let me be clear: I would later learn that man had a lot of game. I have to laugh about it now, women loved him. But maybe that's why this moment mattered.

Maybe it was different for him too. It wasn't love at first sight. It wasn't a fairytale. But it was something. And in a life full of masks and noise, that something mattered.

I gravitated toward people who felt familiar. Many were in and out of legal trouble. I didn't understand it at the time, but now I know, my people were marginalized. And with that came street-level drug sales, and eventually, violence.

***

One Ride Away From Gone

A friend and I took a bus to North Philly. There was a bar that would serve anyone as long as they had the money. Just a place to dance, chill and be served. Two kids with too much freedom and no real sense of danger. We stayed too long and missed the last bus home.

A man who had been wanting to talk to us and dance a lot offered us a ride. No charge. We accepted despite not knowing him. We didn't ask questions, we just wanted to get back. But as soon as we got in the car, something felt off. The alarm kept going off the entire ride, like maybe the car was stolen or something wasn't right. And then he started acting strange. Real strange.

At one point, after driving for some time, he told us that he was not taking us home. He intended to take us some place remote to rape us and would chop us up after. It didn't even sound like a joke, he seemed serious. He bragged and was incredibly descriptive as if it was already done.

My friend was in the front seat, he reached over and grabbed her leg. She pushed his hand away and he slowed. I was in the back seat and realized this was real as he was slowing the car. I leaned forward and told her very quietly "get ready, we're gonna bounce."

I sat back for a moment. I still don't know how I stayed so still. But as the car started to slow down—just a little more—I grabbed my 40 bottle that I had just finished off, and I smashed it over his head. Hard.

We jumped out of the car while it was still in motion, rolled, then ran.

***

Blood, Glass, and Silence

One night, when I was seventeen, I stayed at a co-worker's apartment in Delaware to watch her niece. The niece was barely fourteen but already hardened in ways I recognized all too well. Things escalated—we got into a real fight.

Not an argument. I wasn't an antagonist, but no way was anyone going to attack me and have that be it. From a relatively young age, I believed that fighting wasn't lady-like so if you're gonna fight you put your fists up and fight like a man. This was no different, she tried to claw me which just pissed me off.

A full-on fist fight. We were swinging, and neither of us was backing down. Glass broke. Blood spilled. I held my own. We even smashed a mirror over each other's heads. She got cut up pretty bad. Fists were flying on both ends.

To this day, I don't know what triggered her, but I imagine that is one reason why she was with her aunt and couldn't be unattended at fourteen years old.

Then her uncle came in. A man in his 20's. Instead of stopping it, he pulled a gun and held it to my head. He stepped back with the gun still trained on me. He wanted to let her beat me while he stood there and watched. That changed things, I was frozen. One of my so-called friends, a man a bit older than me, saw the gun and ran out the back door -- just took off, leaving me there alone. No one stepped in. I was on my own.

When I finally got out of there, I had no car. No phone. No help. I walked for miles in the middle of the night, not even knowing where I was going—just trying to put distance between me and that place. Eventually, I found a taxi. It cost me fifty dollars to get back to Pennsylvania.

When I got home, I had a black eye. My parents asked what happened.

I lied. I wasn't about to tell them I'd been in Delaware staying in an apartment full of people using. I wasn't about to talk about the fight, the gun, or how deep I'd already fallen into that world. Telling the truth would've meant exposing everything—how lost I really was.

And no way was I going to tell them how often I was getting high. Not yet. Not then.

***

Stuck With a "Nice Girl"

I was seventeen. My dad traveled a lot. My mom worked hard and drank harder. Still, she noticed who I was spending time with and decided I needed a new friend—a "nice girl."

We were walking into Kmart when a girl, just a little older than me, said hello. My mom would talk to anyone, and this was no exception. She instantly liked her and invited her over. I couldn't believe it. If I had wanted her there, I would've asked. She had a reputation and I didn't want it rubbing off on me.

On January 13, 1994, my mom invited her over for a sleepover, thinking it would keep me home. My parents had no idea I was already using heavily. I might've stayed in, but only because I didn't want to be seen with her.

I hadn't met Claudio yet. I was seeing his cousin, Jorge, who called that night to say he was coming to pick me up for a party. There's more to say about Jorge but I'll come back to that later. For now, just know this: that call changed everything. I told Jorge I couldn't go out; I had company. He asked who. I told him her name. "Really? Why?" he said.

I just replied, "It's a long story." He hung up.

A few minutes later, he called back. "Just ask her if she wants to come out. Someone's guaranteed to get lucky." I rolled my eyes, but I asked. She was eager. Our ride showed up.

Claudio was in the car, but I barely noticed him at first. At the party, I saw him sitting on a sofa with another guy. The girl and I sat on the floor across from them. There was another sofa behind us, but I picked the floor and leaned against it. Comfort was never really my priority.

Claudio and I started talking. We clicked instantly. I kept slipping off to the bathroom, and when I came back, we'd pick up right where we left off.

He didn't judge me. He didn't ask questions. He just talked. It felt like I'd known him forever.

Eventually, Jorge said he and I were leaving. I really wasn't all that eager to go off with him, even though we had been seeing each other. I was way more interested in talking to Claudio.

That connection I felt? I didn't even understand it yet but I knew I didn't want to lose it. Before we left, I went to the bathroom for another line, then went looking for my coat. It was gone. I figured someone had moved it to a bedroom, so I went to check.

Wow! The shock. In the few minutes I'd walked away from the conversation, Claudio and the girl I brought had somehow ended up in the bedroom together.

How the hell did that even happen? I was furious. She had come with me. And Claudio? To this day, I still shake my head at how that happened. As I said, women were crazy for him and he didn't mind. I told him to be careful, muttered something through the cracked door, and left with Jorge—still coatless.

We weren't gone long. We ended up back at Jorge's place, but I was still thinking about the conversation I'd left behind. Eventually, we returned to the party and stayed until the early morning of January 14, 1994.

I sat in the back seat with the girl as Jorge drove Claudio home. And suddenly, it hit me: I didn't even know this man, but I was afraid I'd never see him again.

I nudged her. "Get his number."

She blinked. "Why would I do that?"

"Um, maybe because you just slept with him?"

She looked at me like it was nothing. "Go ahead. Ask."

It threw me. I wasn't trying to chase someone else's leftovers. I was needing to stay connected to this man in a way I had never experienced. The girl seemed genuinely indifferent, like it hadn't meant a thing. That nonchalant "Go ahead" baffled me.

So, I asked. In Spanish. And to this day, I still remember those digits.

Later that day, the girl and I were in the kitchen with my mom. She asked casually if we'd had fun. She wasn't upset that I'd gone out.

Maybe it was because I'd been with the "nice girl" she'd handpicked. Maybe she thought I'd been safe. We told her about Claudio. I was honest.

"There's something about him, and I want to see him again, but not in a romantic way. He was with her," I said. "Can I invite him over?"

She agreed.

Still, I felt the need to prep her. "Don't be afraid of him," I said. "He has some tattoos—one near his eye. But it's not what people think."

Face tattoos come with a lot of assumptions. People see them and jump to conclusions. But they can mean grief, loss, survival, or transformation. They're not always about crime.

In fact, there are programs now offering free removals for people trying to start over. But we shouldn't need clean skin to give someone a clean slate.

I didn't know what would happen next. But to my surprise, he came over. And even more surprising, my mom liked him.

At the time, I was spiraling deeper into cocaine. I worked full-time as a nursing assistant, stayed sober on the job, but the second I clocked out, I was back to numbing. I was young and broken, holding in pain I didn't have words for.

As for Claudio and the girl from that night—it was nothing. He wasn't even supposed to be in Pennsylvania. On January 13, he had just broken up with his longtime girlfriend. He was planning to go to Connecticut, clear his head, get away from everything. But instead, he showed up at the party.

She was a rebound. A one-night thing. At least to him and he didn't reach back out to her. He reached out to me.

It wasn't long after some of those crazy events. He saw me at the party, disappearing into the bathroom to do lines. When I'd vanish too long, he knew exactly what I was doing. But he never shamed me. Never turned away.

He didn't know anything about me, he didn't know of all the chaos that came before him.

I was already deep into the feeling by then—into the rush, the numb, the escape. I didn't know it was trauma. I just knew I could disappear, and nobody would stop me. I didn't understand what safety or love could feel like.

Now I can see it for what it was. Some curve balls were thrown at me. And some? I threw at myself. I can own that. I have to.

And then, just like that, Claudio started showing up every single day. If I wasn't working, I was with him. If he wasn't working, he was with me. No labels. No pressure. Just two people who somehow clicked—and didn't want to let go.

We weren't a couple, yet somehow, we belonged to each other. Despite this, I still had my moments and if he was at work and I was left to my own devices?

Well, things would change.

***

Going Ghost

There were times when I just vanished. No phone call. No explanation. Just gone.

I'd always had this streak in me—something that pulled me toward chaos, toward disappearing when the world felt too loud or too empty.

People used to say I was a ghost. I didn't check in. I didn't explain. I just dipped. And back then, I didn't think twice about it. I could have been at home and just not answering the phone, I could have been working extra shifts at work but I'd be out.

One day, I went to Philly with a couple friends—one who is no longer here, someone who lived by the streets and died by the streets.

We hadn't told anyone where we were going. We weren't doing anything good. Going to Philly usually meant one thing, buy some stuff and pick up a few Latin club mixed tapes while we were there.

Hours passed, and no one could find me. This was 1994, there were no cell phones and I wasn't stopping to make a call to answer my beeper. Everyone could wait.

What I didn't know while I was off not worried about the rest of the world was there was a horrible accident. A small car had driven under a school bus, and three people were killed. News spread fast.

My mom was beside herself, panicked, thinking the worst. All anyone knew was that Amy left in a small car with two other people.

Claudio was already in my life by then, and even though we were still just friends, he was right there—searching, worried, frantic.

When we finally rolled up in the car, Claudio immediately walked up to ask if my friend who was driving had seen me. I stepped out of the back and Claudio just grabbed me, holding me tight.

"Where have you been?" he just hugged me. Hard. Then he pulled back and said, "We have to go see your mom." He wasn't angry. He was scared.

That moment stuck with me. It was the first time I saw what it meant to have someone outside of immediate family care enough to worry. Someone who would show up. Someone who didn't just let me disappear.

It may not have looked like love yet—but it was starting to feel like safety. We'd fall asleep on the sofa, there wasn't much we needed—just each other and the rare stillness we'd carved out in the middle of a chaotic world.

I never asked him outright, but looking back, I wonder if he kept me close on purpose. Maybe he saw the cliff I was heading toward, and instead of lecturing me, he stood quietly between me and the edge. He wasn't forceful. He didn't police my every move. But I can't recall a single time I bought drugs when he was around. He would just shift the course—subtly—without making me feel controlled.

I was still using. Quietly. I didn't do it around him but I wasn't stopping either. I hadn't yet found the strength. I still wanted to numb the parts of me that even he couldn't reach.

He never scolded me. Never yelled. But I could tell he noticed. The way his eyes followed me when I'd disappear for too long. The way his jaw tightened when I came back too quiet. And then one day, he said the words that changed everything.

"I want you to stop using.

I care about you, and I'm not going to sit here and watch you kill yourself. You're going to have to choose.

Me or the drugs.

I'll stand by you. I'll get you help. I'll stand with you while you talk to your parents.

Whatever it takes, we'll get through this together. But I won't stick around if you keep going like this. We can talk to your parents or just deal with it.

Whatever you need. I'm here. But you have to stop."

It wasn't said in anger. It wasn't a threat. It was calm. Certain. Full of love. It was a lifeline. It wasn't an ultimatum. It was love—the kind that wants more for you than you want for yourself.

And it gutted me, because I didn't want to lose him. But I also didn't know how to live without the things I used to keep the darkness at bay. I hadn't yet named the trauma, let alone healed it. I was still running on survival.

He waited—patiently, quietly, consistently. Like someone who knew I could come back to myself if given the chance. Like someone who believed in me, even when I didn't know how broken I was.

Back then, even if I couldn't name it, I knew one thing: I wanted to be clean. Because of him, I wanted to try.

When he saw that I was serious, he knew I wasn't using, everything changed. He never raised his voice. Never picked a fight. He didn't need to. The energy shifted when he was there.

If someone showed up looking for me—usually someone I used with—he would step in. A shake of the head, a wave of his hand. A firm look. No drama. Just presence. "Not tonight."

And they'd leave.

He shut down the revolving door without ever slamming it.

The people who fed my habits started disappearing. Not because I asked them to. Not because I was strong. But because he made it clear they weren't welcome anymore.

And maybe—deep down—a part of me was relieved. I knew those people weren't really my friends—they were just chasing the same high I was. It wasn't real connection.

Claudio was real. He cared. He showed up. And even when I couldn't see my own worth, he saw it for me.

I was tired. Tired of feeling numb. Tired of being caught between wanting to live and trying not to feel. I didn't know how to say that out loud, but Claudio seemed to know anyway.

***

The Call That Wasn't Her

One day, we were hanging out in my parents' living room and I got a phone call. It was someone claiming to be a childhood friend who wanted to meet me across the street. It sounded exactly like her, but something just felt off.

I told her to just come to my house, why wouldn't she just come over since we had known each other all of our lives? She claimed she wanted to stop by real fast so just come outside.

I agreed.

My mom had asked Claudio to go to the store next door to get her something and I told him I was going to meet this friend across the street. I admitted "something isn't right."

He told me to stay home. I wasn't having that, I wanted to know what was up. so I would walk with him to the store and we would meet up with this girl. I told him again, "no, something is off."

He told me again to stay home but I insisted.

As we got off my parents' property, a car pulled up, several girls jumped out, only one of them I knew, a friend I had severed ties with as I was getting clean came rushing at me.

She wanted to fight me for leaving our friendship.

Claudio acted fast.

He was able to separate the other girls from jumping me. I was in a headlock but able to twist myself to get out of it.

I told her "You're a dumbass wanting to fight me for wanting better. I'll fight you but it's gonna be fair and none of this four on one shit."

She simply said "respect," and walked away.

We knew each other well enough to know it likely would have ended with both of us tearing each other up.

Claudio was a little more stern that time.

"You felt something was off, I told you to stay home.

You should have listened—at least to yourself if not me. Stop putting yourself in danger Amy."

Men like him—men who save lives quietly, without applause—rarely get credit. The system never sees them for who they are. It only sees the worst thing they ever did. It ignores the healing work they do in silence, the lives they touch without fanfare.

Claudio wasn't my rehab. He wasn't a therapist.

He was my anchor.

He didn't lecture me.

He made me feel safe.

He didn't force me to change—he gave me a reason to want to.

Even now, after everything, I still believe what he gave me back then—without judgment, without conditions—was the wind beneath my wings.

***

The Night It All Changed

    March 12th. Something shifted in me.

    Claudio had been in my life every day for two months.

    He wasn't just showing up—he was quietly helping me rebuild.

    But still, we weren't together, not in that way. Not yet.

    I started to wonder what was wrong with me. Why wasn't he making a move? Did he not find me attractive? Did he only see me as a friend? He was always respectful, always steady—but I began questioning everything.

    Claudio had a reputation—women loved him, and he could've had anyone. Our connection hadn't started off romantic, but for me, it was becoming something more. He wasn't running around anymore, not since we'd become inseparable. But he still hadn't made a move. And I couldn't read him.

Despite us not being an official couple, every time we walked somewhere, he always positioned me on the inside of the sidewalk. He'd walk on the outside, closest to the street—something I'd only ever seen him do. I didn't know the tradition then, but I know it now.

It was about protection. Respect. Loyalty. That quiet, old-school way of caring.

Looking back, I was already his. And he was mine. I just didn't know it yet.

That night, I decided to test the waters. I swapped my usual jeans and Timberlands for a mini-skirt. I grabbed a 40 and asked him to drink with me. I turned up the flirtation—sitting closer, brushing against him. One thing led to another. We crossed a line we hadn't crossed before. Afterwards—he went to leave. He never left!

It rattled me.

He left around 4 a.m., and I didn't know what to make of it. Was that all it was to him? Did I misread everything? Was I just a challenge he wanted to conquer? The world's longest play?

"Are you coming back?" I asked, trying not to sound desperate. He looked at me like I had asked the dumbest question on earth, and said, "Why wouldn't I?" Then he was gone.

He had been my constant—showing up every day, he was part of my life. So, when he left right after something so intimate, I didn't know how to process it all.

He was steady in a world that had always felt unpredictable. Once he left, I kept replaying everything. Was it something I did? Something I didn't do? My mind raced with insecurity, the kind that crept in before I ever had the words for it.

Eighteen-year-old Amy didn't know how to name the fear of abandonment. She only knew how it felt.

It didn't take long for him to come back. He may have only been gone a few hours, but when he came back, it was like nothing had happened—calm, steady, unchanged. And that, in a weird way, was more confusing than if he had stayed away.

I wouldn't understand why he left that night until many years later. At the time, I blamed myself. I thought maybe I was too much or not enough. I couldn't yet see what was actually unfolding.

But I knew this: Every night, he came over after work, still covered in soot and debris from demolition jobs. He'd head straight for the bathroom. My mom adored that. Not just because she liked him, but because he always left the bathroom spotless. He'd come in filthy and leave the tub gleaming. She used to laugh and say, "He's the only man who comes in dirty and leaves the tub whiter than it started."

He made himself useful without ever trying to impress. That was just Claudio.

Now I can laugh at my younger self—the panic, the spiraling, the inability to see the bigger picture. But that's what makes youth both beautiful and brutal. I was so used to chaos that I couldn't recognize calm.

What I didn't know then—but deeply believe now—is that we were both brought together for a reason. That night we met, that shift in plans, him not going to Connecticut, me still ending up at that party? That wasn't a coincidence. Whether you believe in God, fate, energy, or nothing at all, some things feel too precisely timed not to be part of a bigger plan.

Claudio wasn't just part of my story. He was my turning point.

***

Early Summer – Charlie and the Plane That Wasn't

By early summer, things between Claudio and me had settled into a quiet rhythm. We hadn't defined anything, but we were still together every day.

He was as steady as ever, and I had begun to trust that steadiness more. I still questioned myself sometimes, still wondered if I was too much or not enough—but his presence reassured me more than words ever could.

Then came Charlie.

Claudio showed up at my parents' house one day with him—his boss, his friend, someone I had heard stories about but never met. I was upstairs when I heard the commotion. Charlie's voice carried through the house, playful, loud, full of energy. "Come on! Let's go. We're kidnapping you—don't resist," he yelled up the stairs in this mock-dramatic voice.

I froze.

Was he serious?

Was this a joke?

"Don't worry," he added. "We have a plane waiting." Claudio stood at the bottom of the stairs, smiling—completely unfazed, like this was just a normal day. Charlie was grinning, almost giddy.

And me? I was stunned. For a split second, I wasn't sure whether to laugh or pack a bag. I had never been "kidnapped" before—especially not with a promise of a private plane. Of course, there was no plane.

We were headed to Charlie's place. Pool day. Just a spontaneous little getaway. But that moment stuck with me, and not just because of the dramatic entrance. It was the way Claudio looked at me, the way

Charlie teased him like, "This man can't stay away from you, so we have to bring you with us."

They weren't wrong. We had become inseparable. And even though the plane never materialized, the feeling of being chosen, of being part of something light and fun and impulsive, was real.

Claudio, with all his rough edges, was becoming my soft place to land. And I, despite all my baggage, was becoming his.

We didn't have money. We didn't have a plan. We didn't even have words for what we were. But that summer, we had each other. And for the first time in a long time, that felt like enough.

***

From Sofa to Something More

By the time summer rolled around, Claudio was practically part of the family. He was at my parents' house every day. To them, we were still "just friends"—at least officially. But it didn't take a genius to see how inseparable we had become. If we weren't at work, we were together.

Every time my dad came home from one of his work trips, he'd find us in the same spot: On the sofa, side by side. Morning, noon, or midnight—it didn't matter. We were always together.

Eventually, the suggestion came. Not a confrontation, just a gentle nudge. "You two might want to think about getting your own place," my dad said one evening. My mom chimed in with a more casual tone. "Something simple. One bedroom. Claudio can sleep on the couch."

We didn't correct them. We just nodded.

A junior one-bedroom apartment in West Chester became our next step. It was on the third floor of a secure building with an elevator—which was a luxury in our world. It had a decent-sized living room with enough space for my parent's couch and chair and a card table we used as our dining room table. A small balcony sat off the living room, offering a little outdoor space where we could breathe and pretend we were doing better than we were.

The bedroom had enough room for my full-sized bed, a dresser, and a bureau, and the closet space wasn't bad either. It wasn't fancy, but it was secure. It was private. And for us, it felt like freedom.

My parents gave us some gently used furniture, dishes, towels, basic kitchenware, and the kind of practical things you don't think about until you need them. Claudio wasn't picky, and I was used to making do with what we had. We didn't care what the place looked like—we were just happy to have a place we could call our own.

We were young. We didn't know what we were doing. But we had each other. And in that tiny apartment, we started to figure out what building a life together could look like. At first, it felt like an adventure. Freedom. No parents, no rules. But freedom came with responsibility—with bills, groceries, and stress. Reality moved in faster than we did.

I was working as a nursing assistant, and Claudio, who had done demolition work and roofing, was facing job slowdowns as the weather got colder. He wasn't making much money, and it started to frustrate me. I was young and impatient, and I didn't yet understand the struggles of a working man whose industry depended on the seasons.

***

Our Fire

Even as we settled into the rhythm of living together, Claudio and I were still Claudio and I. We laughed constantly, we joked, we challenged each other—and we knew exactly how to push each other's buttons.

Around most people, I was quiet. Guarded. I watched more than I spoke. But with Claudio, something was different. I could talk. I could laugh. I could let the layers fall away. He made it feel safe.

I had fire in me—passion, emotion, depth—but I didn't let it out easily. Claudio wasn't the kind of man who drew it out with force. He created the kind of space where it rose naturally. Not because I had to defend myself, but because I was finally allowed to be myself.

He was calm. Steady. The opposite of chaos. He didn't shout. He didn't dominate the room. But when he spoke, people listened.

With me, though, he didn't try to lead. He let me unfold.

There weren't dramatic fights or slammed doors. There was just a quiet balance. If I ever got emotional, he grounded me.

If I felt overwhelmed, he didn't try to fix it—he just stayed. That was his power. He didn't need to control anything to protect me. He just showed up, steady as ever, and let me be.

But don't get it twisted—we had our moments. Or, let me say I had my moments.

Back then, there were no cell phones. We shared a beeper. If Claudio was out, he carried it, and I'd page him to call me. One day, he came home with two beepers. I immediately questioned him, and as usual, he leaned into my suspicion.

He leaned against the wall, lowering himself slightly and very slowly as he laughed a bit.

He was bracing for impact.

He held up our shared beeper and said, "This one's for you, my queen." Then he held up the other. "And this one is for the other women."

Before he could blink, I was on him. I dragged him out to the balcony and came dangerously close to throwing him over it. I wasn't playing. He kept saying it was a joke—but I was seconds away from making sure it was his last one.

I wasn't stronger than him, not even close. But that's the thing—Claudio would never raise a hand to me. Not in anger. Not in defense.

He grew up in a world where men fought to survive. But with me, he was always gentle. He knew what he was capable of—and he made sure I never had to find out.

There were plenty of times after that when he'd still push my buttons—just never that far again. I'd jump on his back, hitting him in frustration, and he'd carry me piggyback, laughing until he dropped me gently on the bed and told me to knock it off. One thing always led to another, and, well let's just say our relationship was anything but boring.

Our fire wasn't just passion. It was survival. It was built on trauma and love and humor and pain. But the truth is, neither of us knew that about the other. We didn't know yet how much pain the other carried. We were just two people drawn to something we didn't have a name for.

He wasn't fire like me—but he didn't try to put mine out. He made space for it. And sometimes, that's the most powerful kind of love there is.

***

He Was My Safety Net

It wasn't until years later that I realized just how different Claudio was. He wasn't just another man in my life—he was my safety net.

I want to be clear: I'm not talking about the kind of stability parents provide. I had good parents. They offered me a foundation, especially in my early years. They weren't perfect, but they were stable. They tried to provide a safe home. But we weren't free from chaos.

My grandfather lived with us, and while he wasn't always cruel, he was unpredictable—especially toward me. There were times he'd fly off the handle, and one of those times, when I was fifteen or sixteen, he punched me in the jaw so hard it cracked. He always made sure to do things like this when my parents weren't around.

That day, my mom did the right thing—she called Children and Youth anonymously. But the answer she got shook her: they said if any adult in the household was a danger, they would remove the child, not the adult. So, I stayed. And so did he.

I had a love-hate relationship with Grandpop. He could be a bully—physical, demeaning, cruel. But then he'd try to erase the harm with grand gestures. Not with apologies. With stuff.

He didn't have money, but he had credit cards. And in 1983, when every little girl wanted a Cabbage Patch Kid and they were sold out everywhere, I didn't just get one—I got eight. A guilt purchase. A flashy Band-Aid for a wound he refused to name. He didn't give love—he tried to buy it. And of course, we all know… Nothing says "sorry I treated you poorly" like an army of baby-faced hostages with yarn hair.

There's a different kind of stability we all reach for as we get older—the kind that shapes how we love, how we trust, how we build lives beyond the walls we grew up in. That's the kind of stability Claudio gave me. He didn't just calm the storm—I think he may have rewired something in me.

Long before Claudio and I were ever together, I had a boyfriend who, for the most part, seemed decent. But he had a temper. I can't blame him; his father was incarcerated most of his life and he lived with his grandmother.

There were a few times he got pushy, but the last time I saw him, he threw me against a tree. A fight broke out between him and one of his best friends who wanted to stand up for me and in the midst of it, I remember just walking away. I didn't scream. I didn't cry. I just left. And I never went back.

Looking back now, that moment was a shift. It marked the beginning of me pulling away from certain friendships, certain behaviors, certain patterns. I started leaning toward something different—even if I didn't know exactly what that was yet.

And then came Claudio.

He never tried to control me. He never made me feel small. Even when my temper flared—when I got loud, overwhelmed, or just didn't know what to do with all the chaos inside me—he never raised his voice. He didn't meet fire with fire. He met it with stillness. With calm. With something that felt like safety in a world that rarely gave me any.

That doesn't mean he let me walk all over him. Claudio was strong—strong in ways that didn't require yelling or force. There were moments when I was so full of rage I didn't know where to put it. I'd punch at his back, try to physically shake off the storm I was drowning in, and he would just carry me. No anger. No retaliation. He'd lift me, hold me, and set me down gently. He knew how to deal with me—how to *handle* me—without ever fighting me, without ever raising a hand.

He was the epitome of what a strong man looks like.

He was the anchor. Sometimes he was the calm ocean that kept me from burning myself alive. Around most people, I was quiet, guarded. I watched more than I spoke. With Claudio, something was different. I could talk. I could laugh. I could let the layers fall away.

He made it feel safe.

I trusted him with my life. I still do. In fact, besides my father, Claudio is the only man I've ever truly trusted.

That trust didn't come from grand gestures or big promises. It came from the little things. Like how he never disrespected me. How he never pushed me to be anything but myself. How he stood by me, even when I wasn't easy to stand beside.

At the time, I didn't have words for that kind of loyalty. But now I do. It was love—the kind that doesn't need to announce itself because it's already known. But we were young. And there were still things we didn't understand—things neither of us knew how to say.

Once we had our own place, I started inviting friends over more regularly. It felt like the grown-up thing to do, even if I wasn't acting like much of an adult.

At eighteen years old, freedom came with a heavy learning curve. I had a few close female friends who would come by our apartment, and sometimes, I'd leave them there when I went to work. I didn't think anything of it. To me, it felt normal—just life. But Claudio saw it differently.

With his beliefs, a woman leaving her man home with other women—especially ones who weren't family—wasn't something that sat right. It was about respect; about boundaries he held for himself. Still, he didn't make it an issue. He just let it be.

He was quiet. Disappointed maybe. But he didn't push. We didn't talk about it. We didn't talk about a lot of things we should have.

That's the part of being young no one really warns you about—how even when love is real, it's not always well communicated. You can love someone with your whole heart and still not know how to meet them where they are. You can be loyal to the core and still fumble every single conversation that matters.

But Claudio and I? We were trying. Even in the silence. Even in the chaos. He was the calm in my storm.

***

Chapter 2: In the Palm of My Hand

Getting clean wasn't easy. Even after moving in together, I was still young, still surrounded by people I thought were friends. Many of them still used.

One night, someone I trusted came to our apartment. By then, I had stayed clean from cocaine, but I woke up the next morning to find a "gift" waiting for me. When I went to put on my shoe, there it was—a small $20 bag of cocaine tucked inside. It was an unrequested temptation.

Just as I was trying to process what was happening, Claudio walked out of our bedroom. I was sitting on the floor, staring at the bag in my hand. I was frozen. I'll admit it—part of me wanted to use it. Before this, I hadn't come across any. It had never been within reach, and now, suddenly, it was real. Right there in my palm, almost begging to be sniffed.

Claudio took one look at me and laughed—not out of humor, but disbelief. He thought I had gone back to using. Thought he'd just caught me about to relapse, ready to throw it all away. I told him I had just found it, but even I could hear the weakness in my voice. He didn't yell. He didn't accuse. He just stood firm.

"If you don't want it, then flush it," he said.

I held it out to him. "You do it."

He shook his head. "No. If you really don't want it, you'll do it yourself."

I told him I couldn't. That I couldn't just flush it. He just looked at me again.

"If you really don't want it, you'll find the courage. I will help you but I won't do it for you." There was no softness in his voice—just strength. Controlled. Steady. Real.

Tears welled up in my eyes. He didn't budge. He didn't comfort. He just waited.

Finally, I broke. I nodded. So, he walked with me to the bathroom, and together, we flushed it. Together, we let it go.

That moment was intense, the relief of flushing it, conquering something I could have so easily fallen right back into, the support he gave, it was a flood of emotion. And Claudio was Claudio, he just took me into our bedroom and held me as I wept on his shoulder.

That was Claudio. The man who didn't just love me—he *held the line* for me when I couldn't hold it for myself.

I didn't know then that I would be the one trying to save him someday. The one who'd become a voice for men and women labeled beyond redemption. All I knew was that this man saved me.

***

What Came Next

After flushing that bag of cocaine, things settled—for a while. We were solid. I didn't relapse with the coke. I did one day smoke some wet without him knowing. Just like the coke, the wet, also known as a Sherm, which is a cigarette dipped in embalming fluid, had an opposite effect. Most people who smoke sit around quietly, whereas it gave me energy. It made me feel like I was floating outside of myself. I remember only part of that day, but I recall vacuuming the floor and dancing.

I didn't tell him and I didn't do it again. My story isn't about pretending that I made all the right choices. Far from it! But it's my truth, and the reality for so many others.

Healing doesn't come from perfection; it comes from telling the truth. Even the ugly parts. Especially the ugly parts.

***

Well-Meaning, Misinformed

I was taking birth control at the time. Quietly. Consistently. I never made a big deal out of it. I took it more for regularity than actual birth control. But one day, Claudio saw me take the pill and looked at me like I had just taken poison.

"You don't need to put that junk in your body," he said with a wave of his hand, heading into the bathroom like it was no big deal. I was stunned. That was not the reaction I expected. When he came out, I tried to stay calm. "Claudio, I have to take this or I'll get pregnant."

He barely paused. "Nonsense. It's not that easy to get pregnant." I stared at him in disbelief. Did he really just say that? I wanted to laugh. "Okay," I said, trying to keep a straight face, "so are you going to use protection?"

He gave a short, amused kind of laugh—like ha ha, you're joking—and said, "No. But you don't need to be putting that synthetic stuff in your body." It wasn't controlling. He wasn't trying to dictate my choices. He genuinely believed it wasn't healthy.

Seriously, he went from my man who refused to wear protection to a holistic healer in a split second. In his mind, he was looking out for me. And like most disagreements between us, it didn't spiral. We talked. We communicated very little. And we ended up back in bed.

That was our rhythm. Any tension we had always melted away the same way it showed up—fast, loud, and then quiet again. We were young—me barely an adult, him still in his twenties—but we thought we had it all figured out.

***

Chapter 3: The Dream: A Sign Before the Test

In early November 1994, Claudio had a dream. It was after we had spent some real quality time together. I felt different—like something had shifted. Something deeper had taken root between us. I couldn't explain it, but it felt like we were bonded in a new way.

That same night, in the middle of the night, I felt him reach over and gently shake me awake. His voice had an edge of panic to it. "I had a dream…" he said. I was groggy, barely processing. "What was the dream?" I mumbled, rolling over. "I had a dream…" he repeated, his tone serious, almost urgent.

Now I was annoyed. I just wanted to sleep. "Okay, Martin," I grumbled, referencing Martin Luther King Jr. "What was the dream?" And then he said something that made absolutely no sense at the time.

"The eggs were swimming."

I blinked at him. "What?"

"The eggs were swimming," he said again, dead serious. I rolled my eyes, turned over, and went back to sleep, thinking, this crazy man is waking me up to talk about swimming eggs? Something about the way he said it stuck with me.

I didn't know it then, but he did. Claudio had sensed it—before either of us knew the truth.

***

The Glow That Gave It Away

I still hung out with my friends. I wasn't the perfect little housewifey, not even close! And Claudio never asked me to be. Though I was almost always at our apartment with him, one day I decided to go to my friend's house. When I got there, a couple of guys from my pre-Claudio days were there. Just friends—always had been.

I'd grown up as the only girl my age in the neighborhood. My best friends from the time I was little were all boys, and we grew up like brothers.

I rode dirt bikes, wrestled in the grass, and got into fistfights when it came to it. We didn't play house or pretend to be teachers—we played rough. I still have the memory of getting shot in the butt with a 50-pump BB gun. Of course, I had to retaliate.

To me, being around guys was normal. They were just friends. No more, no less. But Claudio's old-school mindset didn't really work like that. To him, a woman in a room full of men—especially if he wasn't there—meant something different. I hadn't known the guys would be there, but they were.

One of them looked at me a little strangely. "What did you do to yourself?" he asked. "You've always been pretty, but you're glowing, Aim." I laughed, brushing it off. "Nothing. Same old me." Then another guy spoke up. "Nah, something's different. You're gorgeous."

Before I could say anything else, my girlfriend burst out laughing. "Uh oh," she said, pointing at me. "The Puerto Rican men are all about that glow. When was your last period? You've got to be pregnant."

The room fell quiet. My heart did too. Pregnant?

I hadn't even thought about it. But then the realization crept in like a slow wave. I had always been irregular, so missing a period wasn't unusual. But now that it had been said out loud—"When was your last period?"—I started thinking harder. I couldn't remember.

And just like that, the thought rooted itself in my brain.

Pregnant? No way. That couldn't be. I was eighteen, barely an adult, and if this was true, I was staring down some serious adulting. What would I tell Claudio? What about my parents? They still thought Claudio and I were just friends and that he was sleeping on the sofa. That whole 'we're just friends' thing? About to crumble fast.

I wasn't glowing. I was panicking. There was maybe a small twinge of excitement, but mostly, it was fear. Fear of change, fear of responsibility, and a very real fear of having to explain myself. Yet, somewhere under all of it, a strange sense of destiny lingered.

To make matters worse, I don't even remember how I got to my friend's house that day. But I definitely couldn't get home. I didn't drive, and she lived way out—at least 40 minutes from West Chester.

As usual, Claudio came through. He showed up with his friend to get me. And he was... not pleased. I had been gone all night. In his world, that was unacceptable. I should have been home—with my man. Period. He didn't raise his voice. He didn't cause a scene. But the energy was different. That silent, brooding kind of disappointment. The kind that said everything without a word.

And there I was, riding in the back in silence, stuck between two racing thoughts: Am I pregnant? And... how do I even begin to bring this up?

Claudio had told me to stop taking the pill. He said I didn't need to put synthetic hormones in my body, waving off the seriousness of it like it was a vitamin I could do without. I don't think he truly believed I'd get pregnant just like that. But now, I couldn't stop thinking about the dream he'd had not long before—the one that made no sense at the time. "The eggs were swimming."

And maybe… they were.

***

The Pharmacy Test

As usual, my friend and her friend ended up back at our place. We decided to walk into town for a bit, just to get out of the apartment.

As we were passing a small pharmacy, my friend suddenly stopped in her tracks. "There's a pharmacy," she said, giving me one of those side-eyes that came with a silent laugh. She didn't need to say more. Between her excitement that I might be pregnant and her frustration that I hadn't taken a test yet, the message was loud and clear.

I walked in and bought the test, more curious than anything else. We headed back to the apartment, just the three of us. "Go on, get it done… Mama!" one of them teased as we walked in. I rolled my eyes, grabbed the test, and carried the bag home.

Once home, it didn't take long. The double blue lines appeared almost instantly. I stepped out, holding the test like it was radioactive.

Their eyes widened. Then they screamed in excitement.

That's when we heard the door open. Claudio was home.

Panic took over. I darted back into the bathroom and locked the door. Of course, he immediately asked where I was. My friends were giggling and I could hear the curiosity in his voice. "She's in the bathroom," one of them said. "Been in there for a while," the other added, laughing.

He knew something was up. His knock on the door was gentle. "You okay?"

"I'm fine," I said.

"Let me in."

"No... I can't."

He paused. "Amy... please. Open the damned door."

Eventually, I opened the door. I couldn't hide it anymore. I told him. It shouldn't have come as a shock. But I still felt blindsided. Not because it was impossible. But because it was real now.

We walked into the bedroom together. I sat on the bed. He sat next to me, still absorbing it all. "How?" he asked. I blinked. "What do you mean, how?" He looked at me, half-shocked. "Every chance we get, we're on each other..."

That made me laugh, despite the nerves. "Exactly." Still stunned, he reached for the phone and immediately called his mom. He spoke rapidly in Spanish—I couldn't make out a word. Then, suddenly, he handed me the phone. "Mami wants to talk to you."

Her voice came through, full of warmth and authority. She was speaking to me in Spanish, and I had no clue what she was saying. Eventually, I realized she was asking if it was true. "Yes, Mami," I said. "It's true."

There was a pause. Then, in her very broken English, she said something I'll never forget:

"You no take the baby out. You keep the baby." Not a discussion, just a straight-up Catholic Puerto Rican mic drop. My throat tightened. "Yes, of course." And that's when it hit me. I may have been eighteen, barely an adult. But if this was real, I was about to face some serious adulting. I wasn't just Amy anymore.

I was going to be someone's mother.

***

The Elephant in the Room

We didn't really talk about the pregnancy. It was the elephant in the room—unspoken, yet impossible to ignore. I was excited, nervous, and terrified all at once. But more than anything, I was just really excited.

Still, my parents didn't even know that Claudio and I were a couple. I had been living in my own little world, building a life with him, but somehow, I had never actually told them the truth. Now, I had a lot of explaining to do—but I wasn't ready.

I wanted to make sure everything was okay with the pregnancy first. Then I'd tell them. At least, that was the plan.

I made the mistake of calling my sister. She was ten years older than me and had always been the talkative one—the type to blurt things out without warning. When I told her, her response was immediate: "You have to tell Mom." I told her I would, just not yet. That wasn't good enough for her. "You tell her, or I will," she said. I was furious. This was my news, not hers. It wasn't her place to make that decision for me.

I wasn't a child. I didn't live under my parents' roof. I worked. There was no "having to tell." I had a weekend trip planned with my mom to go to New Jersey, but after that conversation, I backed out. I was convinced my sister had already told her, and I wasn't ready to deal with it.

***

The Morning That Gave It Away

The morning my mom came to pick me up, Claudio and I were still in bed together—and that was a problem. She had a key to our apartment. When she knocked and I didn't answer, of course she let herself in. I was already panicking. Claudio and I were under the covers, giggling like teenagers. We could hear her moving through the apartment, but then suddenly—

BANG! BANG! BANG!

She was banging pots and pans together.

"WAKE UP!"

There is absolutely nothing that says "Good morning, pregnant sinner!" Like your mother banging pots and pans as you and your unborn baby's father hide under the covers. I froze. Claudio's eyes went wide. We just stared at each other, caught between laughter and actual alarm, waiting to see what would happen next. Would she come storming into the bedroom? Would she try to open the door? We held our breath. But she didn't. It got quiet.

We waited another twenty minutes, just to be sure she was really gone. When I finally got up, the apartment was silent. She was nowhere in sight. I never went to New Jersey. And later, I found out—my sister had told her.

***

A Stolen Moment

I don't even remember exactly how I knew that she knew. There wasn't some dramatic confrontation, no screaming, no tears. It just became clear. Maybe it was the way she looked at me, the way she spoke just a little differently, as if she was processing something she hadn't expected.

She didn't freak out. In fact, if anything, she seemed shocked—but also a little excited. But that didn't change the fact that the moment had been stolen from us. Claudio wasn't happy.

We had planned to share the news on our own terms, when we were ready. We were adults. This was our child, our future—and that moment should have belonged to us. Instead, my sister had taken it away. I felt it too. The frustration. The resentment.

It wasn't just about my mom knowing—it was about control. About the fact that something so life-changing had been taken out of our hands. But what was done was done. The secret was out, and now, there was no going back.

***

Chapter 4: Thanksgiving and a Painful Lesson

As Thanksgiving approached, I found myself on crutches, nursing an infection that had taken over my ankle—another impulsive, "living in the moment" decision that, unsurprisingly, Claudio wasn't thrilled about.

I had gotten a spur-of-the-moment tattoo before I even knew I was pregnant. It wasn't some back-alley, homemade disaster—it was done at a legitimate shop by a professional artist.

But even professionals have demons.

The artist had gone too deep, working far too long on my ankle. He chipped the bone and left me with an open wound that refused to heal. I ignored it at first, but the pain eventually became unbearable.

It all came to a head while I was at work. The nurses took one look at my ankle and insisted I leave immediately to go to the hospital. Problem was, I didn't have a car—and I could barely walk.

So, Claudio did what Claudio always did. He showed up. On foot. The second he saw my leg, his frustration over the tattoo vanished. No lectures. No "I told you so." He just scooped me up, slung me over his shoulder like a sack of potatoes, and carried me out.

I felt like a child again—helpless, ashamed, and carrying the consequences of another reckless decision.

It wasn't a short walk. He carried me down the hill from the nursing home, up another hill past our apartment, and straight into the ER. Now, don't get me wrong—he was still annoyed. He asked the same question he'd asked the day I got it: "*What were you thinking?*" Claudio had tattoos himself, so he wasn't new to the healing process.

He could see immediately that something was very wrong. The hospital staff was horrified. I'll spare the details—but it was bad. Really bad.

Worse than the pain was the fear. This was 1994. HIV was rampant, and dirty needles were a death sentence. The nurses raised concerns immediately. What if the artist hadn't cleaned his tools? What if I'd been exposed? The room spun. I hadn't even thought about that, because I saw him use a clean needle. Yet, this infection was so bad, no one believed me.

I was tested. Then tested again. And again, over the next year. I kept telling myself: It was a real shop. A real artist. It had to be fine. But in those days, there were no guarantees. And waiting for those results was pure hell. Every single time.

That tattoo stayed with me—not just on my skin, but as a reminder of how fast something impulsive can leave a permanent mark.

***

Thanksgiving: The First Family Gathering

Claudio had gone down to see his mom for Thanksgiving, and my dad came to pick me up. It was surreal—knowing that, for the first time, Claudio and I were no longer just "inseparable friends" in my parents' eyes. Even as he made time for his own family, he never once left me hanging. He showed up for me—always.

This would be the first time we were all in the same room, and the truth was out in the open. He wasn't just my best friend anymore. He was my boyfriend. He was the father of our unborn child. It was a big deal.

There was no more pretending we were just roommates. No more dodging questions. Everything had changed. Claudio planned to come to my parents' house later that day, but I had no idea how things would feel now that everyone knew.

It wasn't just Thanksgiving dinner—it felt like a test. And I had no idea how it was going to go. My mom knew Claudio and liked him. My dad? Not so much. He didn't know him well. Between his constant travel for work and his distance from anything emotional, he never showed much interest in our relationship. But now, he couldn't ignore it.

***

A Father's Questions

The questions started before we even got pulled away from my apartment complex door.

Not the small talk kind. The serious ones. The ones that hang in the air like a weight. "What are you going to do?" he asked. He didn't say the word—but he didn't have to. I was eighteen, pregnant, and still limping around on crutches. This wasn't something to pretend away. It was real. And I didn't hesitate. "I'm keeping the baby."

He looked over at me like he was trying to read between the lines—trying to see if I was serious, if I was scared, if I really understood what that meant. I did. As overwhelming as everything was, I knew what I wanted. This child was mine. Ours. And even though I had no clue what motherhood would actually look like; I already knew I wasn't walking away from it.

My dad could be blunt. Loud when he wanted to be. I braced myself for that version of him. But instead, he nodded. "We'll help however we can." That was it. No lecture. No argument. No guilt. Just support. Quiet, steady, and exactly what I needed to hear. In that moment, everything felt a little less heavy.

I didn't know how hard things would get. I didn't know what would happen between Claudio and me. But I knew I wasn't alone.

And sometimes, that's enough to get you through the next step—even when you can't see where it's leading.

***

The Thanksgiving Test

Dinner was quiet when Claudio arrived. Not tense, not cold—just quiet. The kind of quiet that settles in when people are trying to act normal while adjusting to something very new. My parents had always known Claudio as my friend. The guy I spent all my time with. The one who arrived filthy and left a bright white tub. The one who made my mom laugh.

But now?

Now he was my boyfriend. Now he was the father of their future grandchild. There was no going back to casual. The dynamic had shifted, and everyone at the table felt it.

Claudio walked in like he always did—calm on the exterior, respectful, steady. He greeted my parents, sat where he was told, made conversation when prompted. He was nervous, and he wasn't overly comfortable either. He knew this dinner wasn't just about turkey and mashed potatoes. It was about showing up. About being seen as more than a name they'd heard thrown around or the man who had once slept with their daughter on the sofa.

My dad, as expected, didn't waste time. At one point during dinner, he looked directly at Claudio and asked, "What do you plan to do, son?" His tone wasn't angry—it was measured. But it carried weight. Then came the real question. "Are you going to marry my daughter?"

I held my breath. Claudio didn't flinch. He looked him in the eye and answered with quiet confidence: "I intend to someday. But having a baby isn't a reason to get married. I'll be here, and I'll be a parent—no matter what."

It was the right answer. Maybe not the one my father had hoped for—but the honest one. The respectful one. Claudio wasn't making empty promises just to ease tensions. He was telling the truth.

He was in it. With me. For real. And in that moment, even without a ring or a plan or the traditional steps people expect—you could feel it. We were already a family.

***

A Father's Warning

At some point that evening, my dad and Claudio disappeared. I didn't think much of it at first. I was in the kitchen helping my mom clean up, assuming they'd stepped outside for a smoke or maybe just needed a break from the awkward energy at the table.

But then Claudio came back in through the back door—face pale, eyes wide, expression unreadable. Right behind him was my dad. Something had just happened. That much was clear. Claudio didn't say anything. He just looked at me, shook his head slightly, and let out a breath. It wasn't fear in his eyes—it was disbelief.

Later, I found out what went down. While I was helping clean up, my dad had taken him to the basement. No warm chat. No bonding moment. Just my dad, being exactly who he had always been—direct, protective, and not one to waste words. "If you ever lay a hand on my daughter," he told Claudio, "You will never have to worry about the police again." *Straight like that.* No hesitation. No metaphor. Just a promise.

Looking back, I should've been shocked. But I wasn't. That was my dad. It was how he showed love—especially the kind he didn't know how to say out loud. What surprised me more was Claudio's reaction. He didn't argue. He didn't puff up or take offense. He just... took it. Silent. Steady. Like he understood it came from a place of protection, not hate.

That's when I knew—Claudio wasn't just strong, he was grounded. He didn't feel threatened by my dad. He understood him. Maybe even respected him for it.

My mom realized what was going on and didn't miss a beat. With the kind of sharpness only a mother can pull off, she turned to my dad and said, "You talked to the wrong one, John. She's the one who'll beat the hell out of that boy—and he'd never hurt her." I cracked up. Because she wasn't wrong. Claudio just smiled, shook his head again, and went to sit down.

No one said the word, but that day marked something bigger than just a holiday. The pretending was over. The lines had been drawn—and we were standing on the same side. It was our first real family holiday as a "we." It was messy, awkward, a little tense—and somehow, still perfect.

Not perfect in the fairy-tale way. Perfect in the this-is-my-chaotic-life-and-we're-making-it-work kind of way.

***

Chapter 5: Three Damned Words

Claudio's work in demolition was seasonal. As the weather cooled, the jobs dried up. With that came the slow, creeping pressure of bills, groceries, rent—and a baby on the way. At first, I wasn't worried. I was still working full-time, and we were making it work. But I started noticing things. Claudio wasn't picking up extra jobs. Maybe there weren't any. Maybe he was trying and just not saying much. But from where I sat— young, impatient, already carrying more weight than I understood—it felt like he wasn't trying hard enough. And the resentment built.

I didn't know how to talk about that pressure, let alone how to handle it. I was tired. I was overwhelmed. I was immature. And one day, I snapped. "Get out, get a job, or go sell drugs."

Three damned words... "Go sell drugs." I didn't mean them—not really. I wasn't asking him to become a dealer. I just wanted him to do something. Anything. I was drowning, and I lashed out. The words came fast, sharp, and careless. And they would come back to haunt me in ways I couldn't begin to imagine. Claudio didn't yell. He didn't argue. He didn't throw anything in my face. He just got quiet. And that's the thing with Claudio. When he's hurt, he doesn't explode—he absorbs. And sometimes, that silence says more than any outburst ever could.

Before I knew him, he'd had a few run-ins with the law—nothing major—but he wasn't into selling drugs. That wasn't who he was. When we met, and all the time we were together, he was out of trouble. Focused. Committed. Grounded.

And then I said it. Even now, I think about those words. I know damn well they played a part. My frustration, my anger—they pushed Claudio toward choices he might not have otherwise made. Because he went out to sell drugs, he crossed paths with Jeff. And I've never stopped wondering... If I had just kept my mouth shut, would things have turned out differently?

People often use the phrase "if words could kill." Well, the reality is—those words proved lethal. I didn't expect violence. I never heard of anyone dying from marijuana. I never heard of anyone being killed over weed. I didn't really want him to sell drugs. I just wanted him to bring money home—and fast. And that's what came out.

There was no real thought. No plan. No plotting to become a drug dealer. I viewed it through the eyes of a child. People I knew sold it. People I knew bought it. It didn't seem like a big deal. Not really. Not yet.

I wasn't stupid. I wasn't reckless. I was just young—and broken—and still believing that jail was something people came home from. I never imagined violence. I never imagined anyone getting hurt. I didn't even think he'd go to jail for selling. There was legitimately no thought involved in those words—just pressure and panic and the need for money. It wasn't strategic. It wasn't serious. It was just one of those things people said—especially in the world I grew up in, where so many people around me bought or sold weed like it was nothing.

I didn't see the danger. I didn't think about the consequences. I just snapped. Thirty years later, those words still make me want to cry. Thirty years later, I still carry them inside me—quietly, painfully, and without a way to take them back. I didn't know Claudio's full story back then. I didn't know the weight he already carried—how abandonment and instability had shaped him long before I came into the picture. We were close, but not that close. Not yet. I hadn't shared all of myself, and neither had he. But looking back, I see it more clearly now.

My words didn't cause everything that came next—but they cracked something open. They struck a nerve I didn't even know existed. And while I can't undo them, I've spent decades carrying the weight of that moment.

***

The Wrong People, The Wrong Choices

Claudio wasn't lazy. He was a provider. He took care of me, and he wanted to take care of our growing family. But the pressure of responsibility was mounting, and we both felt it. The struggle to stay afloat—the weight of survival—it was suffocating.

Somewhere along the way, he crossed paths with the wrong people.

As I mentioned earlier, when I met Claudio, I was actually seeing his cousin. I had known his cousin for a couple of years, and to the outside world, he came across as the "good one." He didn't live in poverty. He came from a two-parent home, went to a better school, kept himself looking respectable. On the surface, he was clean.

But I saw through it.

I had my own experiences with him that no longer matter, but I regret never telling Claudio the truth. I didn't want to come between him and his blood. I didn't want to risk losing him by saying I didn't trust his cousin. So, I stayed silent. But the truth was, I noticed things. The way he carried himself. The way he talked. He used to keep the smallest little gun tucked in his pocket—like he was playing a role. He wanted to look like power, even though he lived a more comfortable life than most of the people around him.

I wish I had said something back then, told him more about who his cousin really was. Because both Claudio and his cousin ended up selling drugs. And before I said those three damned words, Claudio wasn't involved in it. I will forever regret that moment—Go sell drugs—because that's when everything started to change.

Claudio kept the streets away from me. He didn't bring it into our home. If he was doing something out there, he did it out there. Our apartment was safe. No late-night banging on the door. No people hanging around. No deals in the kitchen or whispers in the hallway. He protected that space—and he protected me.

Even when things started shifting, I had no idea how deep it had already gone. And looking back now, I see something I missed then—he didn't want to be doing it.

There was one day, in the middle of all of it, when Claudio came home and handed me a stack of money. I don't even remember what I was complaining about—probably bills, groceries, stress—but I remember my tone. Sharp. Frustrated. Accusing. He looked at me and said, "I have some damned money. Some things are more important than money, Amy. You know what? Here's the money." And right in front of me, he tore it up. I was stunned. He literally ripped the bills apart and let them fall.

And me?

As embarrassing as it is to admit, I broke. Full-blown crying temper tantrum—on the floor, like a child. I was exhausted. Angry. Terrified. I didn't know how to fix any of it, and it was easier to fall apart than face it. Claudio just looked at me and said, firmly, "You need to stop that—it's not good for our baby."

Then I spent hours taping those bills back together.

At some point, Claudio and Jorge met Jeff—the so-called mastermind—while selling drugs. Jeff had a plan. He told them about a shipment of marijuana they could intercept and flip for profit. He was also trying to sell Claudio a gun.

At some point, while looking for Claudio on the street, Jeff came across Claudio's cousin instead. It's unclear exactly where Claudio was—he may have been home at the time, or nearby—but I wasn't aware of any of it.

Claudio's cousin told Jeff he'd take the gun for him. And just like that, Jeff handed it over for next to nothing. I had no idea any of this was happening.

While I was inside our apartment or busy at work, going about my day, things were already unraveling outside—conversations, transactions, and choices being made that I'd later be forced to make sense of. Nothing like that ever happened in front of me. Claudio never brought any of this home—not to my face, not in our space.

Looking back now, with thirty years of clarity, I see it: Those three words—Go sell drugs—set off a chain reaction. I wasn't serious. I was angry. I was eighteen, scared, stressed, pregnant—and lashing out. But words have weight. And sometimes, they land harder than we ever mean them to. And those words—spoken in frustration, in a moment of panic—became part of something much bigger.

Something life-altering.

Something life-ending.

***

Chapter 6: The End of Innocence

December 12-13, 1994

By December, I was getting morning sickness regularly, and it was getting worse as each day went on. On December 12, 1994, we were supposed to go to Philadelphia—Claudio, his cousin, and me. But I was so sick that day. I told Claudio a few hours earlier that I wanted us to just stay home together. I didn't want to go out. I just wanted to be alone with him, and he agreed. I felt so relieved.

Later that evening, Claudio's cousin came by, and so did Jeff. Claudio stayed with me in the living room, while Jorge and Jeff went into my bedroom. At that point in my life, I didn't have much. If someone wanted to use my room to talk, that wasn't a big deal. They were close, and I didn't question it.

Once or twice, Claudio got up for just a few seconds—just long enough to ask if they needed anything, like a drink—and then he came right back to me. I thought that was it. I thought we were staying in.

We were going to have the night together. Then, as if the night had already been decided for him, Jorge called out, "Let's go." Claudio responded, "I'm just staying here tonight." But Jorge repeated himself—firmer this time. "Let's go. We won't be out long."

I was upset. He had just told me we were staying in. I had let my guard down. I was pregnant, sick, and emotional. I jumped up, threw on my coat, and followed right behind him. I didn't want to be left alone, and I didn't want to be lied to. I figured he was going out to meet girls, and my insecurity took over.

It wasn't about trust—it was about fear. I was young and pregnant and unsure of everything. Claudio got into the passenger seat. Jorge was driving. I jumped into the back. Before we left the apartment complex, Claudio turned and told me to get out of the car. I refused. He turned to Jorge and said, "Just stop the car," but Jorge didn't.

I didn't know where we were going. The plan had originally been to go to Philadelphia, but that wasn't where we were headed. I didn't ask questions. I was just along for the ride.

They spoke Spanish, as they usually did, and neither Claudio nor Jorge seemed nervous. We ended up following Jeff's car and made a stop at a Wawa. Jeff tossed something into our window—something small, handed directly to Jorge. I didn't ask what it was. I didn't think it had anything to do with me. I just remember thinking I was with Claudio. I wasn't alone. And I still felt sick.

We continued driving and instead of continuing South on the 202 toward Philly, we turned around heading back in the North direction and eventually pulled into the Sentinel Motel in Delaware County.

Once we arrived, Claudio and Jorge got out of the car. I stayed put in the backseat. I couldn't see a thing. Then I heard banging. I know now, this was banging at the door.

And then—two loud bangs, which I know now to have been gunshots going through the door.

A few moments later, Jorge ran to the car and threw a heavy bag into the back seat. It hit my stomach. I was pregnant. It wasn't gentle. I didn't know what it was. I didn't even try to look. I was frozen. It was a heavy bag, that much I knew. But there were no signs of what had actually happened.

Claudio got back in the car next. He was speaking Spanish then in English, he asked Jorge, "What did you do?" He asked again, louder. "What did you do?" His eyes were wet, he was crying. Jorge didn't answer. He drove calmly, without emotion. The silence in the car was heavy, tense. I leaned forward and asked Claudio, "What happened?" It was the first time he ever raised his voice at me. "Just sit back and be quiet!" I sat back, stunned. Claudio was scared. That much was clear.

This wasn't some act. This wasn't just street stuff. He was shaken, confused, trying to get answers from someone who refused to give them.

Claudio had been my calming force. He never lost control, never yelled. But when he asked Jorge what happened and I could see he his eyes were wet, he was holding back tears, he was scared and in disbelief, something inside me knew—we were in deep. And something terrible had just occurred. When we got back to our apartment complex, Jeff was already there. Claudio got out of the car and asked, "Is everyone OK? Did anyone get hurt?" Jeff answered without hesitation, "no, just a bloody nose getting hit with the door."

Claudio sighed. "Oh, thank God."

I still did not actually know what happened. I only knew what I heard and what I could understand was very little. I was still unhappy with Claudio that we were even out that night. Any relief that was there when Jeff said no one was hurt was short lived because the truth was about to unravel. And nothing would ever be the same again.

That night was a blur of emotions—confusion, fear, uncertainty. When we got into our apartment was when I saw it—the marijuana. A lot of it. They dumped it from the bag, spreading it out as if assessing what they had just taken. Jorge didn't stay long. He was ready to leave for the night, and I was just there, sitting on the sofa. Watching. Before he left, Jorge took some of the marijuana for his personal use. I didn't ask any questions. I just sat there, silent.

It wasn't until we went to bed that Claudio and I finally spoke. We just laid together but it was different. There was no intimacy, but it was still as if he was trying to protect me.

"What happened?" He was quiet for a moment before answering. "I don't know," he admitted. "We robbed someone." I was shocked. But more than that, I was worried. Because Claudio wasn't okay. He wasn't celebrating. He wasn't relieved. He wasn't proud. He was upset. Unsettled. And that scared me more than anything.

I never saw a weapon that night. Not before, not after. I didn't even think about it at the time. My only thought was of Claudio—his fear, his worry.

As we lay in bed, trying to fall asleep, I heard the distant sound of a helicopter. At first, I didn't think much of it—our apartment complex was directly across from the hospital, and helicopters weren't uncommon. But this one felt different. It was flying low. Hovering. The sound wasn't fading away like it usually did. Instead, it lingered.

Claudio held me close, his body tense against mine. Neither of us said a word about it. But I could feel it—he felt it too. Something was wrong. I just didn't know how wrong.

Not yet.

The next day felt normal. At least, as normal as it could be. We slept in late, and I went to work for my usual 3–11 shift. Nothing felt off—nothing seemed out of place. I took care of my residents, moved through my routine like any other night. It was just another shift. Just another day.

As planned, Claudio and his cousin picked me up after work. We had already decided we would stay at his mother's house that night.

With Christmas approaching, we wanted to take his little brother shopping, and since he was deaf, Claudio wanted to make sure he picked out exactly what he wanted. I was still battling morning sickness, and since we didn't have a car, staying the night at his mother's house made things easier. His cousin could drive us across town, cutting down on how much I had to walk in the cold December air. It all made sense.

It was a good plan. They got me from work after my shift and took me to a place to get something to eat. That night, we curled up together on a pull-out bed at his mother's house. I wasn't thinking about the previous night. I wasn't thinking about helicopters or heavy bags or the tension in Claudio's voice. I was just happy to be with him. For a few hours, at least, life felt simple again.

But it wouldn't last—because soon, everything would come crashing down.

***

December 14, 1994

At around six in the morning on December 14, 1994, a sharp whistling cut through the quiet. It wasn't random. It wasn't just someone out on the street. It was a warning. I didn't know that then. I didn't understand what it meant. But I would later.

We were in a neighborhood where the police didn't come—not unless it was SWAT. And sure enough, the pounding on the door followed.

The chaos erupted in an instant. Claudio's mother opened the door, and before I could even process what was happening, they flooded in—guns raised, shields up, shouting commands. They ripped Claudio from the bed in nothing but his boxers. I barely had time to react. They didn't touch me, but they had their weapons trained on me.

In that moment, I was just frozen—eighteen years old, pregnant, with guns pointed at me. One of them barked at me to get up. I hesitated. "Can I put my pants on?" "Get up," they repeated. I asked again, my voice calmer than I felt. "Please, can I put my pants on?" Maybe it was the way I asked. Maybe it was the reality of the situation finally hitting them. They agreed, but with one warning:

"Move very slowly." I reached for my pants with trembling hands, my mind racing. Claudio was already gone. And my world was about to change forever.

I stepped outside the apartment, my breath visible in the cold morning air. The SWAT officers who had just been laser-focused on me now seemed to lose all interest. I understand it now—at that moment, they were stepping into an unknown situation in a neighborhood that didn't welcome them. They didn't know what they were walking into. Anyone could be a threat. And for those first few seconds, I had been just another unknown variable.

But once they realized I was unarmed, they barely acknowledged me. I was just there. By this time, all the children in the neighborhood were up. Several of them had been at Claudio's mother's house when this was all happening. They saw guns pointed at me and their uncle being dragged from the apartment in his boxers.

I remember just kind of wandering around, not able to stay still. One officer finally turned to me and asked who I was, if he could speak with me. His tone was different from the shouting and chaos of moments before—more measured, controlled.

He started asking questions. Where had we been the day before? What had we been doing? My stomach twisted. I knew something was wrong—beyond anything I could have ever imagined.

While I grew up going to schools that taught about Officer Friendly and "the police can be trusted," my teenage years showed me differently. My friends came from places the police didn't care about, and they were not a friend of the marginalized. I learned that anything you say can and will be used against you—and I also learned that what you say not only can be used against you, but twisted.

So, I simply said, "We were in Philly." I stuck to where we planned to go, rather than where we actually were. I didn't actually know the full truth. I knew we had been in a car. I knew there had been a robbery after it was done. I knew we had a lot of marijuana. But I didn't know anything beyond that. I hadn't been part of the planning. I hadn't been part of any conversations before or after. But I did know one thing: talking to the police was probably not the smartest move.

I asked the officer if I could leave—if I could just go home. He told me I could—but that my apartment was being searched.

"If they're still there when you get back, you'll have to wait outside until they're done," he said.

Claudio's sister drove me. The ride was quiet. I stared out the window, my mind racing with every possible scenario, every worst-case outcome. But nothing prepared me for what I saw when I stepped into our apartment.

It was as if a bomb had gone off. The sofa was flipped upside down, cushions thrown everywhere. Drawers had been pulled out; their contents scattered across the floor. Closets were ransacked. Every inch of space had been torn apart in their search. But of all the chaos—of all the destruction—one thing stood out the most. A bowl. A spoon. Someone had helped themselves to my cereal. In the middle of tearing apart my home, flipping my world upside down, one of the officers had apparently taken a break to have a snack.

The empty bowl sat in the sink, a few remnants of milk clinging to the sides. The cereal box was left sitting on the counter as if someone had casually poured themselves breakfast before going back to searching for evidence. It was such a small, absurd detail in the middle of something so huge. And for a moment, I just stood there, staring at that stupid bowl of cereal, completely numb.

I don't really remember how my parents found out. I think I had to go and tell them—had to show up and say the words out loud, had to somehow explain that Claudio was arrested and my world had just been flipped upside down.

I couldn't stay at my apartment. It was an absolute disaster. And beyond the physical mess, I was in no place—mentally, emotionally—to even begin to deal with it. I didn't even know if I legally could. Was it a crime scene? Was I allowed to touch anything? Move anything? Clean up the wreckage they left behind? Or was it just my mess now—mine to deal with, mine to sort through, mine to be left sitting in?

I had never been involved in the law before. I didn't know the rules. I didn't know what was coming next. All I knew was that everything had just changed. And there was no going back.

The days leading up to Claudio's preliminary hearing are really a blur for me. I had done some Christmas shopping alone before all of this happened—before my world flipped upside down, before I had to figure out what life looked like now. I had picked out a few things for Claudio. A nice leather coat. A bottle of cologne I loved to smell on him. It was called Incense, and even now, after all these years, I can still remember that scent. But he wasn't coming home for Christmas.

My dad took me to the mall to return it. Claudio was in prison for attempted murder. And his preliminary hearing was set for just before Christmas—December 21st. There was no sense holding onto those things. And that would become painfully clear at the hearing. While Claudio and his cousin were both being held for attempted murder, which was already an incredibly serious charge, everything changed the morning of the hearing. We learned that the victim, Matthew DiMaggio, had died.

I don't know how to explain what that felt like. It wasn't okay. A man was hurt, and now he was gone. I wasn't numb. I wasn't detached. I felt it. Because no matter what else happened, no matter how tangled this had all become, a person had lost their life. And nothing could undo that.

Looking back now, I believe that the out-of-place helicopter we had heard that night—the one that flew low and seemed to linger—wasn't just a coincidence. It wasn't just another routine flight to the hospital across the street. It was him. It was Matthew DiMaggio being transported to a larger hospital, a desperate attempt to save his life. And it hadn't worked.

No one had talked to me. No police questioning. No follow-ups. I went to work and focused on getting through each shift, looking forward to any moment I could talk to Claudio. I was staying at my parents' house, barely leaving. I was incredibly sick—so sick that even the medication prescribed to help with the relentless morning sickness only seemed to make it worse. I wasn't gaining weight. My body was exhausted, my mind was overwhelmed, and I was just trying to survive one day at a time.

***

Chapter 7: Arrested Twice
January 6, 1995

I had the day off, but sometime in the afternoon, the phone rang. It was work. "The police were here looking for you." My stomach dropped. They hadn't come to my parents' house. They hadn't even tried to contact me where I was actually staying. Instead, they walked right into a nursing home filled with elderly residents and started asking for me.

Why?

I wasn't hiding. I wasn't avoiding them. They knew where to find me. But instead, they chose to go there—my workplace, where vulnerable people depended on me, where I had built trust, where I was supposed to be safe. I could understand if they had tried my home and had no other choice. But they didn't. That told me everything. They weren't just looking for me. They wanted to make a scene.

Once I was told the police were looking for me, I didn't wait. I called them. They wanted me to come down to the station for questioning. My dad took over the conversation, asking if he could bring me down around 5 PM. They agreed. He also asked if he could accompany me during questioning. Again, they agreed. At least, that's what they said. We arrived at 5 PM, and I was met by Trooper George Ellis of the Pennsylvania State Police Homicide Division and Detective James McGee of the West Chester Police Department. And just like that, everything changed. They completely lied to my dad. They would not allow him to sit in on the questioning. The rationale? I was over 18. Technically, they hadn't lied—he had been allowed to bring me there. But the moment we walked in, it was clear that was as far as his involvement would go. I was on my own.

During the search of my apartment, they had found the marijuana. The apartment lease was only in my name, which meant that—regardless of how it got there—I was now directly responsible for it. I wasn't selling drugs, but I was close enough to be charged. That's the thing about the system—it doesn't always need guilt. Sometimes, it just needs proximity.

I was questioned for what seemed like an eternity, recorded by audio. Then, I was placed in a holding cell until my arraignment that night.

I remember being hungry. I knew my mom was making lasagna, and all I wanted in that moment was a plate of her food. Of course, that wasn't happening. They weren't about to let me eat while I was in custody, and I was told that I would most likely be released on my own recognizance (ROR) or with no bail. That was something they were truthful about.

I was taken before the district justice, and just as they had said, I was released on my own recognizance. Pending a court hearing on January 24th, I was able to go home.

By this point, I no longer had my job. The nursing home had let me go—it was too much for them to deal with, having someone facing criminal charges working with their residents. People talk about innocence until proven guilty, but the truth is, even before a trial, the punishment begins. I was pregnant, sick, and suddenly unemployable—all without a conviction.

I was incredibly sick. This wasn't just morning sickness; it was an all-day battle. No medication helped. I wasn't gaining any real weight, but my body had definitely changed since the last time I had dressed up.

***

January 24, 1995 – The Court Hearing

You might think I spent every day leading up to this hearing terrified—that I was sick with anxiety, dreading the unknown. But the truth? I was okay. Maybe it was my age, my naivety. Science tells us the human brain doesn't fully mature until at least 26 or later—was that why I wasn't afraid? Or was it just who I was?

My parents, on the other hand, were a nervous wreck. They had no idea how this would play out, but I stayed level. I was concerned. But I also knew I hadn't committed a crime. I hadn't planned this. I hadn't pulled a trigger. I hadn't even known what was happening until it was already over.

My mom handed me a long green skirt, something comfortable but appropriate for court. I don't even remember what shirt I wore. What I do remember is that my mom wanted to make sure I was presentable, that I looked like myself. She believed, just like my dad, that I'd be coming home. How wrong they were.

I felt awful for the family of Matthew DiMaggio. A man had lost his life. A family was grieving—and nothing could ever make that okay or bring him back. I was just confused, and not trying to diminish the loss, but trying to wrap my head around everything. The father of my child a murderer? No. I knew him, I knew his heart. And whatever happened that night didn't begin or end with malice.

I was fortunate. The world needs to be clear about that. I had two parents who worked hard, who owned their home, who were able to remortgage it so they could afford a paid criminal defense attorney. After my first arrest on January 6th, I was no longer on my own. No one was going to speak to me without going through my lawyer.

The magistrate district court was small, within walking distance from my parents' house. My dad and I arrived together. My mom went to work as usual. After all, this was just a hearing, right?

Inside the courtroom, my lawyer, Rob, led me to the right side, where we sat together. My dad took a seat behind me. The state police were there. The local police, too. And as the questioning went on, my attorney's expression changed. He turned to my dad and said words I will never forget:

"You need to take all of her jewelry. I'm getting this over with."

I handed my jewelry to my dad and was taken by my attorney into another room. I was read my charges and my rights, but the whole thing felt like some twisted performance. Trooper George Ellis made the sign of the cross at me and said, "You are now under arrest for the murder of Matthew DiMaggio." My ears rang. I heard the words, but they didn't feel real.

Murder? Me? It was surreal. A spectacle. Almost theatrical in the way it played out. I stood there, absorbing the words, absorbing the weight of what they had just done.

I walked out of the courtroom, handcuffed. My attorney, Rob, was right beside me, but so were the police. The second we stepped outside, cameras flashed. My instinct was to turn away, to shield my face, to make myself invisible. But before I could, Rob's voice cut through everything, sharp and commanding. "Don't do that!"

I froze.

"Hiding your face is a sign of guilt. Look right at the camera."

I don't know if it was fear, or shock, or just sheer obedience, but I did as he said. I didn't hide my face again. I have no idea what my face showed them—whether they saw the fear, the disbelief, the sheer impossibility of what was happening. But I looked. I didn't turn away.

And then, I was led away in handcuffs. In Pennsylvania, pregnant women aren't cuffed behind their backs, and for that, at least, I was grateful. It was a small mercy, but a mercy nonetheless. They walked me out of the courthouse, past my father, past the officers who had been there since my questioning. Past whatever life I had walked in with that morning.

I was placed in the back of the Pennsylvania State Police car. The door shut, locking me in. A trooper—one whose name I can't recall—sat in the back seat with me. He didn't say much, and neither did I.

The ride was mostly silent. But at one point, I laughed. Not out of humor. Not out of joy. But out of sheer disbelief. I glanced over at the officer sitting next to me, and that's when I saw it—his pant leg had lifted just slightly, revealing Bugs Bunny socks. Here I was, accused of murder, on my way to prison, and this man was wearing Bugs Bunny socks. It was ridiculous. Absurd. A moment so out of place in what was happening that my brain just couldn't process it.

Eventually, we arrived at the Media State Police Barracks.

Processing.

Fingerprinting.

Mugshots.

I was handcuffed to a bench, and I sat there for what felt like hours. Time blurred. People came and went. Then, I was transported again.

***

Chapter 8: Jail, Pregnancy and Prison Golds

From Freedom to the Gate

I remember the moment the car stopped outside the prison gates of Delaware County Prison. The check-in. The slow, mechanical groan of the gates as they slid open. The car rolling forward. The gates closing shut behind us. That sound—the heavy, final clang of the metal locking me in—was a sound I would never forget.

Inside, the process repeated. More photos. More questions. I was placed into the holding area. And just like that, my freedom was gone.

***

Stripped and Processed

The holding cell wasn't what people imagine when they think of jail. There were no violent outbursts. No threats. No one trying to start a fight. It was just women, sitting, waiting. Some talking. Some silent. Most of them were older than me. Some asked questions—What are you in for? How far along are you? You don't look like you belong here. I didn't have many answers. I didn't belong here. But it didn't matter. I was here.

After what felt like an eternity, I was taken out of the holding cell and moved to another area. The delousing shower. That's what they called it.

It wasn't about cleanliness. It was about control. It was about stripping you down—physically and emotionally—to remind you that you are no longer a person, but an inmate, a number: 95-0434C

I was ordered to strip. Every piece of clothing I had on was removed. I stood there, completely naked, surrounded by female officers.

Then, the command. "Squat and cough." I hesitated. It didn't matter. They repeated it. "Squat. And. Cough." I did as I was told. A gloved hand hovered beneath me, waiting—checking to be sure I wasn't hiding anything inside me. I had never experienced humiliation like that before. This wasn't about contraband. It was about humiliation. And this is what thousands of pregnant women still face in county jails across the country—many of them pretrial, not yet convicted. The criminal legal system is built to dehumanize—especially for women. Pregnant, traumatized, or not, you are treated the same: like property, not people.

Before all of this, I had been incredibly modest. I wouldn't even go to the bathroom if Claudio was nearby. Even when we made love, I wanted the covers pulled over me or the lights off. He celebrated my body, but I had always been reserved.

My first time in jail was humiliating. Yet, humiliation is the system's first weapon—aimed particularly at women already stripped of dignity through trauma, poverty, and addiction.

Research confirms what I lived; what thousands of people live: incarceration doesn't heal—it wounds deeper. It doesn't solve poverty. It doesn't undo trauma, it doesn't cure addiction, it doesn't offer mental health treatment. It just hides people away and pretends the problem is gone.

There were no blankets. No privacy. No control. Just strangers touching me, inspecting me, breaking me down piece by piece. And I had no choice but to let them. After the delousing shower, I was taken to another area to see the doctor. It was cold, sterile—just another step in the process of turning me from a person into an inmate.

And that word—inmate—I've come to hate it. It strips away everything human. We don't call people "heart attack-ers" or "hospital-ers." But the justice system slaps on a label that defines you solely by where you are, not who you are. "Inmate" becomes your entire identity. And with that one word, people forget you're someone's son or daughter, someone's parent, someone's person. It's a word that erases context, pain, and potential.

Today, we talk about person-first language—saying "incarcerated person" instead of "inmate," "person experiencing housing instability" instead of "homeless." It matters. Because language shapes how we treat people. And inside that prison, I felt how much the language weighed. Back then, I didn't have the words for it. I just knew I was being erased.

They asked questions about my health history, asked for disclosure if I had any transmittable diseases. They took my blood.

They did a quick physical. But none of it was about care. It was about control. No emotion. No warmth. Just checking boxes, making sure I was processed like everyone else.

Then, it was time for the next stop. Before being moved, I was given clothes—a prison uniform that was a deep gold color. It felt heavy in my hands, not just in fabric, but in meaning. The color differentiated me as someone in maximum-security, separate from the general population. We walked past rows of cells—some with solid doors, others with bars. Past the control room bubble, where officers sat behind thick glass, watching everything like security cameras at a department store.

Then, another set of gates opened. This time, I was stepping into a different part of the prison. Inside these gates, the cells lined both sides of a large room. These weren't the solid doors I had seen before. These were traditional barred cells, just like the ones in the movies and TV shows.

***

Miss Betty and the Bunk

I was put into a cell—where I'd be staying for the foreseeable future. I don't call prison "home." That kind of language can quietly speed up institutionalization, and I never wanted this place to feel normal. Experts say it can start in just weeks. You adjust to the noise, the structure, the constant surveillance—and before you know it, it feels safer inside than out. That scared me. I didn't want to settle into it. I didn't want to make it mine.

Even in the short time I was there, I came out different. To this day, I need a fan to sleep. I need some kind of noise. And if I'm sitting still too long, I'm usually fidgeting with something. The system changes you, even when you think you're resisting it.

As crazy as it sounds, I was excited about one thing—the top bunk. My whole childhood, I had wanted bunk beds, but I never had them. So, if this was my one shot, I guess I'd take it. That excitement was short-lived. A pregnant woman can't be on the top bunk. That was not an option. I had a cellmate already occupying the top bunk. She barely moved. She didn't speak. She just lay there, unmoving, like she was somewhere between sleep and death. But one thing did stand out. On her bunk, next to her, was a massive water cooler. Not a normal-sized bottle. I'm talking about one of those bright yellow water dispensers you see at sports games for the athletes. Just sitting there, next to her motionless body.

***

A Life Inside a Life

The first few days were a blur. I kept to myself, not sure what to expect. But then, out of nowhere, she propped herself up. Like she had been waiting for this exact moment. She stared at me, her eyes locked on me as I sat on the toilet. Then, in a thick Southern Missouri drawl, she barked a command: "You haven't shit in three days. That's not good for the baby you have in there. I want you to sit there and shit right now."

My eyes went wide. This half-dead woman, who had barely moved since I got there, was now watching me, ordering me to go to the bathroom. I was too stunned to react. What the hell had I just walked into?

And so, I did. Right there, on the cold stainless-steel toilet with the sink attached to the back, I did exactly what she told me to do.

And when I was done? She clapped. A full-on round of applause. Like I had just achieved something remarkable. Apparently, Miss Betty wasn't as out of it as I thought. She had come in as an overdose. That's why she had that massive water cooler—they were flushing her system out.

Despite her half-conscious state, she was aware of everything going on around her. She knew I was pregnant. She knew I was just eighteen. And she knew—maybe even more than I did at that moment—that I was looking at a long time in prison. Far longer than I even understood.

***

The Move and the Threat

I don't remember the exact reason, but I wasn't with Betty for long. Maybe it was overcrowding, maybe it was something else, but before I had even settled in, I was moved to another cell. The prison was definitely overcrowded. That much was obvious.

I was limited in where they could place me. The end cell closest to the main gate couldn't have a cellmate—she had HIV and was violent. The end cell farther from the main gate also couldn't have a cellmate—she was schizophrenic and allegedly violent. That left only a few options. I had to be in a bottom bunk—no exceptions. And in cells where they were packing three to a room, I also couldn't be on a cot. So, I was moved a few doors down. A new cell. A new routine.

The reality? Nowhere felt like it belonged to me. I didn't feel like I belonged there—locked behind bars, surrounded by women whose lives had already been swallowed whole by the system. But I also didn't feel like I belonged at home—where the weight of everyone's judgment would be just as suffocating. I was caught between two worlds, and I didn't fit into either of them.

Claudio was in the same prison, but on the men's side. In the beginning, I wanted to write to him, but he was my co-defendant, and that was generally not permissible. Any communication between us was a risk, something the prison would never allow—at least not without a fight. But I wasn't going to just accept it. I appealed to the warden, crafting an argument so airtight, so compelling, that I won. I don't have the paper anymore, but I remember what it said. Something along the lines of: "Claudio nor I are convicted of any crime. We are being detained. Therefore, we still have rights. Claudio is the father of my unborn child and should have the right to know what is going on with us. We still have First Amendment rights."

It worked. I was granted permission. But there was a catch. Every letter would be reviewed. Every word we wrote would be inspected. And instead of going through the regular mail system, our letters would be hand-delivered between the men's and women's sides. Even in the smallest victory, we were still under their control.

I was okay with that. I didn't want to talk to him about our case—I had no desire to write about the nightmare we were trapped in. I wanted to share in our pregnancy.

I wanted to tell him how I was feeling, how our baby was growing, what cravings I had that week. I wanted to talk about our love, about the life we had before all of this, about the life I still prayed we would have one day. If they were interested in reading our love letters? So be it. Let them read.

I had no issues with the ladies in there. They all embraced me as their baby. They were protective, and that would very soon become apparent. These older women saw a baby having a baby—a young, first-time mother charged with murder. There's something about being visibly pregnant in jail. Some women saw it as weakness. But many saw it as something worth guarding. A life inside a life.

When I was moved into a new cell, I was with Katie. We got along well and chatted here and there. I would often sit on my bunk with my back against the cement wall, my knees propped up and my feet on the bed. My legs acted as a desk, and I would turn my head to the side for comfort as I wrote.

One day, we got a new cellie, Leah. She didn't say anything, just settled onto her cot. I was busily writing to Claudio in my usual position when I heard a voice.

"I know how you died."

I ignored it, assuming she wasn't talking to me.

Then, again: "Yo! I'm talking to you. Look at me. I said, "I know how you died."

I looked at her and said, "I'm not dead."

She snapped back, "YES! Yes, you are! My boyfriend, the Bluefish, brought me here on a kangaroo to the morgue. You died of a broken neck. You are dead." At this point, I could feel Katie shifting around on the bunk above me. I had never been to prison before, so I didn't think much of it. I just went back to writing to Claudio, ignoring her ramblings. Then, out of the corner of my eye, I saw this woman lean forward and start tying her shoelaces. Katie's legs suddenly swung off the top bunk, as Leah said in a harsh voice, "There's gonna be a bloodbath in here tonight bitch."

Before I could react, Katie jumped down just as Leah got up. She grabbed Leah and growled, "Bitch, the only bloodbath happening here is yours. Sit the fuck down. Amy, get by the gate—NOW!" Katie commanded with a motherly growl. I didn't hesitate.

Suddenly, the women in all the other cells started banging on their gates screaming for a CO. "It's going down in the pregnant girl's cell!" "CO! CO! Hurry up!"

It took several minutes before the officers arrived. They had me step out while Katie held Leah back, then handed her over.

"Get her the HELL out of this cell," Katie demanded.

Katie and I were both friends with Antoinette, another woman on the block. The COs shook their heads. "We can't move her, but we can move you two. Sortino, Katie* (First name used to protect her identity)—you're going over there with Antoinette*(First name used to protect her identity)."

I didn't care where I went, but at least I was going with my two prison "mamas." I wasn't a fighter. I wasn't an antagonist before going to prison. But I would defend myself if I had to. The difference now was that I had a life growing inside me. I wasn't just responsible for myself anymore. And in this place—cramped inside a tiny cell with people I didn't know, with tensions always running high—I had to be more careful than ever.

***

Forgotten by the System

One girl, Shelley, I mentioned earlier, was in the far-end cell. She became schizophrenic after she snorted a line of cocaine that had something in it—something that altered her permanently. She was waiting for a bed in a mental hospital, but in the meantime, she was locked in her cell for 23 hours a day.

When the COs took Shelley out of her cell, they cuffed her while she was still behind the bars, then shackled her before leading her to the main gate. Once they exited through the gate, they removed the restraints and allowed her to shower and walk around the block. No therapy. No healing. Just confinement. That's how mental illness is handled here.

Shelley would stand at her cell gate when we were out on block and ask me to draw her a picture of Tweety Bird. I couldn't draw to save my life, so that never happened—but I still think of her and her simple request.

***

I'm Goin' Home

Every day we heard the excited scream of a woman yelling, "I'm goin' home!" Usually, it happened multiple times a day. For most of us—aside from that first cell—it wasn't a reality. We weren't going anywhere. We knew it. No matter how loud those cries were, they didn't belong to us.

I can't quite describe my feelings during that time. As long as I was on the block or in my cell, writing to Claudio, I was okay. Something about putting pen to paper gave me control. It gave me purpose. But getting on that phone? That was a different story. The second I heard a familiar voice—someone from home, someone trying to check on me, trying to make me laugh—it was like I couldn't breathe. I felt obligated to call. But those calls felt like drowning.

I'm an ugly crier. Absolutely horrible. And I don't cry often. I can carry a mountain of emotion and still manage to keep a brave face. But the second someone shows me care? The second someone tries to comfort me? That's when it breaks.

When I cry, it isn't soft. It's not a single tear rolling down my cheek. It's full-on, can't-breathe, can't-speak, everything-closes-in-on-me sobbing. All boogied up doesn't even begin to describe it. Talking? That's out of the question. I become a blubbery mess of sounds no one can understand—except one person. Claudio. He always knew how to cut through the noise, how to settle me even when my world was caving in. My parents, they could read me too, but they learned early on that the best thing to do was just let me cry it out and then pull myself back together.

But Claudio wasn't there. And those calls? They were expensive. Timed. Limited. There was no space to fall apart.

One day on the phone, my mom said, "We're going to get you out." But the truth was, I didn't want out. I didn't want to be in a cage, but I didn't want to be out in the world either—not where people had seen my name plastered across the front page of the local newspaper. I didn't want to walk through town and feel the stares, the judgment, the whispers.

I didn't want out. Not back into a world where I was a headline, not a person.

***

A Way Out

I was arrested the same day the O.J. Simpson trial started—January 24, 1995. It was national news. O.J. got a small corner at the bottom of the paper. I took up the entire front page.

I'm not sure how it was arranged, but somehow, I was able to go to my own obstetrician. I wasn't seen by the prison doctor. Instead, I was dressed in a bright orange jumpsuit, shackled at the ankles, handcuffed at the wrists, and transported in a prison van. Just like that, I was marched right through the waiting room lobby to my doctor's office.

During the visit, one officer stood inside the room with me, another just outside the door. I wasn't mistreated in any way—they followed their protocols—and I was grateful. At least to my face, my doctor showed no judgment. He was compassionate, professional. And that small piece of normalcy, of dignity, meant everything.

I remember one day my mom brought my grandfather to visit. It was bittersweet. Here was this nearly 90-year-old man—my grandfather—coming to see his youngest granddaughter in prison.

No words for that.

My dad was desperate. And now, as a parent myself, I understand that sense of powerlessness. He contacted the prison and asked if he could provide me some things. They allowed him to bring a bra and a book. I still remember—The Accident by Danielle Steel. That book made me absolutely obsessed with her novels.

Another time, I was out on the block and Antoinette was braiding my hair. In prison, I discovered Dark & Lovely shampoo and conditioner—it worked wonders on my curls.

That day, she spent hours giving me plaits. How disappointed I was to hear I had court and that I would need to remove all the braids.

I realize I haven't told the story of how we met. When I first went into the unit, Antoinette was sitting at a table smoking. I walked up and asked for a cigarette. She took a deep drag, blew out the smoke, and said, "I don't smoke." I paused, unsure, and just said, "Cool, thanks."

She fell out laughing. "Sweetie," she said, "you shouldn't be smoking in your condition, but I ain't holdin' that against you. Here's your Newport." From that moment, that was it. Her and Katie? They became my people. And I was their baby.

One morning when I woke up, I was extra sick. The sickness was daily, but this morning it hit harder. I sat straddling the bench, one foot out, ready to run to my cell if I had to. Katie came over and sat next to me.

She looked at me and said, "What the HELL is going on? You are soaked!" I looked down and realized I was covered in breast milk—my shirt was drenched. She studied me more closely and said, "Man, we gotta get you up outta here. You're swollen. Your arms are swollen, your face is swollen. Baby girl, something is wrong." I was still early in my pregnancy. This was mid-February, and the baby wasn't due until mid-July.

I don't remember a lot of the events from that time—it's all a blur now—but I do remember one thing clearly: I had the opportunity to yell those magic words, "I'm goin' home." But I didn't. I cried. I wanted to go home. I wanted real care. I wanted to feel like I belonged somewhere, but I didn't. Not in that place. And not outside either. I was stuck between two worlds.

As I was getting ready to leave, one of the officers looked at me and said, "Santiago, stay outta trouble." I looked around, confused. I was the only one there. "Sortino," I corrected her. She waved her hand and said, "Yeah, yeah, whatever. You'll always be Santiago to me. Don't let me see you back here."

***

Understanding Trauma: A Reflection Before the Next Chapter

Some people still flinch at the word trauma. They hear it and think it only applies to war veterans, violent assaults, or horrifying accidents. But trauma is so much more than the headlines. It's not about what happened. It's about how your body, your brain, and your heart responded—and whether you had the support to heal.

Trauma is what happens when something overwhelms your ability to cope. And it doesn't have to be loud or sudden. It can be the slow erosion of safety. The quiet heartbreak of being left out, left behind, or never fully seen.

I've lived through trauma that people recognize—like being jailed while pregnant, losing friends to murder, and watching people I love disappear into prison. But I've also lived through the kind that people don't always name. Being blamed. Being silenced. Surviving while no one noticed I was breaking.

Even my son, Sebastian, has lived with trauma. He was born into chaos—monitored, separated from his father, raised under the weight of a system that stole his dad and judged his mom. People see him and think, "He was just a baby." But trauma doesn't care how old you are. His body remembers. His nervous system remembers. And so does mine.

In the late 1990s, a groundbreaking study changed everything. It was called the Adverse Childhood Experiences Study, or ACE Study, and it revealed that early experiences—like having a parent incarcerated, living with addiction, witnessing violence, or being neglected—could shape a person's entire life. The higher your ACE score, the more likely you were to struggle with depression, anxiety, heart disease, substance use, or even early death.

It shook the medical and mental health world. Slowly, the term "trauma-informed" started to appear. Schools. Clinics. Courts. Some prisons even claimed the title. But the truth is, most of society still doesn't understand trauma. We still expect people to "get over it" without ever asking what it really was.

This chapter you're about to read isn't full of action. It's not the courtroom. It's not the prison. But it's still trauma. It's the quiet ache of abandonment. It's the weight of judgment. It's the kind of pain that doesn't scream—it just lingers.

If you've ever told yourself "It wasn't that bad," or believed your hurt didn't count, I hope this gives you permission to look again. Because trauma isn't a weakness. It's a wound. And healing doesn't come from hiding it. It comes from being honest, being seen, and learning that you never had to carry it alone.

***

Chapter 9: The Hollow Peace

House Arrest and The Hollow Peace

I wasn't free. I still had a trial to face, and I was going to be on house arrest with an ankle monitor. But I was out. My parents had somehow managed to get a loan from their small employer, enough to pull together the bail. And that would prove to have saved my life.

Life truly was uneventful. I learned quickly how many friends I didn't have. Out of all the people I knew, only two stood by me. Just two. That was a hard truth to swallow.

I remember running into one so-called friend who said, "You never put me on your list to visit you in there, so they wouldn't let me in." I had to laugh. "I was in Delaware County Prison, not Chester County," I told her. "There's no list. You could have come anytime." That was it for me. I didn't ask why she hadn't come—she just offered up a lie, unprompted. I had too much going on in my life to tolerate dishonesty. If she couldn't own up to the truth, then I didn't need her around.

A Letter Dated February 16, 1995

(I was in the county at this time).

My love, I am so bored. I'm just sitting here watching t.v. I guess I'll go to sleep pretty soon. There isn't much for me to say because nothing new goes on and I have too much on my mind. I will say, I'm sorry if you were upset about anything I've said. I love you. write back soon. I love you. big hugs and soft kisses. bunches love your girl

"I am Free Because You Love Me"

I was lost in a world where shadows fell
Drowning in storms I could never quell.
But then you came a steady light, Turning my darkness into something bright
I now carry more so much more Not just time, but a life to adore.
Our child grows beneath my heart A piece of you though we're worlds apart.
They call us numbers and lock these gates Write our futures in cruel fates.
But they don't know and they'll never see the way you saved and set me free.
Not with keys or open doors but with love that healed my sores.
You pulled me back when I was gone, gave me a reason to carry on.
Now this little soul will know your name Feel your love despite the chains.
And though they say we'll fade in time I know I'll love you for all time.
Through concrete walls and shattered dreams Through days that pass like silent screams
One truth remains, forever true I am free because I love you.

***

I wanted to speak out, but when you're on trial, speaking is dangerous. Instead, I started to think about the future—about the lawyers, about the system, and even about becoming a lawyer myself. Not a defense attorney, but a prosecutor. Everyone needs a good defense attorney, but society needs good and honest prosecutors. Not those molded into the need for convictions, but those who stand by ethics, who want justice, not just wins. Prosecutors who seek accountability without throwing people away. Who won't rely on false narratives or reward the loudest voice with the best deal. Is that really justice for the victim? I didn't know it then, but that desire to work in law—that was my early fire.

I had so much time to think. Too much time. I wasn't just confined to the house—I was confined to every thought I hadn't been ready to face. Every quiet moment became a mirror.

I'd stare at the ankle monitor and wonder how it had come to this. I'd wonder if people thought I was guilty, or if they just didn't care enough to ask. I'd wonder how much longer Claudio could survive in there—if he even believed I was still with him. There were days I'd stand by the window and imagine what freedom felt like without a condition attached to it.

Even then, Sebastian was changing me. Sometimes I'd place a hand over my belly without even realizing it. I would talk to him softly in those quiet moments. I didn't know what kind of world I was bringing him into, but I knew I wanted better for him. And there were thoughts I didn't say out loud: thoughts of what would happen if I went to prison. Would he grow up never knowing who I was? Would it be kinder to let him believe I never existed? I didn't want him living a prison sentence alongside me. At that time, there was no Ancestry or 23andMe. I thought maybe, if I vanished from his life, he could be raised without the weight of having parents charged with murder. But I never considered adoption. I couldn't bear the idea of strangers raising him. Still, the question loomed: who would raise him if I couldn't? That fear sat with me every day.

Before any of this began, I had two anole chameleons—tiny green lizards that usually thrive in warm southern states. They had done well under my care, but after I was arrested, they were forgotten. My mom eventually told me she thought they were dead. She had taken the cage outside in the cold, unsure what else to do. But days later, as she walked by, she saw movement. Against all odds, they had survived. I couldn't stop thinking about it. How had they made it through? They should have died in the cold, but they didn't. That strange little miracle gave me something to hold onto. If they could survive the impossible, maybe I could too.

Yet through all the noise, I learned the silence of abandonment can be deafening. One night, something else broke through the quiet.

***

Interlude One: The Vision

I wasn't someone who went to church. I didn't grow up in a deeply religious household, and I wasn't the kind of person who quoted scripture or talked about God on a daily basis. Even now, I don't claim any specific religion. I've always believed that faith is personal—messy, private, and different for everyone.

So, before I share what happened, I want to be clear: I'm not preaching. I'm not trying to convince anyone of anything. And I know full well that most depictions of Jesus are just that—depictions. Cultural, artistic, symbolic. I get it. I don't pretend to know what's literal and what's metaphor. All I know is what I saw. What I felt.

This moment didn't come from devotion. It came from desperation. I wasn't asleep. I wasn't high. I wasn't mentally ill. I had no diagnosis, no hallucinations. I was completely sober. And yet, in the silence of that night, I saw something—clear as day.

An image appeared on my wall. The devil. He was behind bars and laughing. And then—Jesus. He appeared without warning and pushed the devil aside. I was terrified. Frozen. Jesus looked at me and spoke:

"You will be OK. You and your baby will be OK." Shaking, I asked, "What about Claudio?"

He replied, "You and your baby will be OK. And one day—a long time from now—Claudio will be too. You won't understand until much later why all of this is happening." And then He was gone. I didn't understand. Not then. But I never forgot those words.

Outside my window, I saw them—tiny gold and silver balls of light, dancing. It felt like something sacred had brushed against me and left a shimmer behind. I screamed for my mother, sobbing that I was going crazy. She didn't dismiss me. She didn't panic. She looked at me and said, "No, you aren't. Those are the angels you saw when you were four. And besides, if you were going crazy, you wouldn't know it."

It sounds like something insane—Jesus and the devil on my wall, glowing orbs outside my window. But it wasn't madness. It was something else. It was something profoundly spiritual, deeply personal, and incredibly intense. It happened during a moment of extreme vulnerability, grief, and uncertainty. And it's not unusual for people to have vivid spiritual experiences in moments like that. We talk about mental health now like it's something separate from spirit—but in that moment, the two were inseparable. This wasn't a breakdown. It was a breakthrough of a different kind.

I was eighteen. Pregnant. Heartbroken. Terrified. And something—call it divine, subconscious, ancestral, or spiritual— showed up for me. My mother's words grounded me. She reminded me of a thread from my childhood, a sacred connection I had long forgotten. That moment, however surreal, became part of my survival story. Even if I didn't feel peace in that moment, even if it didn't fix anything, it planted something in me. A quiet knowing that someday— somehow—I would survive.

When I think back on that moment now, I see it through different eyes—not just as the girl who lived it, but as a woman who helps others survive their darkest hours, too.

***

Interlude 2: Meanwhile, in the Papers

While I was seeing angels and screaming for my mother in the dark, the outside world was building a different kind of narrative.

I was eighteen. Pregnant. Sober. Back on house arrest, trying to survive what felt like the unraveling of everything. The media didn't care about the visions, the fear, or the fact that I was still a kid about to become a mother. They cared about names and charges. About headlines.

Here's some of what the public was reading while I was just trying to keep breathing:

"Murder Counts Upheld for Four in Drug Slaying"

"Death Penalty Not Sought for 4 in Motel Shooting"

"Drug Charges Dropped Against Homicide Suspect"

They weren't just stories. They were assumptions—printed in ink, impossible to undo. The world outside had its version of events. But inside my room, angels danced. And I clung to the one thing no one could take from me: hope.

***

Chapter 10: Born into Chaos

Rh-negative?

During this time, I had a few doctor's appointments. Even though I wasn't gaining much weight, things seemed to be progressing. At one visit, they told me I had a negative blood type and would need a RhoGAM shot. Rh-negative means my blood lacked a specific protein found in most people's red blood cells.

If my baby had Rh-positive blood and any of his blood mixed with mine, my immune system could treat it as a threat, like an invader, and develop antibodies that could harm him or future pregnancies. I had never heard I was Rh-negative before, so I questioned them. Since we did not know what blood type Claudio is, it was more pressing to get the shot. If Claudio was a positive Rh factor, which is the most common, the baby could have had either of our blood types. They assured me—even if they were wrong, the shot wouldn't hurt me. But not getting it, if they were right, could cause devastating consequences. So, I took it.

There wasn't a lot going on. I was still in custody, just doing it at home. Every day at 1 o'clock, I called the parole office to ask if I could go outside just to check the mail. My ankle monitor didn't reach that far, and if I went out of bounds, the bells and whistles would go off. After a couple of weeks of this routine, the officer finally said, "Amy, you call every day at the same time. Just go. If you're not back in 30 minutes, we'll send someone out."

***

Blood and Panic

On May 18, 1995, I went in for an ultrasound. The doctor looked concerned. "It looks like you're losing some amniotic fluid," she said. "I don't want you to worry. We're going to go through the weekend and monitor it. You still have a healthy pregnancy, but we want to be cautious. Go home, relax as much as you can, and come back Monday morning."

That night, I went to the bathroom and thought I felt a bit of fluid come out. I assumed it was the baby pressing on my bladder and remembered what they said. I tried to reassure myself. I had a snack and went to sleep, trusting that I could make it through the weekend.

I woke up around 6 AM on Friday, May 19, 1995. I was really hungry. My dad was in Virginia for work, and my mom was getting ready to leave for her job. I always found comfort in my parents' bed, so I asked my mom if I could go lay down in there once she left. I made myself a piece of toast with peanut butter and went upstairs to watch a bit of TV before dozing off. I laid on my dad's side of the bed, the one farthest from the bedroom door. Around 7:30 AM, I felt sick.

But more than anything, I had this indescribable pain that completely overtook me. I couldn't move. I was stuck on my left side, frozen in place. It felt like I was trapped inside my own body. I tried to meditate or focus my mind—anything to distract from the pain. I wasn't near a phone, and of course, we didn't have cell phones back then. I don't know how long I stayed like that, but suddenly, the pain just stopped. And then came the gush. I reached down and my hand was covered in blood.

I jumped up, ran around the bed to the bathroom, and blood was pouring out of me. I tried to stay calm, but how do you stay calm in that? I sat on my mom's side of the bed, staring at the phone, trying to decide whether to call 911. More blood. Back to the bathroom. I grabbed a maxi pad—completely soaked through in seconds. The reality is I should have called 911, but I was already in a bad state and not making the best decisions. I suppose a part of me felt that calling 911 made it real.

I called my mom at work. Just from the tone of my voice, she knew it was serious. "I'll be right there," she said. Then I called my OB. The nurse told me to come into the office immediately. I told her I was going to the ER because I was bleeding heavily. "No," she insisted, "come here first." I hung up and immediately called parole to let them know I was going to breach my ankle monitor. I needed to get to the hospital.

Just as I was walking out the door, the nurse called back and asked how much I had bled. I told her that in just 15 minutes, I had gone through eight pads. "Go. Go NOW. Get to the ER. Someone will be waiting."

***

Labor and Blood Loss

As we were driving, I turned to my mom. "He's not moving. Oh God, I think he's gone." When we got to the ER, a nurse was waiting just like they said. I walked a few steps inside and felt blood pouring into my shoes, literally squirting out from the sides as I took a step. I have never in my life seen that much blood.

They rushed me upstairs to labor and delivery. I was losing so much blood; they couldn't even find a vein. I was light-headed, and the nurses were trying to undress me and hook me up to the monitors. They found the heartbeat—he was alive.

My OB came in to check me. I was only two centimeters dilated. And he was breech. There was no way I was delivering him naturally. To have a natural birth, a woman should be 9 centimeters dilated, and breech meant he was head up toward my heart. A baby cannot be delivered feet first.

My mom sat in a chair by the wall, trying to stay composed. The doctor looked at the monitor. "We're okay for the moment," he said. "We need to stabilize her bleeding. If the baby's heart rate drops below 110, we move." Then came the numbers: 110. 107. 103. Lower. 96, 93, 72…

A nurse knelt by my mom and whispered, "You might want to say something to your daughter. Things aren't looking good." My mom squeezed the chair and said, "It'll be okay. I'll stay right here." I recall looking downward and seeing the blood drain from her face as she went completely pale.

They were already wheeling my bed out when the doctor handed me a clipboard. "I need you to sign consent for a blood transfusion." I threw it. "I'd rather die now than get AIDS," I said. Only months earlier, there had been a national scandal about tainted blood supplies, and I wasn't about to take that chance.

They rushed me into the OR. At 10:02 AM, my son Sebastian* (name has been altered to protect his identity) was born by emergency C-section. He weighed 2 pounds 15 ounces. Sixteen inches long. Breathing on his own. No one could believe he was breathing, as lungs are just developing at 31 weeks gestation.

Just 31 weeks gestation—two months early. They held him up for me to see—black skin, tight black curls, and piercing green eyes. I couldn't hold him. They had to rush him to the Neonatal Intensive Care Unit (NICU). But I remember staring at him and saying, "That baby is adorable… but where's my son?" I'm Italian. Claudio is Puerto Rican. And that baby didn't have the skin tone of either of us.

The nurse laughed. "I've heard fathers say a baby isn't theirs, but we just took him out of you." They laughed. I didn't. I would later learn that it was trauma that caused the skin color difference.

Claudio called. My mom had gotten word to the prison, and his counselor allowed him to make a call in the privacy of their office—not knowing what news he was about to receive. It took him a moment to understand this wasn't a joke. His voice was a mixture of excitement and fear, and all I wanted was for him to be there with us.

My sister—the same one who spilled the beans to my mom about my pregnancy—came down immediately when she found out what was going on. We're ten years apart and have more differences than similarities.

I've always been quiet, no-nonsense, let's-get-things-resolved. She, on the other hand, seemed to live in a state of constant chaos. Not that she was dishonest or manipulative—it wasn't that kind of drama. But there was always some earth-shattering crisis in her world, and anytime you offered solutions, another obstacle would pop up.

Regardless of all that, she always showed up. And this day was no different. She sprang into action and drove down within hours to be with my mom. She even brought a friend I didn't know—nice enough, but she didn't exactly bring peace to an already overwhelming situation.

I was so incredibly alone in that hospital. I had experienced trauma on multiple levels, already facing the weight of a high-risk pregnancy, a murder charge, and now recovering from emergency surgery. My mom was off with my sister, at least that's how it felt to me.

I could barely move. The sheets were cutting into my lower back. I still had the ankle monitor on. I was miserable.

I couldn't see my baby. I was calling for my mom, asking for gummy bears, for comfort, for anything. I wanted Claudio. I wanted Sebastian. I wanted the nightmare to end. But I only had one number to call. So, I kept calling her. Each time I heard "I'll be back soon," I started to spiral. And when she finally arrived, I was a basket case. I was completely beside myself.

I didn't know what was happening with my baby. I still hadn't seen him hours later. Was he okay? Were they lying to me? I was exhausted, blood-depleted, drugged, and emotionally shredded. My mother, watching me fall apart, turned to the doctor and asked, "Do we think she is going through some form of depression or psychosis? Will this baby be safe with her?"

What she said stung. But what the doctor said next, I will never forget. He looked her square in the eye and said, "Your daughter has been through more trauma than most people can imagine. This baby is not going home today or tomorrow—and neither is she. I think we can wait to jump to any conclusions. I would expect that her body still feels pregnant. She is basically a child herself. These feelings are all incredibly normal, and I would say she's holding it together pretty well in spite of it all."

The practice I used had a policy—all pregnant patients had to meet each doctor so they'd be familiar with whoever was on call during labor. I never had that opportunity to meet the man who would deliver Sebastian, and for once, someone I didn't know gave me this relief. He didn't judge, and for the first time in a long time, I felt that someone was actually on my side.

Looking back, I can see that my mother was concerned. I was in a dark place, and I wasn't acting like myself. But at the time, it felt like a betrayal. Like no one was willing to see me beyond the chaos I was trapped in. When I finally began to talk to her again, I asked my mom, "Why didn't you say anything to me?" She looked confused.

"What do you mean?" "The nurse told you to come say something to me… and you didn't." My mom froze. Her face went pale, her mouth slightly open. "How did you know that?" she asked. I snapped, "I was right there, Mom. I heard her! I heard you!"

She stared at me in disbelief and said slowly, "Amy… you weren't in the room when that happened. You were already in the hallway, being wheeled into the OR."

And all I really wanted through all of this was Claudio, our baby, and a darn gummy bear!

My dad returned from Virginia, and we were able to see Sebastian. Seeing this baby, who could nearly fit into my dad's hand, was overwhelming—but there was an instant connection.

Years later, while going through insurance papers detailing the coverage provided during my hospital stay, I saw it in black and white: Several blood transfusions. I was irate. I had explicitly refused the transfusion. I called my mom furious. As it turned out, I hadn't been in any condition to make that decision—and my mom had signed off on it. There were several things that happened in that narrow window of time that could have changed everything.

The NICU at Chester County Hospital was brand new—less than a year old that morning. Had it not been built, my son and I would have been flown into Philadelphia, and the outcome may have been very different.

I had been charged with second-degree murder, facing a life without parole sentence if convicted—but I had been shown mercy and placed on house arrest. Had I still been in Delaware County Prison that morning, neither of us would have made it. And finally—what haunts me still—I "saw" the nurse speak to my mom… when I couldn't possibly have seen or heard it. Whatever you believe, I'm confident of this: Through all of my challenges, there is a higher purpose for me.

***

NICU and Powerlessness

While Sebastian was born breathing on his own, he didn't yet have the swallow reflexes needed to eat. The tiniest baby I had ever seen was covered in wires, tubes, and IVs. He was being fed through a tube in his nose, receiving only two ccs of milk at a time—milk I had to pump. I had an overabundance, so there was no issue there. In fact, the issue became just how much there was. My milk was in my parents' refrigerator and freezer, and it filled the refrigerator and freezer in the NICU, too.

When I was discharged from the hospital on May 22nd, Sebastian was not coming home with me. His projected release date was July 18th—his due date. This was yet another hurdle. Having a baby didn't erase anything. I was still on house arrest. I was still going to trial.

My daily phone calls to the parole office had to start again. I had to get permission to visit the hospital during my lunch hour. The NICU wasn't just a few steps to the mailbox—it was a longer trip, and they wanted a heads-up every time I went. Any time the phone rang—whether in the middle of the day or the middle of the night—I was on edge. We had a few instances when the hospital called to report an issue. Sebastian was doing relatively well, but there were still some touchy moments. I was there as often as I could be, but that was limited to a few times a day because of my situation.

One day, I went in at my normal time, and a nurse who seemed to really take to Sebastian told me I couldn't hold him. She had already taken him out earlier, and now he had to go back into the incubator. I can't express how livid I was. I waited for him to warm up again so I could hold him, even if only for a few minutes. I was glad he was getting human touch when I wasn't there, but this woman knew quite well what my situation was. I suppose it was a power move—or a rush to judgment. I let her know that unless I personally informed them that I wasn't coming in, they could expect me. And if I was there, I expected to hold my child.

As much of a supply of milk as I had well before Sebastian was born, and in the days following his birth, it eventually began to dwindle. A pump just doesn't substitute for the natural process. We participated in kangaroo care, where I would hold him skin-to-skin, even though he was covered in monitors. The idea was that physical closeness would help him latch and signal my body to respond.

But as it turned out, we had to supplement with formula. That became another challenge entirely. Something in nearly every formula didn't agree with him. He wouldn't just spit up—he would full-on vomit after feeding, which was terrifying considering his already small size. Eventually, we found a preemie/neonatal formula that worked. It was a huge relief.

***

Coming Home Early

He began progressing rapidly. By early June, Sebastian was moved to the NICU step-down unit. It was still serious care, but a little less dependent on emergency intervention. And then, well ahead of schedule, I was finally able to take him home. We didn't expect him to be released from the hospital until July 18, so this was well ahead of schedule and such a relief.

On June 21, 1995—Claudio's birthday—Sebastian came home, weighing 4 pounds, 9 ounces. Bringing Sebastian home didn't feel real. He was so small. His legs were so thin and frail, like a twig that had fallen from a tree. He cried so softly it sounded more like the coo of a dove than a real cry. Finding clothes for preemies in 1995 wasn't as easy as it is today, they were just a bit bigger than the diapers you'd buy in the toy section for a baby doll. But he was home. He was mine. He was safe—for now.

But I wasn't free. I was still under house arrest. Still fighting a murder charge. Still walking through a world that didn't feel real.

***

Postpartum Half Caged

The outside celebrated. People sent gifts. My parents did their best to give us both everything we needed. But there was a heaviness around it all. Sebastian was a high SIDS risk, so he was sent home on a heart and breathing monitor and I was taught infant CPR, a constant reminder of how fragile he was. And the clock still ticked toward my trial date.

I didn't have the luxury of slowing down. But that didn't mean I wasn't spiraling. I was absolutely experiencing postpartum depression, only no one called it that. Not at the time. Not around me. The chaos didn't leave space for healing. I wasn't okay, but I had to act like I was.

There wasn't space for fear. I had to be strong—for Sebastian, for myself, for Claudio, who was still behind bars missing every moment.

***

A Visit Without Me

In order for him to see his newborn son, my parents had to take him. I wasn't allowed. I gave birth alone. I brought my baby home alone. And when it came time for his father to lay eyes on his son for the first time, I wasn't even permitted to be there.

Claudio held Sebastian in a large prison visiting room—under fluorescent lights, surrounded by surveillance, with no privacy and no comfort. Despite Sebastian being close to five pounds, he was still on a heart and breathing monitor, and that monitor had to remain on him for the visit.

I couldn't see how Claudio was with him, but I can imagine. I imagine how he would've been with me—how he would have held my hands and really looked at me. Taken me in. Maybe brushed a fallen hair off my shirt.

Maybe it was a mercy I wasn't there. Because if I had been, I probably would've fallen apart. I was already barely holding it together.

This was the man I loved with all my heart. The father of my firstborn. The man I was running through fire with. He couldn't be there. And knowing the kind of man Claudio was—how dedicated he was to me, to our baby, to our well-being—it broke me in a way that still aches.

Despite his own fear, all he cared about was us. I haven't said it before now, but Claudio had a son from a previous relationship. I've always called him my bonus son, and Claudio loved that boy with all his heart.

This book doesn't not mention him to erase him. It's just that, in that moment, I was eighteen. Claudio and I were dead center in a circle of fire with our newborn, very premature, very fragile, and constantly at risk. And the terrifying question was always just beneath the surface:

If we both went to prison, who would take him?

We didn't know what was coming. Claudio and I were both still facing a sentence of life without parole. But for that moment, there was a quiet joy in the chaos. A fragile peace that lived between the sound of my son breathing and the weight of an ankle monitor around my foot.

***

Chapter 11: Thirteen Jurors and a Lie

Our trial began on July 10, 1995. Make no mistake, this book isn't intended to be an attack on the system, judges, attorneys, police or anyone else. It is not intended to bash the system. It is intended to be about the realities of our system which we call the justice system and that is not just the court system but everything that leads up to it.

***

Jury Selection and a Quiet Death Sentence

I remember juror voir dire—the part where a pool of potential jurors gets questioned, and both sides decide who stays and who goes. Some eliminations are automatic. One woman stood up and said she was friends with someone in prosecutor Daniel McDevitt's family. That alone should've disqualified her. Others were trickier. People who had been victims of crime, or who had family in law enforcement, were often dismissed—but not always. By the end, they aim to lock in twelve jurors and a couple of alternates.

One man stood and said, loud and clear, that he opposed the death penalty. McDevitt jumped in fast: "This is not a death penalty case." But here's the truth jurors don't get told—life without parole is still a death sentence. It just doesn't come with an execution date. There's no last meal, no final words—just time, until the end.

And many jurors don't understand that. Research shows that some think a life sentence includes the possibility of parole. In some states, that's true. But in Pennsylvania? Life means life. No second chances. No exits.

Jurors often aren't even told what their guilty verdict will mean. They might believe they're leaving room for rehabilitation. That parole could be possible. But they aren't told that "guilty" means a mandatory death sentence in prison. The Supreme Court ruled in Simmons v. South Carolina that in capital cases, jurors must be informed if life without parole is the only alternative. But outside of death penalty cases? The system stays silent. And silence isn't neutral. It's manipulation.

When sentencing outcomes are hidden from jurors, when we deny them the truth, what kind of justice are we really delivering? Maybe they thought parole was possible. Maybe they would have chosen differently if they had known.

Maybe they'd ask if the evidence truly justified sending someone to die in prison. But the system doesn't encourage understanding—it encourages conviction.

***

Three Trials in One

Our trial was called "three trials in one." The judge insisted the cases be heard together, even though we had three separate defenses. Jurors were instructed to keep them mentally separate—as if that's even possible. If we had been tried separately, things may have turned out differently. If I had been tried alone, the outcome for me might have stayed the same. But I would have been allowed to testify for my co-defendants. At that time, I would've testified for both. But how can anyone have a fair trial with three separate defense strategies tangled together?

Juries are made up of regular people, not legal experts. They're told not to read the news or talk to others about the case—but what guarantees are there that they won't? Prosecutors build powerful, emotional narratives, often acting like it's their own family member who was harmed. But justice shouldn't be about vengeance. It should be about truth. Instead, innocent people spend decades—or lifetimes—behind bars. And even when the Innocence Project gets involved, even when wrongdoing is proven, that time is never given back.

Claudio was charged with first-, second-, and third-degree murder. Jorge and I were charged with second-degree. At one point, there was even talk of trying all three of us with first-degree and seeking the death penalty.

The whole case rested on the word of a known liar—the primary mastermind. He was the one who gave Jorge a gun, told him a shipment of marijuana was coming in, and set up the plan for a robbery. But I will always say there was a secondary mastermind: Jorge Fraticelli, Claudio's cousin. He bought the gun. He brought the gun. He pulled the gun. That doesn't erase Claudio's role. It doesn't erase mine. But it does reveal a deeper truth that too many people have ignored.

Jorge didn't walk out of that courtroom like I did. He remains behind bars. But he's never taken responsibility. In fact, he's built a polished, sympathetic narrative where he's the one who got "swept up" in something he didn't understand. That story has reached advocacy groups, social media, and communities who have no idea what really happened. For years, I said nothing. I figured the truth would stand on its own. But silence lets a lie grow.

So, I'm saying it now: Jorge Fraticelli was not innocent. And I'm done pretending otherwise. His version of events has hurt people—including Claudio and me—and disrespects the family of Matthew DiMaggio. I'm done watching him shape a false reality.

I contacted Jorge in early 2025. I gave him the benefit of the doubt. Maybe he really didn't remember. Maybe he was truly so high that night that he has no actual recollection. So, I sent him court transcripts, the same pages that are in the appendix of this book, to refresh his mind and asked him to tell the truth. I told him once he was willing to tell the truth, I'd fight just as hard for him as I do for others.

He didn't respond. But he has told others, "I won't let anyone bring me down now."

That's not growth. That's selfishness.

As someone who fights for second chances—who knows survivors and has survived herself—I take offense to his disregard. I don't care if someone was the shooter or just the driver. If they've changed, I'll fight for them. But I will not tolerate lies. I won't stand beside someone who won't even own their role.

Here's the truth: Jorge was eighteen years old, just like me. He wasn't some lost kid. He was using drugs, fascinated by guns, and fully aware of the things he was doing. I remember the tiny gun he carried in his pants pocket months before this ever happened, before Claudio was even in West Chester. And while that wasn't the gun, his obsession was real. Jeff testified that Jorge kept playing with the gun that night. And the judge said it best: if Jorge hadn't brought that gun, Matthew DiMaggio might still be alive.

That's not my opinion. That's public record.

***

A Record They Should Already Know

There are thousands of pages of police reports and court transcripts. It's not possible to share every page, but there are some key points that should be reflected. These are pages that Jorge should be well aware of. Pages that the Board of Pardons and the prison should be well aware of.

If they are making accusations of mistruth, if they want to pretend to retry a case without the courtesy of due process, without allowing the people seeking to share the truth the fundamental right to face their accuser, they should look at the bare minimum, which is the testimony of the state witness / mastermind and the sentencing transcripts. I am sharing pictures of these in the appendix for full transparency.

***

Under Oath: Jeff's Testimony

The following are two excerpts of Jeff under oath:

Q: What color was it?

A: Silver

Q: What did you do with the gun after you got it from Joe Lynch?

A: I brought it to West Chester with me.

Q: Okay, for what reason?

A: Well, 'cause one of the times I met Claudio on the street he mentioned to me that he was having a hard time in the neighborhood, that people were trying to rob him and stuff and asked if I knew where I could get a gun, and I said I didn't think—if I saw one or whatever—I really didn't think I could at the time, it was just good timing that I saw it and knew that he needed it. That's the only reason I picked it up.

Q: Did you buy the gun from Joe Lynch or was it given to you?

A: He gave it to me under the impression that I'd pay him in a couple of weeks or something.

Q: Did you ever pay him for it?

A: No, I never got a chance to pay him.

Q: Now you had some discussions with Claudio Manzanet about a gun. What happened to the gun that you got from Joe Lynch?

A: Well, I took it back to West Chester with me, and I saw Jorge, and I told him, I said if Claudio still wants a gun, I got one. I wanted to trade it for some drugs, and then Jorge told me to follow him, and I followed him back to the Seven Oaks Apartment, and that's when Claudio wasn't around. I don't know where he was, and Jorge says yeah, he wanted it for sure, and Jorge got it off of me and gave me like 20 bucks or something, and he said he would give me some coke for it later.

Q: Where did the actual exchange of the gun take place from you to Fraticelli?

A: At Seven Oaks in the apartment.

Q: Whose apartment?

A: Amy's apartment.

Q: Was anyone else present other than you or Fraticelli?

A: No, Amy was home at the time but she didn't see what was going on. We were in the back room.

Q: Now in relationship to the incident that happened at the Sentinel Motel, when was it that you gave the gun to Fraticelli?

A: About a week or two before that. About two weeks before that.

Q: Now from the time that you gave the gun to Fraticelli until the incident of the night at the Sentinel Motel, the morning at the Sentinel, did you see either Fraticelli or Manzanet in possession of that gun?

A: Yeah, the night of—I guess you said the early morning of when all that happened.

Q: That's the next time you saw it?

A: Yeah.

Q: And who had it then?

A: Jorge had it.

Q: Where was that at?

A: It was at the apartment, Seven Oaks.

Later in his testimony:

Q: Did you have a conversation with either Jorge or Claudio in that room?

A: Yeah.

Q: Would you tell the Court what the conversation was about?

A: I told them that the pot was there and I most definitely knew it was there, and where it was, the hotel and all, and just small talk besides that.

Q: Well, was there any kind of plan formulated when you were there?

A: He—Jorge—was playing with the gun and I told him we didn't need a gun, that he shouldn't bring a gun, and he kept talking about bringing it, and then he was playing with bullets, and then I told him just don't bring a gun at all. Before we left, I was telling him just don't bring a gun at all, and, you know. I was scared about—I knew nobody had a gun there and I told them that.

Q: Describe exactly what you saw Jorge doing with the gun when you say he was playing with it?

A: He was holding it and, you know, putting bullets in the clips and taking them out, and...

Q: Was he saying anything while he was doing that?

A: He just said how much he liked it, that's all.

Q: He thought it was a cool gun?

A: Yeah.

Q: Did you recognize the gun you saw him with?

A: Yeah, it was the same one.

Q: What do you mean it was the same one?

A: The same one that I traded to him a couple weeks ago.

Q: The same .22 Smith and Wesson semi-automatic?

A: Yes.

Q: Now about how long were you in this room having this discussion or conversation with either Claudio and/or Jorge Fraticelli?

A: At least a half an hour. A lot of the time it was just Jorge and myself.

Q: Well, on the occasions when it was just Jorge and yourself, where was Claudio?

A: He was outside the room.

Q: Okay, could you see where he was going?

A: Yeah, he would go like watch TV and hang out by there.

Q: And approximately—about how many times did he leave the room leaving you and Jorge in the room alone?

A: Several times. He would just come in and say, you know, what's up and go out.

***

Weapon, Blame, and the False Narrative

He's told organizations he was the poor kid who got caught up with bad people. That Claudio brought the gun. That he was just scared and high. He's even tried to use my attorney's arguments post-trial. But none of it is true. And I won't let him keep shaping that false narrative—especially when it still impacts my life.

I've had incarcerated people approach me over the years trying to "ask questions." Pretending it was innocent curiosity. But I saw through it—just like I saw through Jorge when we were eighteen. Maybe Jorge doesn't know how aware I am. But I'll share this: he was seeking sentence commutation and met with the Secretary of the DOC. According to what I've been told, the Secretary said, "I'm surprised Amy Sortino wasn't convicted." Jorge's response? "I can't believe it either."

That wasn't thirty years ago. That was recent.

I stayed silent about Jorge for too long. I fumed. I hoped the truth would speak for itself. But it didn't. And now, I am done letting his version stand unchallenged. His lies have consequences. I'm done allowing him to pretend his role was "peripheral." I'm done watching him posture for sympathy while denying the truth.

When I work with the people inside, they know I care more about who they are today than who they were. Whether they were the primary, the driver, or the lookout, I see the full human. But if I won't tolerate lies or manipulation from strangers, why would I tolerate it from someone who still impacts my life? And yes, Jorge still impacts my life. As long as he refuses to tell the truth, both he and Claudio remain trapped. And that's what makes me angriest—his lies aren't just self-serving, they hurt other people. People I love.

I should have gotten out of the car that night. I had no idea any crime was going to happen. I had no role in planning, I was in the back seat, I do not speak Spanish so I had no clue. I did choose to stay in the car, despite Claudio telling me to get out. I was pregnant, insecure, and afraid Claudio was going to meet other girls. But if I had listened to him, if I had gotten out of that car and said, "Don't come home if you leave," I believe he would've followed me.

I believe Jorge would've been alone with his gun. And maybe—just maybe—Matthew DiMaggio would still be alive. If I hadn't uttered those three words months before, maybe—just maybe— Matthew DiMaggio would still be alive.

I own that, I live with it and I will forever be sorry. I just wonder when Jorge Fraticelli will own his central role.

Claudio had a public defender with almost no time to prepare. Jorge had a medical malpractice lawyer—someone completely out of his element in a homicide case. His lack of courtroom experience frustrated my attorney to no end.

I remember my lawyer whispering during trial, "If these idiots don't stop with their nonsense, I'm burying your co-defendants." And every time, I begged him, "No. You can't."

Before I went to trial, the prosecution offered me a deal: testify against my co-defendants, and I would serve five years at SCI Muncy. "You'll be home in time to see your baby off to kindergarten," they promised. I declined. Then they offered full immunity—total freedom—if I testified against them.

My attorney called my mom, filled her in, and then asked me. When I was offered full immunity, my reply back was, "Tell Danny to shove any deal where the sun don't shine. I'll be in court."

My mom cried. She loved Claudio. But I am her daughter. She didn't want me to hurt anyone, but she wanted her youngest child safe from a system she never knew to be so callous.

I was angry. I didn't drive the vehicle. I had no intention of lying to save myself. If standing for the truth meant facing a life sentence, then so be it. Even though my lawyer refused to let me take the stand, it was my decision not to take a deal.

I would not send others to prison to save myself.

But standing for the truth didn't mean I was given the opportunity to tell it. It meant resisting their version of events, refusing to bend to their narrative, and holding my ground under the very real threat of spending the rest of my life behind bars. There was no scenario in which I would have been allowed to take the stand, no moment where my words would have changed the course of the trial.

My only choice was to endure—to stand firm in silence, knowing that my fate had already been decided by forces beyond my control.

As twisted as it sounds, I would have rather my child been raised by my sister or even my mother, allowing him a chance at a normal life, than to have him visit his mother in prison for five years or—God forbid—a lifetime.

I am far from a perfect person, but I have morals, I have values, and there has never been—nor will there ever be—a time when I would sacrifice others' lives for the sake of my own.

I wasn't powerless against just the system, with its woven narrative and its reliance on an admitted mastermind and liar. I was also powerless against my own attorney—a man with decades of experience who had one job: to save me.

Those who are on trial have rights. You have the right to be silent, the right to testify, and the right to face your accuser. But those rights only go so far when your own lawyer decides what's "in your best interest." Once you take the stand, nothing can be undone. Pleading the Fifth may be legal, but it often looks like guilt to a jury.

My attorney wouldn't let me testify. He said they'd rip me to pieces. Yes, I was grateful to have someone who fought for me—but I also felt like he saw me as just a naive girl with no say in how my life was defended. I had no voice. No power. No control. Maybe he was right. But not being allowed to speak—being silenced by the very person defending me—was oppression.

Because even when everything was on the line—even when it would've helped me—I couldn't bring myself to harm them. I couldn't lie to save myself. I wasn't going to take a deal. I couldn't play their game.

The courtroom wasn't built for people like me to speak. It was built for people to speak about me. Around me. Over me. But not to me.

The prosecution used theatrics—like bringing in an empty gun case. No weapon was ever found. But that case was introduced, quietly planting seeds of doubt. It never had to be explained. It just lingered.

Even after the jury acquitted me, the judge couldn't resist making a final dig. At sentencing, he said, "Ms. Sortino knew what was going on... she was fortunate, I guess, that a jury saw otherwise."

That line has haunted me. Not because it held truth—but because it didn't. I wasn't allowed to testify. I wasn't allowed to speak. And yet here was the judge, declaring what I "knew" as if he had been inside my head. As if the truth was his to dictate. I had no voice in that courtroom, but somehow, I was still blamed.

That's what people don't understand—an acquittal doesn't erase the harm of being accused. It doesn't protect you from the weight of a judge's opinion. That one sentence stayed with me for years. And it's part of why I speak now—because I didn't get to then.

Most people—even lawmakers—don't realize how easy it is to be convicted of second-degree murder in Pennsylvania. You don't need to hold a weapon. You don't need to cause a death. You just need to be nearby when someone else does. Another reality? There doesn't even need to be evidence against you. The word of an admitted liar is evidence enough.

If someone dies during a robbery—even of a heart attack—that's second-degree murder. If you hand someone a flashlight during a break-in, and someone dies? That flashlight becomes your life sentence. That's the felony murder rule. And that's what happened to us.

It doesn't matter if you didn't know. It doesn't matter if you didn't want it to happen. It doesn't even matter if you tried to stop it. If someone dies while a felony is in progress, everyone involved is punished the same.

And in Pennsylvania, that means life. No parole. No second chances. Just death by incarceration.

I can live with the consequences of my actions. I have. I've owned my truth and rebuilt from the ashes. But what I will not do is stay silent while others rewrite history to protect their image or gain sympathy under false pretenses. There's another reality at play. If you can't admit you played a role, if you minimize what you did and you are given a second chance, what will stop you from repeating the same behavior? And this is exactly how the Parole Board or Board of Pardons will view things.

Here's the kicker, that application process, the Board, they only want the narrative they have been given, what the courts have said. So, when a person like Claudio is telling the absolute truth, they would rather what was written decades ago than actual closure for the family of the victim, they are making it more difficult for all involved by not accepting that things are not always as they may seem.

If we want a system based on truth and rehabilitation, then we have to be honest about our pasts—even the worst parts. We don't get to cherry-pick which parts of the story we tell. We don't get to pretend we were innocent just because we don't like the way the truth sounds.

For years, I tried to protect Jorge by staying silent. I thought I was doing the right thing. But silence enables lies. And lies destroy lives.

So, this is me—finally—saying everything I couldn't say back then.

Not for revenge.

Not for attention.

But because the truth matters.

Because growth demands honesty.

Because justice demands clarity.

And because my son, Claudio, Matthew's family—and even Jorge—deserve a truth that isn't bent, buried, or bought.

***

Chapter 12: Acquitted, Not Innocent – Part One

My two Hispanic co-defendants were found guilty and sentenced to die in prison. I sat through that trial. I heard all of the evidence—or lack thereof. I heard the primary witness consistently put the gun in our co-defendant's hands, yet they kept pushing it onto Claudio, who was older and had a criminal record, versus our co-defendant, who was just eighteen.

It seemed they took the easy way out. To get a conviction, they didn't go for the truth—they went for the easiest possible win.

The mastermind testified that he was facing 27 ½ to 55 years. The reality? He was sentenced to two years. Let me repeat that. A man planned a robbery of a large amount of marijuana, had a stolen gun which he sold to Jorge Fraticelli for a few dollars' worth of drugs, set up his so-called friend to take the marijuana, went back to the motel to clean up a mess, patched bullet holes, then went to the police to point fingers. He pointed to Claudio and Jorge, and his story consistently changed.

It seems his deal kept getting better and better as his story evolved. It took over 30 days to even name me as a person. The jury was under the impression that he would serve significant time in prison.

This was misleading—and if proven, it would constitute prosecutorial misconduct. The reality? Delaware County is hiding the records.

There is documentation of when the deal was made and what it was, but they refuse to furnish it, claiming the records are "limited access." How? The law clearly states that only non-violent offenses can be marked that way.

There's something called a Brady violation. That's when the prosecution knowingly withholds information that could have changed the outcome of the trial. Well, post-trial, we became aware of a psycho-social evaluation showing that Jeff was so high the night of the crime he was in a drug-induced psychosis and couldn't distinguish reality from hallucination. How did the court respond? "Too late." It couldn't be used on appeal.

So, let's lay this out. One man planned the entire thing, provided the weapon, claimed he faced 27 ½ years, and was shown by a psychological evaluation to be in a drug induced psychosis—yet he got the deal of a lifetime. He's been home for 28 years.

The Australian national who smuggled the marijuana across state lines, and who could never positively identify Claudio in any lineup, only did time in county prison before being deported after the trial.

He also could never positively identify Claudio. In fact, in the courtroom, he pointed to a blown-up picture of Jorge Fraticelli as the shooter. He described Jorge Fraticelli but when asked if he could point to that person in the courtroom? He pointed to Claudio, who had very distinct tattoos, which his lawyer had him hide from the jury at trial.

Everything I'm stating here is public record (except the pieces the county has chosen to withhold). Whether it's trial transcripts, docket sheets, or sentencing records—it's all there. I've always wondered about my jury. Did they question any of it? Do they have any idea what really took place? If you happen to be one of my jurors, I welcome a conversation. And since I was acquitted, it wouldn't violate any law.

***

Deliberations and Verdict

The verdicts were read. They went in alphabetical order, so Jorge was read first, Claudio second, and me third. Jorge and Claudio received guilty verdicts.

When they got to me, I was acquitted on all charges. Each "not guilty" slammed into me like a freight train. I wasn't sure I even heard them right at first. Then I saw Claudio's face—the devastation written all over it—and I knew it was real. My knees nearly gave out, and I briefly blacked out onto the shoulder of my attorney.

I was acquitted. Free. But Claudio wasn't. The man I loved—the man who stood by me, who fought for me in his quiet, steady way—was found guilty of second-degree murder and related counts. He would be sentenced in September to die in prison.

The gavel came down, and so did my entire world. The system had split us apart in ways I couldn't have imagined. It told the world he was a monster and that I was a survivor. It told the world he was beyond redemption and I was redeemable.

It was a lie. And it was a lie I had to live with.

Claudio never showed an ounce of anger toward me for my acquittal. Not once. He told me he loved me. He was relieved that at least I wouldn't be trapped behind walls. But I carried the guilt like a second skin. I still do.

During deliberations, I recall a juror asking, when they came back with a question regarding the case, "If we hurry up and get a verdict, can we get out of here?" That's how important three lives were to the jury... getting their time back. They didn't deliberate for weeks or even days. Twelve people who didn't know us, who had barely looked at us during the trial, now held our lives in their hands.

***

Sentencing

Claudio's sentencing was set for September. I wasn't required to attend. I wasn't even supposed to be part of it anymore. But in my heart, I couldn't stay away. He wasn't just a case number or a defendant. He was the man who had held my hand when no one else would. The man who fought for my soul even as the world tried to erase him.

I sat in the back of the courtroom, quiet, unseen. The judge handed down the mandatory sentence: life without parole. No chance of freedom. No second act. No acknowledgment that people can change, that one moment doesn't define a lifetime.

I watched Claudio stand there, absorbing a punishment that would never end. No matter what anyone said, no matter how much time passed, that day changed both of our lives forever. The justice system didn't just take his future. It took mine too.

The world thinks it's easy to separate yourself from someone after a conviction. They think it's clean, black and white, guilt and innocence. But love doesn't work that way. Truth doesn't work that way. Nothing human does.

Claudio was gone, but he was still with me—woven into my DNA, into every step forward, every breath I took. I had survived the trial. But surviving the aftermath was something else entirely.

***

Jorge Fraticelli

Now let's talk about Jorge Fraticelli. I want to be clear—I hold a lot of disgust toward him. He's one reason I'll never step foot inside SCI Phoenix as an advocate. He is the main reason the father of my son—an amazing man who dedicates his life to helping others—may never come home. Not just for the 30 years he's already spent inside, but through the entire commutation process, and in any potential future legislation involving second-degree murder.

Don't get me wrong—I know this was a horrible tragedy. I know that better than anyone. I also know it was a preventable tragedy. I don't believe Jorge wanted anyone to die. I believe he was a young, immature punk who used drugs and may not fully remember what happened that night. But to put the blame on everyone else? To lie to advocates and groups who fight for justice? That's where I draw the line.

Despite my disgust, I do not believe Jorge should spend the rest of his life in prison either. It was not intentional. I'd back him on that in a heartbeat. But if he cannot take responsibility, then maybe he needs to sit down and think—really think—about all the lives he helped destroy and continues to this day to harm.

***

The Weight of Acquittal

I was acquitted of all charges and allowed to live my life in society—but what does freedom really mean? The shadow of this case has followed me for 30 years.

I walked out of the courtroom legally free, but there was no celebration waiting for me. No hugs. No high-fives. No parade of victory. Just a quiet exit, like I was slipping out the back of a nightmare I never agreed to enter. The courtroom let me go, but the judgment never stopped—not from the people around me, not from society, and certainly not from myself.

Everywhere I went, my name followed me. It lived in whispers, in awkward handshakes, in the way people tilted their heads when they recognized me from the news or courtroom sketch. People assumed I got away with something. That I was lucky. That I had somehow slipped through the cracks of a system built to destroy. But they didn't see how hard I fought to survive. They didn't see the cost. They didn't know how close I came to losing everything.

And Claudio? He didn't walk out with me. He was convicted—life without parole. The father of my son would never come home. Life without parole isn't just a sentence; it's a slow death. It denies the truth that people can change, that healing is possible, and that redemption matters. And that truth haunted every moment of my so-called freedom.

I was acquitted. Claudio was not. That reality still haunts me. My name may have been cleared in court, but I never stopped carrying the weight of what happened—my three damned words said months before any of this, his sentence, the silence that followed, the relentless injustice. The system let me go, but it kept him. And nothing about that has ever felt like justice.

I had to keep going. I had a child to raise. A life to rebuild. But everything felt like it came with an asterisk. I wasn't just Amy. I was Amy who'd been on trial for murder. Amy who walked free when others didn't. Amy who some believed shouldn't have walked at all. Every birthday, every holiday, every milestone our son reached—Claudio was missing from all of it. And I could never forget why.

***

Staying Connected

After Claudio was convicted, he was processed into the Pennsylvania state prison system and sent to SCI Camp Hill, where every incarcerated man starts—evaluated, categorized, and eventually placed. I don't remember how long he was there before being transferred to SCI Mahanoy, but that's where we would have the most visits.

I don't even remember the first trip to SCI Mahanoy. Maybe I've blocked it out. Maybe it was too much to hold onto—the weight of everything, the emotions, the exhaustion of being a new mother.

All I know is, those visits became part of our life. Me, Claudio, and this fragile little boy between us, doing our best to hold onto something that was never meant to survive inside prison walls.

Sometimes I made the trip with Claudio's sister, other times with my mom. The drive to SCI Mahanoy was long, especially with a baby. Sebastian didn't handle it well—he'd cry, get sick, or be overstimulated by the time we arrived. The visits took a toll on all of us, enough that when I went with my mom, we'd often stay overnight in a hotel just to break the trip up. What should have been a day visit turned into a two-day event.

Prison isn't made for children. And it certainly isn't made for families. But it was the only place we could see Claudio. Mahanoy did have a small play area for children and vending machines to get food to share. There was nothing natural about it.

Walking through security, holding my baby to go see his father who would have to watch us leave without him. Sitting in a fluorescent-lit room with guards watching, emotions carefully restrained. The walls were painted in soft colors, maybe to make it feel less harsh—but it didn't matter. The reality couldn't be softened.

Sebastian would cry. Or sleep. Or just cling to me. Claudio tried to stay present, to hold it together—to smile and savor the time, pretending, for a few hours, that we were just a family spending time together. But prison doesn't allow you to be a family. Not really. It doesn't just steal years—it steals moments. The ones you can't get back. The ones you can't recreate in a room filled with rules and echoes.

We tried to hold onto each other through letters, phone calls, and photos. But the truth was, I was raising our son on the outside, and Claudio was learning about him through secondhand stories. He missed everything—the first smile, the first steps, the first time he said "mama." And I missed having someone to share it with. I was doing it alone. Still tethered to Claudio through love, but separated by steel gates, watchful eyes, and a sentence that didn't belong to either of us.

I tried to hold on. But things became hard—harder than I expected. I wanted to help him. I wanted to fix it. But the world was not on our side.

People didn't want us together. Even those closest to me whispered in my ear, filling my head with doubt. The pressure from both sides was relentless. Claudio had people in prison telling him I'd move on. I had people on the outside telling me I needed to let go. Every visit, every phone call, every letter was another battle against the world trying to tear us apart.

***

The Loss That Broke Me

In 1997, everything changed. My neighbor was murdered. It wasn't just any neighbor—it was a boy I had grown up with, someone who looked up to me like a big sister. He was only sixteen years old, his life stolen in an act of senseless violence. The grief was unbearable. It wasn't just a loss; it was a trigger—a moment that made me reevaluate everything.

For years, I had fought to help Claudio. I had loved him, believed in him, stood by him despite everything. But now, the loss of the boy I called brother—combined with the pain of not even being allowed to attend his service because of my past—broke me. People believed I had something to do with his tragic death. Another pain. Another judgment.

I looked at Claudio the way the world did. Not as the man who had saved me from addiction, not as the person I loved, but as just another murderer behind bars. I hated myself for thinking that. But I couldn't stop it.

I remember one of the last times I visited Claudio in prison, still trying to hold onto something between us despite how much the world had changed. I was angry, broken from the loss of my friend. The grief had hardened into rage, and in my pain, I let it consume me.

"If you ever come across the people who did this," I said, my voice shaking, "have someone kill them." The words left my mouth before I could even process them, and the moment they did, Claudio looked at me like I had become someone he no longer recognized. It was the first time I saw true disappointment in his eyes—not because of the system, not because of the trial, but because of me.

He had always been my protector, my savior, my best friend. But in that moment, I realized I had let the darkness win.

Claudio—the man the world labeled a murderer—was horrified by what I had said. And that was when I truly saw the gap between who he really was and how the world chose to see him.

Despite my darkness, I knew Claudio to his core. I knew him—but I couldn't separate the two truths. That moment showed me how easy it is to absorb what society teaches us: that a conviction erases a person's complexity. That once someone is labeled, they're no longer allowed to be seen in full. That's what we do to the incarcerated—we strip away who they are and lump them into one faceless category.

Even though we had already begun to grow apart, this was the moment when the final break started to form. I wanted nothing to do with anyone in prison.

I couldn't separate Claudio from the people who had taken my friend. The idea of fighting for him, of advocating for someone convicted of murder, felt impossible now. My heart was still tied to him, but my mind had begun to drift far away.

I was raising our son. I couldn't work for a full year after Sebastian was born due to the SIDS risk, but I went back as soon as I could. I was no longer home 24/7, and people were telling Claudio I was moving on. That wasn't true. I was falling apart, but there was no one else. He was my heart.

***

Breaking Point

Despite being together outside the prison walls for less than a year, Claudio and I had stayed connected through years of separation—letters, visits, and phone calls. But I was falling apart. Slowly. Quietly. I was breaking into a million pieces.

I was still living with my parents, working full-time at a jewelry store, and trying to raise our son. I wanted nothing more than for the nightmare to be over—for Claudio to come home, for us to be a family. But life wasn't playing fair.

Inside, Claudio was hearing whispers. That I was moving on. That I wasn't loyal. People were feeding him stories, twisting the truth. And the truth was: I wasn't moving on. I was falling apart.

Then came the man from my past—a longtime acquaintance, someone Claudio had always disliked. He wasn't a partner, not in the romantic sense, but I suppose I clung to him because he knew me at my lowest. He had been the one to call and tell me of my friend's murder. He heard my screams of despair. Maybe I needed someone who had heard that pain up close.

One day, he asked to borrow my car while I was at work. I knew better. I gave it to him anyway. He didn't come back.

He stole it.

I called my friend Carlo for a ride home. He couldn't help search, but he got me home. I went out alone, on foot, searching until I found my car and the man. I cursed him out and left. Sebastian was with my mom in New Jersey. I thought it was over.

It wasn't.

Weeks later, I was home with Sebastian and a close girlfriend when the same man knocked—then barged in. He refused to leave. "You're taking me to the airport," he said. "Or I'll slice your fucking throat." He rifled through drawers, looking for a knife.

My friend quickly grabbed my son and got him out of the room. I stayed calm and said, "I'll Walk. Just don't let my son see anything." He walked me outside, the knife low at his side.

My friend followed with Sebastian, strapped him into the car seat, and jumped in. It wasn't the smartest idea to have Sebastian in the car, but she couldn't stay at my parents' house either.

I wasn't in any frame of mind to call the police for help, nor did I trust them. I still lived by the street code—the unspoken rule that you don't snitch, you don't involve the cops.

We sped toward the airport. I drove over 100 miles an hour at one point. I couldn't believe this was happening with my baby in the car. I dropped him at the gate. I didn't wait to see if he boarded a plane. I didn't care. I just wanted him gone.

I never told Claudio.

We were still together, technically. But I didn't see the point in explaining. I felt like I'd been loyal through everything: fire, prison, judgment. If he couldn't trust me by now, what else was there?

The visits grew tense. The love was still there, but it was buried under grief, fear, and broken trust. The last time I saw him, I said: "You're throwing me away. You're listening to people who won't even be there in five years. Ten. They don't love you like I do. But if that's what you want—fine. You'll never see or hear from me again."

And I walked out. Without looking back.

It was the unraveling of something that was once so strong—not because of a lack of love, but because of everything life had thrown at both of us. The pain of being doubted, the exhaustion of always having to prove myself, the weight of grief and judgment and trauma—it all pulled us further apart.

And somewhere in all of it, I was just trying to survive.

***

Spiraling

There was a time—after the trial, after Claudio was sentenced, after I had Sebastian—when everything in me came undone. I wasn't raised in church. I didn't pray before bed or attend Sunday services. But when I was pregnant, I had a vision. It happened in my bedroom.

I wasn't high. I wasn't hallucinating. I wasn't dreaming. I was fully sober and wide awake when I saw something I still can't explain—Jesus and the devil, right there on the wall. Jesus told me everything would be okay. That Claudio would be okay too. And I believed Him.

But the years passed, and nothing felt okay. Claudio and I were falling apart. I was raising a baby alone. I was drowning in shame, grief, and exhaustion. One night, I walked across the street from my parents' house—forty in hand, pills already in my system. Not enough to end it, but enough to numb the pain.

I sat down in the field and looked up into a clear, silent sky. The air didn't move—not even a breeze. I begged aloud, "Show me you're real. Show me something. Anything. Come back." I stood up and screamed into the night, threw my nearly empty forty, and cried until my body gave out and I collapsed in the grass.

I wanted a sign. A crack of thunder. A sudden wind. A flicker in the stars. Rain from a cloudless sky. Anything. But nothing came. And that's when I quit God.

I didn't stop believing because of logic. I stopped because of silence. People love to say God doesn't give you more than you can handle, but I was already past my breaking point. And the God I had once seen in my bedroom—the one who promised I'd be okay—felt long gone.

Somewhere around late 1997 or early 1998, I wrote Claudio a poem. Something I probably never sent:

Without You, But Because of You

They unchained my hands, but not my soul.
Left me standing, half, not whole.
You saved my life, yet lost your own,
Now I walk free, but I walk alone.
The world is wide, but it feels so small.
Every shadow, I hear your call.
They say I should heal, that time will mend,
But how do I breathe when I lost my best friend?
I see the old path, calling me near,
A whisper of numbness to quiet the fear.
But I remember your hands, steady and strong,
Pulling me back when I had no song.
I owe you more than a shattered goodbye,
More than these tears that refuse to dry.

You gave me life when I wanted to fall,
So I'll keep fighting through it all.
Not just for me but for the love we knew,
For the child who carries a piece of you.
I am lost, I am breaking, but I still stand,
Because you saved me with your hands.

***

The Prison After Prison

Before this—before the car was stolen, before I lost control—I had mostly stayed home. I didn't go out much. I worked. I raised my son. I kept my distance from anything or anyone that might tip me over the edge. But this was the point where I finally broke.

Maybe I had been good at hiding it from my family. Maybe I was good at fooling myself. But I started going out. Drinking. A lot. I drank more and more.

I had met Carlo through another acquaintance, and he quickly became a dear friend. When he first met me, I think he had an interest, but I wasn't there for that. Friendship was all I could give. No more, no less. He became my unlicensed therapist—someone who listened to every mad ramble and knew just how broken I truly was. If I was going out to drink, he was driving. That was non-negotiable. He made it clear: there would be no drunk driving.

He became my safe ride home. All he ever wanted in return were pastelillos, and his only rule was "no green olives." I can't tell you how many nights he gave me space to just be—the shattered, unraveling mess I had become. He wasn't a negligent friend; he was just helpless in the face of someone falling apart in slow motion.

He knew I still loved Claudio—deeply. That nothing could take that from me. But he also knew that nothing could ever be the same again. So, he did what he could. He watched out for me. He made sure no one got too fresh. He got me home safely. He let me fall apart, but never let me completely fall.

One night, though, he snapped. "Jesus Christ, you HAVE to straighten up," he said. "Or I'm going to find Claudio and somehow, he's going to get through to you. You drink too much. You're killing yourself."

I was furious. How dare he bring up Claudio? Claudio was mine. No one else had the right to speak his name—not like that. For better or worse, Claudio was off-limits.

Carlo was the support system I needed at the time. The person who made sure my son didn't end up with a father in prison and a dead mother. And he stuck around—until things started to move too fast.

Another poem I wrote—undated, but likely from around this time:

Why Not Me?

I swore I'd stay strong; swore I'd hold on.
But I caved, I'm gone.
Bottle to my lips, fire down my throat. A taste of the past in a poison coat.
I feel nothing, just empty air. Numb hands, numb heart, too much to bear.
They said I'd be free, that I'd start anew. But what is freedom if it's not with you?
Why not me? Why did fate decide? Why did they open my cage while you're trapped inside?
I'd trade this sky for the cell they gave. Lie down in your place, take your days in my grave.
I need your voice, your steady hands The only one who understands.
Tell me this pain has an end somewhere. Tell me you'd still be proud I'm here.
But we haven't talked not in days, not in weeks
You don't even know how deep this cuts how much I need.
I yearn for you, but shame keeps me still. I trade the coke for the drink and the pills.
No one sees me, no one knows, not even my mother, who claims every woe.
She takes the pain and makes it her own. Never leaving space for me to mourn.

Only you know me, the real me, the raw truth. The scars, the weight, the shattered youth.
You saw me drowning and pulled me through, and now I'm alone, without my rescue.
You think there's another, that I let you go, that my heart has wandered, that I've lost what I know.
But there is no other, there never could be, only you because you are everything to me.
I thought I could fight to get you free but I am so broken. How can I fight let alone win?
Will you even love me when I bring you home again? I'm not who I was, I don't like who I am.
I'm slipping, I'm breaking, I don't understand. Would you see the girl you once believed?
Or just a stranger too lost to retrieve? I need to know before I drown.
If I could save you, would you still want me around?
Even in this wreck I've become, I know my heart still beats for one.
For you only you, through all this pain My love for you has never changed.
I love you in the way the sun meets the sea. Bound, unbroken, destined to be.
No walls, no time, no fate could erase, the love that still holds me in your embrace.
I swear, I swear, I'll find my way, I'll fight through the dark, push past the haze.
I'll try to pull myself up, break through this pain. My heart is broken, my shame runs too deep,
The weight of it all is too much to keep.
I want to fight, to bring you home, But I am too lost, so I leave you alone.
I let the world take me, I let myself fade, buried in silence, in choices I've made.
I want to save you, but I can't save me, So I let you go… while you still need me.

***

Interlude: The Shifting Ground - Spiraling Forward

There's a strange kind of grief that comes when you survive something you thought might kill you. A strange kind of loneliness when you walk free but leave part of yourself behind. The world outside expected me to be grateful. To move on. To rebuild. But survival wasn't triumph—it was hollow. It was standing in the rubble of everything I loved, unsure which way to step. And every time I tried to step forward, the ground shifted under my feet.

I missed Claudio. I hated Claudio. I wanted to fight for him. I wanted to forget him. Some days I dreamed of visiting, of holding his hand across a cold steel table. Other days, I swore I'd never set foot near another prison again.

Grief isn't linear. Healing isn't clean. And love—real love—doesn't vanish just because life rips it apart. For a long time, I floated between two worlds. The one where I was a survivor. And the one where I was still bleeding inside.

I wasn't sure where I belonged anymore. I only knew I wasn't done. Not with the past. Not with the future. Not even with him. I didn't fall all at once. It was piece by piece. Some days, I held it together just enough to fool the world. Other days, I couldn't even fool myself. I was still going to work, still raising my son—but inside, I felt like a ghost in my own life.

I missed Claudio every time I breathed. I hated what was happening to me, and that I couldn't fix any of it. The loneliness was deafening. I had pushed away the man I loved, and I wasn't even sure he would want me back.

I was haunted by the courtroom, by Claudio's sentencing, by the way the world kept moving forward—by the sense that everyone else got to live peaceful, ordinary lives while I carried the weight of a story no one wanted to hear. I couldn't bear the guilt of being free while he remained caged.

Eventually, I stopped writing. I stopped visiting. It wasn't out of cruelty—it was out of pain. I convinced myself that if I let go completely, maybe I could heal. But letting go of someone who shaped your very survival isn't healing. It's amputation.

They said I should grateful. That I had my freedom. That I had my child. But freedom didn't feel like freedom without Claudio. It felt like wandering. Like pretending.

Like smiling when your heart is still in handcuffs. Even as I tried to rebuild, something in me remained broken.

And no matter how much time passed, no matter how far I drifted, a part of me still whispered his name.

***

Chapter 12 – Part Two: The Wrong Kind of Attention

One day, I got incredibly sick and needed a prescription filled. I looked awful—sweatpants, messy hair, and a pale face—but the pharmacy tech flirted with me anyway. I hadn't been with anyone since Claudio, and I guess I enjoyed the attention.

Later, I told a friend about it. She called the pharmacy and asked the guy if he remembered the sick girl with the long curly hair. He said yes. "Give me her number," he told her. And that's how it started.

What seemed innocent quickly turned into something much darker. At first, Rick was charming. Smooth. Attentive. I was drawn to the validation, to the feeling of being wanted. But after we moved into an apartment together at 5th and Venango—in the heart of North Philly's Badlands—his true nature emerged. Our home was attached to the back of Rick's father's business. Locked gates. Barred windows. Once inside, it felt more like a prison than a home. And it became one.

Rick was violent. Not immediately—but inevitably. First, it was controlling words. Then isolation. Then fists. At 5'5" and 125 pounds, I was no match for him. He was nearly six feet, 190 pounds, and all rage. The bruises weren't always visible. But the damage—the damage ran deep.

And still, I stayed. Not because I didn't want to leave, but because Rick made it clear what would happen if I did. He threatened me often—but the worst was the threat no mother should ever hear: "If you leave, I'll kill your son." He didn't scream it. He didn't make a scene. He said it calmly, coldly, like it was a fact. And I believed him. I had experienced enough death and loss to know the danger wasn't just words. But no one would hurt my son. Not while I was alive. I would have died for him without hesitation. And if staying meant keeping him safe for one more day, then I stayed.

***

The Prison Inside the Walls

Rick didn't hit me right away. Abuse rarely starts with fists. It starts with words. With rules. He told me who I could talk to. Where I could go. What I could wear. He made me feel like I was lucky just to be loved. And I believed him.

When the physical abuse started, I convinced myself it wasn't that bad. I had survived worse, right? I had survived a murder trial, survived raising a baby alone, survived being judged and abandoned. I could survive this too.

Survival, though, isn't the same as living. I wasn't living. I was trapped. No one saw it. Or if they did, they didn't say anything. I had become an expert at hiding pain.

***

The Threats That Kept Me

Rick didn't need to scream for me to understand the danger. He didn't need to punch a wall or throw a plate. He only needed to speak—calmly, coldly, like he was stating a fact. "If you leave, I'll kill your son." That was the line. And it worked. Because I believed him. I had already experienced enough death, enough loss. I didn't think he was bluffing. And I wasn't about to test it.

But the cost of staying wasn't just bruises or broken ribs—it was the slow, internal bleeding of who I was. And the more afraid I became, the more I started to disappear.

***

The Blood on the Stairs

I didn't really have friends. Most people from my past disappeared after the trial. The two who stayed were living their own lives, and our friendship was the kind that could go a year without talking and still pick up where we left off. Carlo had been a real friend—he called several times—but I was afraid to answer.

No one truly knew what was happening. I was at that age where I didn't see my parents daily. They knew where I was living, and Sebastian was with them more often than not. He was safe. I went to work. I commuted an hour each way to keep my job at the jewelry store. If I was late getting home—stuck on I-76, trapped in traffic—I paid for it. Physically.

One day, we pulled up to our apartment and saw a man lying on the steps. The deep red paint on the stairs looked wet. I remember how it glistened—thick and dark, like fresh blood. "Oh my God," I said. "Is that man dead?" Rick and his friend jumped out of the car. They poked him with their feet. He didn't move. Then they started kicking him—and stole his wallet. I screamed for them to stop. Later that night, I was beaten badly for challenging Rick's "way of getting money."

That day marked a shift in me. Not the kind of shift that leads to action—not yet. But something inside me cracked. Watching them rob a man who might have been dead—or might have died right after—and knowing I lived with someone capable of that without remorse… it shattered another piece of whatever will I had left.

Rick was a textbook abuser. He told me, more than once, that if I ever left, he would kill my son. And I believed him. I had already experienced enough loss. I didn't think he was bluffing. No one would hurt my son. Not while I was alive. I would have died for him without hesitation. And if staying meant keeping him safe for one more day, then I stayed.

I suppose my parents were getting an idea of what was going on. They reached out to Claudio. They even sought an attorney to get partial custody of Sebastian—not to take him from me or from Claudio, but to prepare. It wasn't if something happened to Amy. It was when. They wanted to be sure their grandson wouldn't end up a product of the system. They promised Claudio it wasn't to take Sebastian from him. And they meant it.

But as I was unraveling further—more fearful of Rick—I was afraid. Afraid that if Rick found out Sebastian had seen Claudio, there would be more issues. I was separating further. From them. From Claudio. From myself. I still have a letter from Claudio. He had no idea what was going on. I'm strongly paraphrasing here, but he said something like, I hope you're not letting anyone put their hands on you. You're better than that. I know you have a boyfriend, but there's no reason for him to be jealous. He has you, and I don't. Any real man would respect that the father of their girl's child wanted to be present. I'm not a threat.

The reality is—I wanted Claudio. Every day. Especially on the days I took a beating. Even if he hated me, I knew he would have marched into that house, picked me up, and gotten me out. But I also didn't think I deserved to be rescued. I had a death wish. I didn't care what happened to me. But no one—no one—was going to hurt my son. Not while I was breathing.

This wasn't a relationship. This wasn't survival. This was rot, and I was living in the middle of it. I still stayed. Not because I wanted to, but because I didn't know how to leave. Because every time I thought about it, I remembered his threat: "If you leave, I'll kill your son."

***

The Rules of Survival

Abuse teaches you rules—unspoken ones. Rules that shift constantly, that you only learn by bleeding. I didn't learn them all at once. I learned them through trial, through error, through bruises. Don't laugh too loud. Don't talk to the wrong person. Don't wear the wrong thing. Don't have opinions. And above all—don't make him feel small.

When a friend cut my hair above my shoulders, Rick lost it. "Your hair is too short!" he screamed, as if I had committed some betrayal. Another beating followed. That's how it worked. Every change in appearance or behavior was a risk. I stopped being a person and started being a mirror—reflecting only what he wanted to see.

I learned to watch his moods like the weather. I could feel a storm coming before a word was spoken. I could sense when a joke would be taken as disrespect. I became hypervigilant, calculating every move, every word, every silence. These were the rules of survival: Stay small. Stay quiet. Stay hidden. And never forget the stakes.

***

The Day I Could Have Died

One night in March 1998, I told Rick I needed to go home because my grandfather was dying. As if the situation wasn't hard enough, my sister-in-law called, berating me for not being there to help. "How selfish can you be?" she snapped, completely unaware of the nightmare I was living in. The guilt weighed on me. But even if I wanted to leave, I couldn't. Rick didn't care. His response was to lift me off the floor by my throat, split my lip, and sexually assault me. Then he told me I wasn't going anywhere.

For months, I lived in constant fear. The beatings. The control. The isolation. Every day was a gamble. Every night, a battlefield. I never knew which version of him I would get, or how long I'd survive it.

And then, one September day, it got worse. Rick lost a video game and blamed me. He dragged me into the kitchen and slammed my head into the counter so hard my vision blurred. Before I could react, his fists connected again and again. I tried to shield myself, but it was useless. He had too much power. Too much rage. When I collapsed, he kicked me—my ribs, my back, my head. Anywhere he could reach. Then he grabbed me by the hair and dragged me down the cement stairs into the locked driveway.

The bricks tore into my skin as he slammed my head against the pavement. I felt myself slipping away, unsure if this was the moment it would all end.

By some miracle, Rick's father was walking up the block and saw everything from the other side of the gate. He fumbled with the lock but couldn't open it. In a panic, he ran through his shop, out the other door, and screamed at Rick to stop. Rick wouldn't. His father had no choice. He pulled out his legally registered gun and aimed it. "If you don't stop, I will kill you." Rick finally froze—panting, sweating, a monster caught in the act. I barely registered the moment. I was in and out of consciousness. My body was limp from exhaustion and pain. Rick's father didn't waste time. He yanked his son away and turned to me.

"You can't stay here. He'll kill you,"

***

The Escape

Rick's father led me inside, sat me at the small kitchen table, dampened a clean rag, and handed it to me. "You need to clean up. Your parents. You need to call them." I wanted to move. To respond.

But I was numb. The weight of everything was crushing me. Then he said something that jolted me awake: "Before you go, I want you to get a hit in. He hurt you so bad, I want you to take a shot." Rick was sitting on the toilet.

I stormed in and punched him twice in the temple. It wasn't the smartest thing to do, but for a moment, it gave me back a sliver of power. I didn't wait to see his reaction. I turned away, walked out of the bathroom, and never went back.

Walking away that day didn't erase the fear. It reminded me of something I'd seen not long before when an older couple was driving down 5th Street in a brand-new Mercedes. They were well-dressed, clearly lost—and they had no idea how lost they really were. I was coming out of the bodega when they rolled down their window and asked for directions. I yelled, "Lock your doors, roll up your windows, I'm coming!" I was relieved they'd asked me—someone with no ill intent—but I was terrified for them. It doesn't take long. If you don't live there, and you're not there to pay into the local street economy, you're a target. They were no exception. From the corner of my eye, I saw the guys coming—looking for their next opportunity.

I was holding back tears as I gave them directions as fast as I could: "Put your windows up, keep your doors locked, go. Roll at the stop sign—do NOT stop. Get to the red light, make a left on Erie, then a right on 9th, and get the HELL back on the highway. Don't stop until you're out of this area. If you need more directions, stop at a gas station—up there, not here. Please, just go." Of course, that was another beating in store for me. But there was no way I was going to stand by and watch that couple get robbed or worse. It was what it was.

When my parents arrived to get me, it brought another level of fear. I felt relatively safe knowing Rick's father had my back, but he couldn't defend me—or them—from everything. They didn't belong in that neighborhood. And by then, neither did I. At that time, they were all I had: my mom, my dad, and my son. As they sat waiting while I loaded the few things that mattered, I was terrified.

On the way home, my dad asked why I hadn't told them how bad it had gotten. There was no answer that would make sense. No way to explain how someone who had once been strong had been broken into pieces over time. How I had no care for myself. How I truly didn't feel like I deserved better.

Back at my parents' house, I barely moved. My body ached and was swollen. My ribs were bruised. Every breath reminded me of what had happened. But for the first time in a year, I was safe.

Safe, but not free. The nightmares started immediately. Every time I closed my eyes, I was back in that apartment. Back in that driveway. Feeling his fists. Hearing his threats. Sleep didn't come easy. And when it did, it was filled with panic. My body was healing, but my mind was still trapped. Trapped in the aftermath. Trapped in the silence. Trapped in the shame of what I had endured.

And on top of that—I was still emotionally entangled. I was the girl who stood trial accused of murder. I loved a man convicted of murder. I carried such rage toward the man I had once loved so deeply he didn't even know it. I wasn't present in his life anymore, and the more I fell apart, the more I wanted to see him. But the more I knew I couldn't let him see how broken I was.

The destruction didn't stop when I walked out of Rick's apartment. I carried it with me—into the sunlight, the silence, the pills, the people, the places that felt like escape but only dragged me deeper into the dark. And Rick wasn't going to let me go quietly. He started showing up at my job at Lord & Taylor, lurking just outside. Security always saw him. I was always escorted to my car. But for months, I wondered—what about the times I wasn't under the watchful eye of the cameras?

***

Changing Course

At the end of October 1998, I took the test for my GED and enrolled in a technical vocational school. I had to find a way forward. I started in an associate degree program for Computer Systems Technology, focused mostly on hardware repair.

But the program was new, and no classes were available during the times I needed. I was offered a free audit course in Network Engineering instead—and it turned out to be a better fit. I switched programs, trading the degree path for a diploma. Ironically, I earned more credits than required for an associate degree and ended up receiving two diplomas instead.

I was balancing school, work, and motherhood. On the surface, I was doing everything right—but something was still missing. There was a lingering emptiness that no diploma or job could fill. I wanted to feel something—anything.

Despite my progress, I hadn't shaken the habits that once numbed my pain. The emotional scars from Rick, from the trial, from years of feeling broken—they hadn't healed. I had survived things that should have killed me more than once.

So many women in prison are survivors of trauma, just like me. Some killed their abusers—something I could have done. Even as I fought to build a future, I was still haunted by my past. I didn't just want to live—I wanted to feel alive.

Before graduation, a group of friends from school planned a weekend trip to Rehoboth Beach. It was meant to be a break from stress, a chance to escape reality, even just for a night.

The plan? Get high on the beach and forget everything else. I had been talking to a guy—nothing serious, just someone I spent time with. He was part of the group going to the beach, and for once, I looked forward to something not tied to survival or obligation.

The night started like any other. We sat in the sand, talking, laughing, letting the sound of the waves fill the silence between us. I took ecstasy, chasing a sense of euphoria, connection, release. And for the first time in years, I felt it.

I ran my fingers through the sand, mesmerized by how it slipped through my hands, each grain textured and alive. The ocean waves moved in time with my heartbeat. Everything felt magical. The sky, the breeze, the hum of the moment—it was all overwhelming in the best way.

Then someone passed around a blunt. I took a few hits, unaware of how the mix would hit me.

Suddenly, everything shifted. The magic turned to panic. My heart raced. My body overheated. I started vomiting—hard—and couldn't stop.

The guy I had been seeing vanished. But one friend from school stayed with me the whole night, holding my hair back, keeping me safe, making sure I didn't choke. Making sure I didn't die.

I don't remember much beyond that. Just the sunrise, and the clarity it brought: if things had gone worse, would anyone have cared? Would they have left me?

That question stuck with me. I had craved connection, but now I saw how alone I really was. After that night, I tightened my circle. I kept only the people I trusted. But the need to feel hadn't disappeared.

Most of my free time was spent with my instructor and his longtime girlfriend. We took ecstasy, blasted music that felt like it shook our souls, and escaped.

We'd do each other's hair, dress up, laugh at things that weren't funny. It was temporary happiness. A break from reality.

One night, I tried to return to my old ways.

I had an 8 ball of cocaine—3.5 grams. I sat at a small table, ready to snort a line, and stopped.

Claudio. Always Claudio.

Even in his absence, his memory shined through. I remembered the power he gave me the day I flushed that 20 bag from my shoe.

I didn't touch it—just tasted a trace off my finger, testing purity. But I didn't use. Not really.

Somewhere deep down, I knew this wasn't sustainable.

I was a mother during the week, but weekends were mine—and I knew that eventually, one of those weekends might take me away for good. A part of me believed Sebastian might be better off without me. But an even smaller voice inside whispered: *you're all he has.*

My parents were amazing, but aging. His father was in prison. He had no other family.

And then came the night everything changed.

We got high like usual—music, food, laughter, escape. I stayed over, as I always did, planning to head back to Sebastian in the morning. I went to shower while my friend was in the bathroom, doing her hair. I still felt the ecstasy, but this time, it wasn't right.

I stepped into the shower. The curtain had fish on it. Suddenly, they started moving. The entire room spun. I leaned against the wall and slid down slowly, a deep, guttural sound escaping me as everything went black.

When I came to, I was in bed, my pulse faint, my body limp. My instructor had rushed in after his girlfriend screamed for help. He threw something over me to cover me and carried me out, panicked, trying to cool me down, hydrate me, keep me alive.

That moment changed everything. It's one thing to chase a feeling. It's another to nearly lose your life trying to find it.

I was done. Maybe not all at once. Maybe not with some dramatic declaration. But something inside me shifted that night. I wasn't going to die for a feeling.

***

False Stability

By May 2000, I was done with school. I had spent the past two years balancing full-time classes, working multiple jobs, and raising Sebastian—exhausted, stretched thin, but standing. I earned two diplomas, one of them summa cum laude. I didn't walk across a stage or toss a cap into the air. I just kept moving forward because I had to.

Not long after graduation, I was offered a job at a large regional bank. It wasn't glamorous, but it was professional. Steady. A path forward. I needed a fresh start—something completely new. I didn't want to be anywhere near the places that reminded me of Rick, the trial, or the life I had barely crawled out of. So, I moved to South Philly, to a quiet neighborhood called Girard Estates.

I shared a house with another woman and her daughter. It was a comfortable setup—having another adult in the house made things feel a little less lonely, and our children got along well. My housemate had a traumatic past of her own and was in recovery, so there was no alcohol in the house.

That wasn't an issue for me.

I always had an odd reservation about drinking at home or drinking alone—I just didn't do it. Any alcohol in my kitchen was only for cooking or dessert recipes. It felt like a fresh start, a step into independence with a built-in support system.

The neighborhood was different from anywhere I had lived before—rows of houses, tree-lined streets, and a sense of community that felt unfamiliar but safe. I loved walking Sebastian to school in the morning, riding the subway to work, and coming home to a peaceful block where families looked out for one another. On the surface, everything seemed good. But inside, I still felt alone.

Not a day went by that I didn't think of Claudio. I had spent years trying to push him out of my mind, trying to move on. But he was always there, always a part of me. I enrolled Sebastian in St. Monica's School—not because we were Catholic, but because it was safe. That's all I ever wanted for him. Safety. Stability. Something I hadn't known since childhood, but was determined to give. We had what looked like a real life, but the past never completely let go.

***

The Phone Call That Never Came

One day, on impulse, I reached out. And Claudio called me back. I remember sitting on the stairs of that little house when I heard his voice again.

It hit me like a wave—love, sadness, guilt, anger. I still missed him. Still felt connected. But I never told him.

I waited for his next call. It never came. Years later, I found out my housemate had been taking his calls and telling him I wasn't home. At the time, I had no idea.

***

September 11, 2001

I was working in a Philadelphia skyscraper when the news broke of the September 11th terror attacks. Planes had crashed into the Twin Towers. The subways shut down. No one knew what was happening. Panic swept through the city.

I had to get to my son.

At his school, parents were lined up in fear. We were less than a mile from the oil refineries. A nun blocked the door, insisting the children were safer inside. My rage exploded.

"That is my son. You are not keeping him here. If you want to dictate what to do with a child in a crisis, then have your own—oh wait, you chose not to! Now give me my son!"

By the time we made it home, another plane had gone down in Pittsburgh. My father called, begging me to leave the city. Hours later, after sitting in traffic, I arrived at my parents' house—only to be reminded why I had left.

My mother was drinking. An argument exploded. I turned around and left. My housemate had also fled the city. I was alone. Philly had never been so quiet. No planes. No cars. Just a stillness I hadn't felt since childhood. And with that silence came the memories. The loneliness. The weight of it all.

***

A Step Toward Independence

When things began returning to some kind of normal, my housemate and I finished our lease and parted ways. I moved to a house just two streets over—this time, alone with my son. Another step toward full independence. Another attempt to rebuild on my terms.

The house was mine. The responsibility was mine. For the first time, I was creating a home just for us. The change was bittersweet. While I had more control over my environment, the sense of isolation crept in again. The ghosts of the past didn't care where I lived. They followed.

***

Searching for Something

While I had given up ecstasy, I hadn't stopped searching. I just traded one escape for another. I drank—boy, did I drink. Not every day, but weekends were mine.

During the week, it was Vicodin. Small pills. Small relief. I still showed up for work. I took good care of Sebastian. I paid the bills. I smiled when I had to.

My parents adored Sebastian, and most weekends they took him, giving me space to live freely—or self-destruct quietly, depending on how you looked at it.

By 2000, I was 24 years old. I had a stable job, a beautiful little boy, and just enough freedom to destroy myself without making headlines. I wore normalcy like armor, but inside, I was unraveling thread by thread.

I had a good friend who lived in Delaware County with a spare bedroom. That's where I spent a lot of weekends. Sometimes we'd all go out to a bar, dance, lose ourselves in the music and the noise. But more often, it was just a small group of us—my friend, his girlfriend, and a few other close friends. People who understood trauma. People who didn't ask too many questions.

My friend had been through things too, and he had one non-negotiable rule: if I drank, I didn't drive. That bedroom was mine. The door locked. No one came in. I was safe. At least physically.

He didn't know everything. He had a vague idea about Claudio—that he was in prison, that I still cared—but I didn't open up much. If the subject came up and made me uncomfortable, I shut it down with a look or a joke or a sudden need to grab another drink or go play a round of beer pong.

This was more of a party house, yet it was a safe place. One night, we all went out with a group of friends. I had started taking shots before we even left the house. That night, I didn't pace myself. I didn't care. Something had triggered me—I couldn't have told you what—and by the time we got back, I was a mess. Sloppy drunk. Sitting on the grass. Vomiting. Trying and failing to keep it together.

And then, for the second time in my life, another friend looked at me—really looked at me—and said, "My God, I don't know the man, but I'm going to find a way to talk to your son's father. You are killing yourself, Amy." And for the second time, I snapped.

"Don't you dare."

It was strange—the way people who truly cared about me could see what I refused to face. Somehow, they knew Claudio was still the only person who had ever truly gotten through to me. Even from the outside, they saw that his presence—his influence—still mattered. That he still had that power. And the truth?

They were right.

As much as I wanted to hear his voice, to feel the grounding calm he always brought—what I really wanted was impossible. I wanted him to magically appear, to sweep in like some twisted fairy tale, throw me over his shoulder, and say, "That's enough. You're done. You're going to stop this."

But that was a dream. A fantasy I clung to when the silence became too loud. It wasn't even about romance anymore. It hadn't been for a long time. I loved him, yes—but what I missed was something deeper. I missed the way he saw me. The way he showed me I could be strong, someone worth saving. He had been my best friend. My anchor. The man who saw through every mask I wore.

What I really wanted wasn't love—I wanted redemption. I wanted to be fixed. I wanted him to fix me. I wanted the father of my child to grab me by the shoulders and say, enough. Be better. Do better. For him. For us. For you.

And if something came of that—if we found our way back to each other—so be it.

I wasn't chasing a relationship. I was chasing a version of myself that had slipped through my fingers. A version I wasn't sure I could ever get back on my own.

Deep down, I didn't believe I could fix myself. And a darker truth whispered beneath it all: maybe Sebastian deserved better than what he was born into. A better life. A better start.

And maybe that didn't include me.

***

A New Connection in an Unexpected Place

By late 2001, I had moved into my own home with Sebastian. Life, on paper, looked stable. I had a steady job, a routine, and full control over my environment for the first time in years. I was finally standing on my own. But still—something was missing.

The past hadn't disappeared, and neither had the loneliness. It was quieter now, woven into the background, but it lingered. It always did.

That's when I decided to try something I had never done before: online dating.

Back then, it was still considered odd—even experimental. But I was curious. I had spent so many years avoiding relationships, not because I didn't want love, but because I wasn't sure if I could handle it. I didn't even know if I could feel it. But something inside me wanted to try.

That's how I met him—a police officer who worked for a major city college. The irony hit hard. A man who wore a badge. A man trained to enforce the same system that had swallowed up Claudio. It felt surreal, like I was flirting with the enemy. And yet, I was intrigued.

Despite everything that should have made us incompatible, there was a strange, easy connection. He was confident, polished, steady. There was no label, no expectations—just something new to explore. And at that point in my life, that was enough.

I was drawn to the structure he represented. His routine. His clean-cut world. He didn't seem haunted. He wasn't burdened with ghosts. I wanted to believe I could live in that world too—that I could belong there. That I could be someone different. Someone who didn't flinch every time a past memory came knocking.

But it didn't take long for cracks to appear. Our time together became predictable. Always on schedule, never spontaneous. I wasn't his girlfriend. There was no commitment, so I had no place to question things. Still, I couldn't ignore the feeling that I was just one of several options. That I was being kept in rotation.

Then one afternoon, he was cleaning his service pistols—calmly, routinely, like someone washing dishes. When he finished with one, he looked at me and said casually, "Hold this while I clean the other." I laughed, half-nervous, half-freaked out. "I don't know if I can touch that thing," I said. "I have an arrest record." He stopped, turned, and asked, "Were you convicted?" "No," I replied, suddenly feeling twelve years old again. He nodded without hesitation. "Then that's over. It's in the past."

Just like that.

His response stunned me—not because it was profound, but because it wasn't. No judgment. No hesitation. No deeper digging. Just acceptance. Coming from a cop, that moment struck something in me. He, of all people, could have seen me as damaged goods. But instead, he gave me a glimpse of something I hadn't let myself imagine in years—maybe, just maybe, I could move forward.

Christmas of 2001 came, and I found myself at his house surrounded by his friends, a few members of his family. I felt like an outsider, but not in a painful way—more like someone visiting a life she might have lived in another universe.

We exchanged gifts. I remember being surprised by how much he spent on mine. It was a normal evening. The kind of normal that had once felt out of reach. And for a moment, my doubts faded.

But the illusion didn't last.

***

The Holiday Illusion

I tried reaching out, worried something had happened—he was a police officer, after all. My mind jumped to the worst: a shooting, an injury, a tragedy. Days passed. Then weeks. Then months. Silence.

And then, just like that, he called. "Hey, come over," he said, as casually as if we had just spoken the day before.

I should have slammed the phone down. Demanded answers. But I didn't. I had nothing else going on, and part of me—the lonely, wounded part—still wanted to believe in something. So, I went.

He welcomed me like no time had passed. No explanation. No apology. Just expectation. It took everything in me not to scream. I kept the peace. I played along. It was all just a strange time. I liked this guy—but it wasn't love. I wasn't introducing Sebastian to him, and even if things worked out, he had a Fila Brasileiro dog which would have loved to have me or anyone it didn't know as his dinner. This man had vanished for months, and now here he was, acting like I should just fall back in line as he cooked me a meal and baked a cake with the dog safely in the basement.

Maybe he thought I would. But something in me had changed. And honestly, I wasn't okay.

I wasn't drinking heavily—I saved that for the weekends—but I was still drinking. We continued on for several more months, seeing each other regularly. It became more of a routine—predictable, scheduled, familiar. I often cooked for him and brought him food when he worked late or pulled doubles. We had more time sitting side by side, him in his police car, me in mine just talking. It didn't seem strange at the time. If anything, it felt like we had found our rhythm.

Until, of course, he disappeared again. Gone. Just like before. No warning. No goodbye. I was done. It didn't matter if he ever called again, there was no turning back. There was one man, only one who ever had my heart and if I wouldn't have taken it from him, I wouldn't take it from a fool.

By that point, I was no longer working in the city, I was getting promotions. Making friends. Building a new kind of identity for myself inside the corporate world. For the first time in a long time, I was being seen for something other than my past. I was becoming someone—someone reliable, respected, even admired.

As strange as it sounds, maybe I needed him to disappear one more time—for good—so I could finally see what I had become on my own.

***

The Pop

So much for stability. I went on a ski trip, and a single mistake cost me dearly. I wasn't some advanced skier out there taking moguls for fun, but I could handle black diamonds. I liked the thrill of the unknown, especially on trails I hadn't tried before. One of my more experienced ski buddies used to say, "If you can ski on Pennsylvania ice, you can ski anywhere with powder." He wasn't wrong.

This was our annual trip to Elk Mountain. It was always a good time—rowdy in the best way. A charter bus left from Delaware, packed with regulars who knew how to party. The back of the bus was our crowd: mimosas, Bloody Mary's, Jello shots, snacks. People skied buzzed, but they were pros at it. The kind of people who could handle the edge because they had lived on it.

I had already done a couple of black diamonds that morning. My buzz had worn off. I wasn't reckless—I was actually headed back to the lounge to warm up. As I came off the lift and started down, I was flying—quick right, left, right. I came up on a slower skier and went to pass him when a snowboarder wiped out right in front of me.

I shifted hard to avoid him. That's when it happened. One ski popped off, just like it was supposed to. The other didn't. My leg twisted under me—ass over head—and I heard the pop... The pop. The one athletes talk about. The one you don't forget.

It wasn't just pain—it was the sound of something giving way. Something that wouldn't snap back. I finished the rest of the hill on one ski, my knee screaming the whole way down. I hadn't planned to drink anymore, but I needed something to dull the pain.

By the next day, I was at the orthopedic office: torn ACL, prescription for Vicodin, physical therapy, and talk of surgery if things didn't improve. They started with x-rays, then the MRI, then physical therapy. But nothing changed. I could barely walk. The pain didn't fade—it intensified.

My leg was unstable, and the smallest movement felt like fire. Everything changed. I couldn't stay in South Philly. Our bathroom was upstairs. Walking Sebastian to school on crutches? Impossible. And anyone who's ever lived there knows—once you find a parking spot, you guard it with your life. I couldn't keep up with that. I had no choice but to move back in with my parents. Sebastian was thrilled. I was not. I had finally begun carving out independence. A space of my own. And now here I was again—back in the house I had once escaped.

Still, I tried to manage things responsibly. I took my pain meds exactly as prescribed. One tablet every four to six hours—never more than that. I was proud of that. But the pain was relentless. Eventually, they switched me from Vicodin to Percocet.

Before surgery, they handed me a waiver. If I agreed, they'd use a cadaver ligament. The risk was low—1 in 1.6 million for HIV or hepatitis—but I couldn't do it. My gut said no. My luck had never been good. I refused.

The surgeon agreed to use my own tendon, grafted from my thigh. It was a more complex operation, more painful, longer to heal—but it felt safer. They drilled into my tibia. Cut into my thigh. Built me a new ACL from my own body.

And the aftermath was brutal. I was completely immobilized for over a month. When physical therapy finally started, my leg was locked. Atrophied. Two therapists had to force it to bend. I'd pop a Percocet before every session and still end up crying.

The pills I was legitimately taking for pain turned into something more. I had a good job. I showed up. I did what I needed to do. But behind that version of me was a woman who needed a few pills just to function. Not to get high, not to escape—but just to feel normal. It was like what they say about heroin addicts—after a while, they're not chasing the high anymore. They just don't want to be sick. That was me. I took pills so I wouldn't fall apart, so I could hold it together, be a mom, clock in on time, smile when I had to.

It wasn't about getting lost. It was about surviving. Everything I had fought so hard for—stability, freedom, momentum—was slipping out from under me again. The independence. The illusion of control.

I had built a fragile peace, and one wrong turn on an icy slope shattered it.

And that's where the next part of the story begins.

***

Running

I could barely walk—I was on crutches—but inside, I was always running.

I hadn't had a real relationship since Rick. And if you want to call that a relationship, go ahead—but let's be real: that was captivity, not love. It took me years to understand that what I was chasing wasn't a new beginning.

I was chasing someone I could never replace—Claudio. Before prison, he was everything to me. And the truth is, that probably never changed. Despite the distance. Despite the silence. Despite the bars and years between us. He was always there, a presence in the background of every decision, every ache, every heartbreak.

I've often wondered: what if he never went to prison? Would we have stayed together? Would we have struggled through the years, arguing over money, fighting insecurity, but still holding on? Would he have listened to those three words— "Go sell drugs"—and ended up murdered on the street, leaving me a widow instead of a survivor?

I'll never know. But I do believe that our beginnings—those fragile, fiery, complicated beginnings—catapulted me into a different future. One I might never have reached otherwise, even with all the setbacks and pain along the way.

Over the years, I've reflected. We laugh now about the balcony incident and how I used to press his buttons, but the deeper question always lingered: "You would have lost your mind if Claudio ever treated you like Rick did—so what was wrong with you?"

The answer is painfully simple: Claudio would never lay a hand on me. He was gentle. He was playful. He was strong—not just physically, but emotionally, in ways I didn't understand until much later. He protected me, even from myself. And deep down, I knew it.

I was tired of running. Tired of being tired. I was healing from knee surgery and still on pain meds, so I wasn't drinking. I was focused on work, slowly rebuilding my life. I had no intention of hurting myself—I wasn't chasing death.

I just wanted to stop hurting. To feel something, or to feel nothing. That tug-of-war had been my reality for years.

Did I want to feel? Or did I want to go numb?

That's when I met Ken*(Name altered to protect the identity of my children.)

He worked with me. We'd step outside together during breaks to smoke, share light conversations filled with humor. There was nothing serious between us—just ease. Familiarity. A sense of calm I hadn't known in a long time.

One night, a mutual coworker invited us out for drinks with a group. I said yes. I wanted to be responsible, I was taking pain meds and that is a no go with drinking. I took one early in the day then held off. I had a safe ride to and from the place. Ken was there, and the night took off—rounds of shots, loud laughter, the buzz of temporary escape. I wasn't even feeling the drinks mentally.

That is, until the cool September air hit my face outside.

I had a safe ride home. But Ken had driven himself. Even in my drunken state, I knew he shouldn't drive. My ride and I tried to convince him to come with us, but he refused. We argued. He got in his car and drove straight into a DUI checkpoint.

***

The DUI that led to a relationship.

When I found out the next day, I felt awful. I had been buying rounds of drinks, never thinking it would end this way. I offered to drive him to and from work during the time he'd be without a license.

At first, he said it wasn't necessary, but I insisted—with boundaries. I'd stay in the spare bedroom, and there was never pressure. Still, the interest between us was clear.

I respected him. He was a hard worker. No prior legal trouble. A single father who had raised two daughters. That mattered to me. He understood responsibility. He understood boundaries.

Ken was different from any relationship I'd ever had—even Claudio. There was no chaos. No fear. No criminal past hanging over our heads. He had no record. He had a steady job and a house in the suburbs. There were no street corners, no whispered warnings, no sense of danger lurking in the background. It was calm. Stable. Safe. And for me, that was entirely new.

We started talking more. Went on a date. But afterward, I left abruptly—I had to get home to Sebastian. He was always my first priority. I didn't explain much, just left.

Ken misunderstood. He thought I had no interest. I thought he had ghosted me and he thought I ghosted him. For two months, we didn't speak. We both assumed the other had moved on.

But the truth was simpler: miscommunication. When it came time for Ken to officially surrender his license, I reached out. "Hey," I asked, "do you still want me to give you rides to work?"

Regardless where I stand with a person, I am always true to my word. I've lived a life where there have been times my word is all I have.

He was relieved. That ride meant the difference between keeping his job or losing it. I went to stay at his place, we talked through the silence, and we laughed about it. The misunderstanding had been just that.

We took it slow. Really slow. But eventually, we were seeing each other regularly. We dated for two years before I even considered introducing him to Sebastian. My son wasn't going to meet anyone I casually dated. He deserved more than confusion or false hope.

My dad had always stepped in—taking Sebastian fishing, skiing, kayaking, doing all the "guy stuff" with him. And he never blurred the lines between grandfather and father. He just showed up.

Both of my parents gave Sebastian the strongest beginnings. And I made a promise—he would never meet "some guy" just because I was lonely. He had a dad. Even if he didn't know it, he had a dad who loved him to pieces.

When I finally did introduce them, Sebastian did what kids do—he said exactly what was on his mind. We were outside, watching

Ken dig up a tree. Sebastian turned to him and said, "You'd make a good dad."

Ken smiled. "I am a good dad."

Sebastian blinked. "How would you know that?"

Ken chuckled, "I have two little girls—well, they're older now."

Sebastian's face changed. His voice got quiet. "But… don't you want a little boy?"

And there it was. My son was dad shopping. And I had no idea.

***

A New Kind of Family

Things were getting more serious, and in May 2005, Sebastian and I officially moved in with Ken. Sebastian was turning 10, and we all went on a trip to Florida and the Bahamas.

He was still very innocent-minded for his age, still small for his age too. He was ecstatic when I told him I was taking him to Disney World for his 10th birthday—just the two of us—while Ken and his youngest daughter went to Epcot.

Underneath it all, I wasn't okay. My knee injury had led me into the worst addiction of my life. The difference was, this time I had a doctor who knew my history and believed that prescribing me pain medication was better than me finding it elsewhere.

I was taking 12 to 15 Percocet a day. Every month I got a prescription for 380 Percocet. I needed it just to get out of bed in the morning. I needed it to feel awake, to function. People thought I was high if I hadn't taken it.

Most people check for their keys, wallet, and glasses before leaving the house. I checked to make sure I had my Percocet.

***

Pregnancy, Sobriety, and Loss

In 2006, I got pregnant. Incredibly unexpected. A huge surprise. At first, I was in absolute shock and not excited. I was moving on in my career, Sebastian was 10 going on 11, and my dream of having more children with Claudio was over.

I knew the Percocet was no good for a pregnancy, so over the course of several weeks I tapered myself. No program. No intervention. Just me—I simply paced everything and got down to just a quarter of a pill a day and stopped. Ironically, my last day of using was June 21, 2006—Claudio's birthday. There was no plan; I wasn't even in contact with him at that time. I didn't realize the significance of it until years later. I was incredibly proud of that and felt that it was due in part to being more stable in life. For the first time in years, I was on the path to becoming truly sober.

***

Fighting for my Nothing

I called the OB/GYN letting them know I needed to be seen. After such chaos with my pregnancy with Sebastian, I needed to be sure everything was okay. This office would not see me until I was three months pregnant.

When I finally went, the doctor did an ultrasound and, despite being bigger than I ever was when pregnant with Sebastian, they determined the fetus had absorbed itself. I was at a place of being truly excited to welcome a new baby—and then, here I was, devastated.

I fought for my nothing for three more months, believing the doctors were wrong. How could my stomach be growing and my blood work show I may have not one, but two fetuses, for this doctor to tell me there was none?

In August 2006, the doctor said, "Amy, if you do not have the procedure to clean you out, you will give birth to nothing. There is no baby, and this can cause you to never have a child again."

Under duress, I agreed. Immediately following the procedure, I was in excruciating pain. The doctor prescribed me—you guessed it—Percocet.

I was determined not to get hooked again.

***

The Missed Sac and Silent Grief

Three days after the surgery, we should have known something was wrong. I had pain so unbearable that I ended up in the ER. If I thought I was devastated before—hearing there was no baby—it was worse when the doctor finally rolled in at midnight, after I was hemorrhaging, to say they missed some during the prior procedure.

"What do you mean you missed some? You said there was nothing!"

"Your sac was empty. It is possible there was another unviable fetus we didn't see, but now we need to deal with it." To say the least, I was crushed. I would never have an abortion, and this man is standing there basically telling me that I had. My primary care doctor was livid. He said, "Amy, sue them. Sue the hell out of them."

All I could do was live with it. I carried that grief silently, buried under layers of hurt, disappointment, and resignation. I was tired of drama and courts, so I never pursued going after them.

***

Are You Shittin' Me?

Several days later, Ken asked me to marry him. I was speechless at first. He looked embarrassed and said, "Say something?" I said, "Are you shittin' me?"

I was never expecting someone to ask me that. I responded, "Sure, okay." Not the typical response, but that's what it was - it was real. Afterward, as we drove along, he said, "Well, don't you want to know anything, like the date I have planned?"

I just laughed and said, "Oh please, you have a date? Oh my God. I'm not sure I can marry you—I think I'm still married to Claudio." He said, "What? How?" I said, "Well, when I was arrested, I put Claudio as my husband and he did the same, and the DOC always referred to me as his wife." He assured me, "No, a common law marriage can be overridden by a real marriage with a real certificate."

I didn't look any further into it, but clearly, Claudio was still with me. In my heart, he always would be.

***

The Mystery Ailment and the Unexpected Turn

For the first time in almost a decade, I was sober. I didn't drink. I didn't use anything. I was climbing the ranks at work. I was finally stable.

In April 2007, an opportunity came up: a position at an insurance company doing IT audit and ethical hacking. The pay was better. The commute was shorter. I resigned from the bank and took the leap.

I was doing well—until my old boss from the bank called. "Amy, you know more than anyone here. You can do the work of two people. I want you back." At first, I declined. Then he sweetened the offer: senior manager title, big pay raise, my own office, full tenure as if I had never left. I agreed to apply.

The recruiter must have googled me and was brazen enough to warn me, "When you get to the conviction section, if you've ever been arrested, say yes—even if you weren't convicted." I pushed back. "An arrest isn't a conviction."

He agreed but explained that people who said "no" and had arrests show up on background checks were terminated. Reluctantly, I followed his advice. I got the job. But two months later, HR called me in. They brought up my old arrest. It would stay sealed in my HR file, they said—but still, it stung.

It was November 2007. My life seemed stable. The wedding was coming. The holidays were ahead. And then everything changed.

***

Collapse

One November evening at Walmart, I suddenly felt dizzy. Sounds around me distorted, like underwater screams. I lowered myself to the floor, terrified. I don't know how long I sat there. Somehow, I got home and collapsed into sleep.

The next day, I went to work—and it happened again. And again. I was slurring words. Flipping sentences backward. Losing track of time. Driving became terrifying.

It wasn't anxiety. It was something else. Something wrong. I drove myself to my primary care doctor 40 minutes from work. They did an EKG to verify I wasn't having heart issues. My doctor said "honey, this is anxiety. You have so much going on in your life, it will settle soon. For now, let's get you a shot to settle you down and a prescription for Xanax."

I asked if I could drive after the shot, he chuckled and said "believe me, you've taken enough Percocet in your life to tranquilize an elephant, you'll be fine." Off I went with a prescription for Xanax.

He was right, it didn't do too much but it calmed me. However, my issues were so bad, I needed to take one just to go into a meeting. It didn't stop.

The Holidays passed and I was no longer blowing money as I had been, the job was no longer new. I begged my doctor for answers. Test after test—everything came back normal. They theorized mini-seizures. Put me on anti-epileptic medication. Hospitalized me for nearly two weeks to determine what type of seizures I was having and try to determine what was causing them.

What did they find? Nothing! No epilepsy. No seizures. No answers. But they did see abnormal brain activity. My brain waves were covered in spikes—unusual patterns that had some of the best doctors genuinely stumped. It wasn't consistent with any known form of seizure. The activity was there, but it didn't fit anything they could explain.

I was a medical mystery.

***

Holding It Together

I lived in fear of episodes—forgetting where I was, losing words mid-sentence. I couldn't drive far. My world shrunk. But on the outside, I was functioning: paying for my own wedding, keeping Sebastian stable, holding down my job.

And Ken didn't make it easier. Even though he contributed the bare minimum financially, he acted like I owed him. Every gesture came with a debt of gratitude. If I needed a ride somewhere, he made it out to be some grand favor—like I should be amazed and thankful. It chipped away at my hard-won independence. Not only that, it was terrifying. How could this be happening every single day, and no one knew what it was?

I paid for the wedding. I had withdrawn money from my 401(k), covering every cost myself. All these things should have been red flags. Everything was screaming, run—don't walk. But I wasn't about to listen to that thought.

My mom gently warned me: "Save some money. You don't need to do so much." I snapped back: "I'm only getting married once—and I'm going to do it however I damn well please."

She knew exactly what I meant. I was moving forward—not moving on.

***

The Ache That Remained

I loved Ken. But no one—ever—could replace Claudio. I didn't dwell on him. But he was still there. A silent ache. I had accepted that we would never have the life we dreamed of, but I never gave up the hope that he might come home.

Even if it wasn't to me. Ken was rarely present outside of work. I told myself it was normal. But deep down, I knew: my life was stable—but it wasn't whole. I was preparing to say "I do" while carrying a grief no one else could see. I had rebuilt everything, but a piece of me was still missing. And it always would be.

***

The Wedding That Wasn't Meant to Be

I moved the same as I had been moving. About a year before the date Ken picked, he said, "Shouldn't we be planning a wedding?" I looked at him and said, "Oh, you were serious?" I started planning. I withdrew all the money from my 401(k) and began piecing together a fairly pricey wedding from that point forward.

On my wedding day, my maid of honor pulled me aside and said, "Aim, you do this, I want you to know—it's okay not to. You and I both know Ken is a decent guy, but your heart is locked in that prison." It blew my mind that she even knew. I didn't talk about Claudio. Ever.

I got teary-eyed. I got angry. And in that moment, I said aloud into the air, "Fuck you, Claudio. This should have been you." And then... I went and got married. The entire time the priestess was speaking, a voice inside me kept screaming: "Say no. Be friends, be partners—anything but married." But shaking, feeling as though I would pass out, I said yes.

There were things about Ken that were nice. But the things that mattered—the time spent together, the intimacy, the emotional connection—weren't there. I settled. Yes, we enjoyed each other's company. But the reality was, I don't think we ever connected the way a married couple should.

***

The Name Change

In 2009, Sebastian came to Ken and me. He wanted to change his last name. He wanted to feel like we were one family unit. Ken agreed, and we contacted an attorney. Everything would have been simple—except Claudio had to give permission.

The lawyer said he would draft a letter and send it to him. At that moment, I snapped. "You will do no such thing. If he is getting something in the mail, then he deserves to hear from me. He deserves to know his son is okay. He deserves to know even I am okay. He may hate me right now, but I know him. I am the mother of his child—and he will want to know we are both okay."

I wasn't going to let Claudio get another blow out of nowhere. It wasn't just trauma that lived between us—I realized I still cared deeply for him. Despite not talking in years, I still felt the need to protect him. I tried to tame it but he and I had been through so much, I was not going to have him receive one more letter from the courts.

The attorney said, "If you have permission from your husband to contact him, I see no issue." I replied, "We are in the 2000s. I do not need permission to reach out to the father of my son."

So, I reached out by mail. I was a nervous wreck. I explained that we were doing well, that I had gotten married, and that our son wanted a sense of belonging, that he was getting older and carrying his last name in our small town was just putting a target on his back. I knew it would hurt him. But all Claudio had ever wanted was for his son—and me—to be okay. And he agreed.

It felt so final. I grieved inside. I wanted what was best for Sebastian. But it felt like I was erasing Claudio—and it hurt. I felt torn between two worlds: my son's needs and Claudio's unspoken loss. But it was Sebastian's idea. And if it meant that much to him, I couldn't stand in the way.

***

Sebastian's New Request

After the name change was finalized, Sebastian decided he wanted to meet his father. Go figure. He had wanted to shed Claudio's name—and now he wanted to know the man behind it. Once again, I reached out to Claudio.

At the time, Pennsylvania prisons were overcrowded. Claudio—along with many others—was transferred between Virginia and Michigan to open up space. For this, I did speak to Ken. I believed Claudio needed to be prepared—that the little boy he last saw was now growing into his own person. His voice was deeper, he had his own interests, they needed to have something real to talk about. Ken agreed.

But then he made a comment I will never forget: "Don't get pregnant." Wow. That was the biggest slap in the face I had ever felt.

I had never, in all the years I'd known Ken, even discussed my past, he had no interest. I wasn't going to see Claudio to reconnect intimately. I was going to talk about our shared son.

Did Ken feel inadequate? I'll never know. But that comment stunned me. It shattered a fragile trust I didn't even realize was so delicate.

The truth was, Ken had never really been part of our family. We were married on paper. But inside the home? He was rarely there. Not abusive. Not cruel. Just... absent.

***

The Visit That Changed Everything

In March 2011, I finally made plans to visit Claudio in Michigan. By that point, I traveled often for work. I had a nice office and was a senior-level manager for my business segment at the bank. I had finally gotten clean, and I was further along in life than I ever imagined I would be. Quite honestly, I was further along than I believe most people thought I ever would be.

We had a beautiful visit. We talked—really talked—as we never had before. We were nearly sixteen years older and far more mature. There were tears, there were laughs, and there was total honesty. For me, it was a gut punch. There were moments I felt like I couldn't breathe. There was no chaos. No anger. Just complete forgiveness—from both of us.

We talked about our losses. I told him how much I had wanted a boy when I was pregnant with Sebastian. I was still that girl who didn't get all girlie and, while I wanted a healthy baby, I had hoped for a son. But I also admitted something else: I had always wanted a girl with him, too.

***

The Contrast Between Systems

Muskegon Correctional Facility in Michigan was actually a pleasant place to visit—not just for me, but apparently for the men as well. From what I observed and what Claudio shared, the staff treated people like human beings, and in turn, the men behaved like human beings.

There were vending machines on the block. The officers understood that prison was about removal from society, not about staff inflicting punishment. The men were allowed to use the phone regularly, from early morning until late at night. They had staff they could talk to. It was humane.

They went out of their way to be accommodating to me, knowing I was traveling by plane and taxi and wanted to be sure I felt welcome, that our visit went without issue. The superintendent even reached out to me before and after the visit!

This was the complete opposite of Pennsylvania, where the system doesn't just warehouse people—it breaks them. The Pennsylvania DOC thrives on perpetual punishment, allowing certain staff to break down the human spirit unchecked.

Don't get me wrong—there are some amazing correctional officers in Pennsylvania. That's who they are as people. But the DOC doesn't cultivate that. It allows the bad apples to keep spoiling the bunch. In Michigan, Claudio had found something rare: a place where he could breathe.

***

What He Didn't Know

We learned more about each other in that one visit than we ever had before. Claudio already knew he helped me get off cocaine—but he never knew the reason I was using in the first place. I told him then.

While I had a loving family and a good upbringing, there was an older person—not part of the family—who made sexual advances toward me at a young age. He tried to touch me and wanted me to touch him. I never told anyone. I felt ashamed. I feared people wouldn't believe me.

The fear of losing friends outweighed the urge to speak up. To this day, until this writing, Claudio is the only one I have ever shared that with and I have trusted him with carrying that weight.

Claudio and I spoke openly about my past—my drug use, my history, and the things I had never fully shared with anyone else. I told him something that at the time, I had only recently come to understand myself: I had undiagnosed attention deficit disorder (ADD). When I first tried cocaine, it didn't make me feel high—it made me feel focused. Clear. Like my mind had finally stopped spinning. That's why I kept going back to it.

Despite all the drugs I had used over the years—alcohol, ecstasy, pills—I never touched cocaine again. Because of Claudio. Even from a distance, his presence gave me the strength to walk away from it completely.

What's funny is that back in 9th grade, my school counselor was convinced I was already on drugs. He was so adamant about it that he called my parents and made a huge deal out of it. But I wasn't. Not at that time. His accusations didn't scare me straight—they pushed me away. It was likely then that I was exhibiting the signs of ADD and was just completely missed.

I already drank pretty regularly before school, but drugs? Not yet. And still, I felt tagged. Labeled. Judged. I started to skip school more often, thinking: what was the point of showing up if I'd already been written off as a lost cause? The damage was done before I ever had a chance to prove otherwise.

***

"Give Up" Is Not in Our Vocabulary

I asked Claudio where he was with his case. He got quiet. "I gave up," he said. "I've exhausted all my appeals. There's nothing left to do." I turned to him and said, "Give up is not part of our vocabulary. I want to help you. You should not still be in here."

Same trial. Same evidence, or lack thereof. Same jurors. I was free. He wasn't. And that hurt. No—I didn't wish I were in prison. But I did wish the outcome had been fair.

In almost every other state, he would've at least been preparing for the possibility of parole. Not guaranteed release—just the opportunity to show who he'd become. To show that he was sorry. That he could live differently.

But in Pennsylvania, the answer was no. Life meant life. Life means death by incarceration.

No second chances. No redemption in the eyes of the system. Just permanent punishment.

And taxpayers pay a fortune just to throw people away.

***

Reawakening

I left the visit emotional. Over the years, I had mastered the art of hiding emotion. I didn't let it show on my face—because once someone showed concern, once someone saw me, I'd fall apart. The ugly cry. The kind that overtakes you and won't let go.

When I walked out of that prison, I knew something in me had shifted again. Claudio wasn't just a memory anymore. He was real, present, and desperately in need of help. And in typical Claudio fashion, he was more worried about me than himself. That night, we talked multiple times while I stayed in my hotel room. He asked about me, about our son, about our lives—really asked.

For the first time in a long time, I believe he had hope again. Hope that someone still cared. Hope that someone was willing to fight for him. And deep down, I knew the truth: it was finally my turn to try and save the man who had once saved me.

***

The Cold at Home

When I returned from Michigan in March 2011, Ken was acting strange. He said I was different. But I wasn't—not really. Yes, something had shifted in me. I had a new sense of purpose. A deeper awareness of injustice. A fire to stand up to a system designed to destroy people. But I wasn't running into Claudio's arms.

I was a career-focused woman with a son thriving in school and a future to build.

The truth is, the doubts I had about my marriage weren't new. They had been quietly building for years. Ken's presence had been missing long before that prison visit. He wasn't abusive. He wasn't cruel. He just wasn't... there.

He spent most of his time in the basement or off visiting his elderly mother. I was with him during most of those visits—helping with yard work, grocery shopping, whatever needed to be done. But there was no warmth between us. No connection.

That distance only became more obvious when I found out I was pregnant. The first thing he said was "you made that in Michigan."

***

The Pregnancy That Changed Everything

Claudio called me shortly after I took the test. "Is there something you need to tell me?" he asked. I froze. How did he know? It reminded me of when I was pregnant with Sebastian and he had the dream about the swimming eggs. Somehow, once again, he just knew.

And from that moment on, Claudio was present for everything. He wanted to know how I was feeling. He wanted updates after every appointment. He called constantly—not to interfere, but to support.

He remembered which days were hard for me. When I was sick, he somehow felt it.

I remember one day he called and asked gently, "Are you feeling any better today?" I told him I was. He laughed and said, "Good. I've been sick all day. I've been trying to will it off you." I don't know if that's even possible. But that's connection. That's partnership.

Every appointment, every update—I shared it with him. Not because he demanded it, but because I wanted to. He made me feel like I wasn't alone.

Meanwhile, Ken—my husband—was physically there, yes. He came to Sophie's prenatal appointments. But even then, he always seemed distant. Distracted. Like he was doing what he was "supposed to" do, but his heart wasn't in it. It was such a stark contrast. Claudio, from prison, made me feel more supported, more seen, more emotionally held than the man I shared a home with.

Sophie was born a little early, on January 13, 2012. It was a snowy weekend, and I had been planning to deliver at a major city hospital—University of Pennsylvania—because of my complicated medical history. Our local hospital had shuttered its labor and delivery unit, so if anything went wrong, I had nowhere to go. And Sophie's heart rate had been dipping. Doctors were worried. They made the decision: C-section.

During all the chaos—rushing into surgery, trying not to panic—I wasn't even in communication with Claudio. But early in the morning of January 14, the phone rang. "Did you have the baby, Amy?" he asked. "Yes," I told him. He didn't miss a beat. "I knew it."

Meanwhile, Ken was...busy. Too busy to stay. Too busy to be in the hospital. He had things to do at home. That moment summed up everything I had been feeling.

***

Postpartum and the Peanut Butter Sandwich

During the delivery, I had my tubes tied. I had already been through three pregnancies, and each one had taken a toll on me. Between the C-section and the tubal ligation, I was in a lot of pain—even days after the birth.

When I got home, I was sore, exhausted, and trying to breastfeed Sophie on the living room sofa. I needed calories. I was healing. I asked Ken—my husband—to get me something to eat.

He snorted. "Go make yourself a peanut butter sandwich."

That moment told me everything. I had just undergone surgery. I was recovering, nursing, and doing everything I could to care for our newborn—and that was his response. There was no tenderness. No instinct to care for me. No recognition of what I had just been through. Just cold detachment.

And that was the tone of our marriage: physically present, emotionally absent. I didn't need grand gestures. I didn't need flowers or praise. I just needed kindness. And he couldn't offer even that.

***

Between Two Worlds

I want to be clear—there was nothing inappropriate happening between me and Claudio. We had settled into a place of being best friends, and I was trying to find a way to help him. I never told him how miserable I was in my marriage. I didn't share that with anyone, really.

We talked regularly, until suddenly, in November 2015, he disappeared from my life again. His silence was deafening. Confusing.

Painful. On our last call, he said, "I'll call you later." He hung up—and never did. What happened? Where did he go?

Later, I discovered the truth: Claudio had withdrawn because I'd told him I was happy. He believed that meant happy without him—and he loved me enough to let me go. But that was all a façade.

I was miserable. Ken and I didn't even sleep in the same bed. But I didn't want Claudio to think things were falling apart. Especially with my history of addiction, he would've seen right through me—seen the fragility I was trying so hard to bury under layers of strength.

***

Partnered with Silence, Not a Man

I lived in that house, but I was emotionally on my own. We were legally married, yes—but that was just paperwork. What mattered, what truly defines a marriage—support, connection, presence—was missing.

I paid far more than my fair share of the expenses. Ken complained that he had used the line of credit to pay for Sophie's preschool. Meanwhile, I was the one actually paying. Money was already being withheld from my paycheck for childcare expense deductions. I was paying my own credit card bills. I paid over double what the mortgage was. I bought the clothes. I bought the food. I kept everything going.

***

Emotionally Abandoned

By 2016, Sophie was four. Ken and I didn't even sleep in the same room. The tension was thick. There was no intimacy, no partnership—just two people existing under the same roof.

When he was home, he was in the basement. After his mother passed in 2014, I thought maybe we'd grow closer. Instead, he disappeared even further into himself. It wasn't grief—I understood grief. This was withdrawal. Disconnection. Escape.

He even made snide comments a few times—remarks about Sophie being "made in Michigan." He didn't say it often, but once was too much.

I was exhausted. I worked full-time. I managed our home. I raised both kids. And I was doing it alone. Emotionally, financially, physically—I was carrying it all. I wasn't chasing Claudio's love. I was trying to find myself.

I was trying to stand by the man who had once stood by me—not romantically, but as his former co-defendant, his friend, the mother of his youngest child, someone who had seen me through hell and never judged me. And that kind of connection doesn't fade. It lives in you.

Claudio and I reconnected in a way most people only dream of. He wasn't just an old flame or a friend from the past—he was the father of my son. Someone who had walked through fire beside me. Our bond was deep. Rooted in survival. In truth. In years of shared pain and unspoken understanding.

But we never crossed any lines. Not once. Even when my marriage was falling apart, Claudio never stepped over the boundary. He respected that I was married. He encouraged me to work on it. His presence wasn't romantic—it was grounding.

He was more of a partner than the man I lived with. A partner in spirit. In loyalty. In care. And that kind of connection—built on history, trust, and restraint—means more than most people will ever understand.

Claudio never wanted to interfere in my marriage. He was happy that I was happy—or so he thought. But I finally admitted it: I wasn't happy.

I wasn't being mistreated physically, but I was emotionally abandoned. And I had been for a long time. The truth was, it was already too broken for too long. You can only go so long feeling alone—especially while raising a child in silence.

***

Reconnection and Raw Truth

Days turned into weeks. Weeks into months. By January 2016, I began having this overwhelming feeling—like Claudio needed me. It wasn't logic—it was something deeper. I'd felt it before. Over the years, I always knew when he was about to call. It was a sense. A shift.

I reached out. He called. Calm. Controlled. But with heavy breathing, like he'd been holding his emotions in a vault for months. In a low, firm voice, he said, "Amita... What... do you want from me?"

I was stunned. Shocked. All I wanted was for him to be present. To talk to me again. To be there.

As it turned out, he had taken my words at face value. When I said I was happy, he believed me. Claudio wasn't a homewrecker.

He thought staying away was the best thing he could do. "I had this feeling," I told him. "I felt like you needed me."

He responded with a rhythm in his voice, low and deliberate. "I have always needed you, Amy. What do you want?"

I could practically see the smoke rising from his nostrils. I became defensive, emotional, accusatory. "You said you'd call me back!"

We fought—for three straight days. I sent him messages. He called. I screamed. I was angry, he was composed. I yelled; he barely raised his voice. Honestly, it was mostly me fighting. He was just trying to hold space.

On the third day, Sebastian was driving me to the store. I was yelling into the phone. I asked him to pull over so he didn't need to hear his mother screaming at his father. I got out of the car and continued my tirade. That's when Claudio, in the softest voice, said, "Stop, Amita. Please. I don't want to fight with you." And just like that, I crumbled.

But I never crossed a line. Yes, my heart was cracked wide open, but my focus remained clear. I wasn't trying to reignite something romantic. I was trying to help the father of my firstborn finally have a shot at coming home. Not to be with me—to be free.

This man had saved me, truly saved me, once before. And now, I had a chance to show up for him. We were 21 years older. Wiser. Changed. I wasn't happy in my marriage, but I was grounded in life. I had stability. I had strength. And I wanted to use it to help him.

I'd be lying if I said I didn't love him. I always loved him. Not a single day passed, even in the worst moments—even when I was angry that he hadn't been part of our lives—when he wasn't burning in my heart.

We had a connection like nothing I've ever known. Sometimes, I'd just know—know that the phone was about to ring. That he needed to talk. Or that I did. I could close my eyes and feel it. Something inside me would reach for him—like some strange internal radio frequency—and within minutes, the phone would ring. Even Sebastian saw it. One day, I said out loud, "Claudio's going to call. I need him to call." I closed my eyes. And minutes later, the phone rang. Claudio's voice came through, playful, familiar: "You rang?" We still laugh about it. Who does that? Apparently, Claudio and I.

After the hiatus between November and January, we had to talk—really talk. Claudio admitted the back and forth was too much. He couldn't keep swinging between connection and silence. We either needed to be friends or nothing. Not this rollercoaster. He was right. What we had was deep. Meaningful. And once we had that heart-to-heart, once everything was out in the open and there were no more games or second guesses, we never looked back. Since that conversation, we've never missed a day of being solid. The only time we don't talk is if the prison is locked down.

***

When the Mask Slipped

Despite the connection Claudio and I shared—despite how unhappy I was in my marriage, even feeling alone—he encouraged me.

He encouraged me to get things right with my husband. He reminded me that I married him and that I should put in what I could to stay married.

Claudio is pretty old school in many ways, and it reminded me of back in the decades before I was born—when no matter how bad a woman felt in her marriage, her mother or some other close adult would say, "Make it work."

Claudio was well aware of my anxiety, the spacing out. He, of course, was well aware of my history, and he didn't want me off on my own. He wanted me to be safe. He wanted Sebastian and Sophie to be well adjusted.

I am sure he knew that by this point, I probably would have run off with him if he came knocking on my door. He was to me what my heart needed. A partner. A best friend. Someone who knew me like no one in this world knows me.

He was my emotional safety net. The one I would ask the tough questions of. The one I would seek guidance from. It was odd, talking to him, sharing with him the issues I faced and hearing him try to be objective. He never bashed Ken. He guided me in trying to get things right.

That is, until one day I asked a favor of him. He didn't want to do it, but I begged. "Please, I need to see what happens. You've had a lot of time to think. Just once—write me a letter that is inappropriate to send me." I told him what to write. A lot of content about love and sex, of course.

He was apprehensive. He sat on the letter for over a week. I was getting annoyed.

"Please, Claudio. Just send the damn letter—or letters—will ya?"

I planned to place the letters in places to test Ken, to see his integrity. And if I found out he was snooping around—would he act? Would he try to reclaim his wife?

I received the letters. I left them out—on purpose. I even put one in my purse. I had always suspected Ken was snooping through my things. This would confirm it. But that wasn't all.

He didn't say anything at first. The first thing he did was abuse his authority at work to look into my small, personal bank account—not the shared one, mine. Something he had no legal right to do. And something that could have gotten him terminated if I wanted to make a scene. He even printed out papers from my bank account—evidence of his own deceit. I was furious.

He began an irate tangent. He was telling me I was crazy. "Leave the people in prison alone. They are trash. They are where they belong."

How could any human being turn a blind eye to suffering? If you have the ability to make a change and refuse to do so, that says everything about you. I started to ponder my own past—the realization that twelve strangers once decided my fate, and they could have easily gone the other way. It cut deep.

People in society don't care. The system doesn't care. Well, damn it—I do. I don't just fight for Claudio. I fight for every man and woman the system has tried to throw away.

Rather than talk to me, or try to understand who I was, Ken jumped straight into attack mode.

When I was honest about wanting to help Claudio come home, he lashed out. He demanded to know why I would waste my time on someone who had been in prison for over twenty years. He accused me of being naïve, foolish. Said Claudio would never come home. Said I wasn't smart enough to see it.

And then he made a real threat: "You know, I have a friend who's a guard at Graterford. He can make people disappear." It was chilling.

But it also showed me everything I needed to know. He called Claudio a snake. A womanizer. Said I was a puppet and Claudio was the puppet master. He went on a tirade—about raising Claudio's son, about betrayal, about Claudio's upbringing. He made crude and disgusting racial jabs.

The irony? In all the years we'd been married—even before that—Ken had taken Sebastian out maybe twice. He wasn't raising Claudio's son. He wasn't really there at all. The man who stepped up as a father figure was still my dad—Sebastian's grandfather.

I asked for marriage counseling. Ken refused

***

The Final Unraveling

I continued to live in the house. I was still legally married. But it was miserable. I was at a point where I was terrified to be alone. I still wasn't able to drive regularly. I was still having massive episodes that no one could figure out.

By 2019, I had reached my breaking point. I worked long hours, managed leadership-level responsibilities, and raised both of my children. But because I worked from home, Ken treated it like I had unlimited time—as if I was just lounging around, doing whatever I pleased. That couldn't have been further from the truth. I was dedicated. I worked with integrity. And even simple things—like cleaning off a dish after I cooked—somehow still fell on me.

I couldn't take it anymore. I talked to Claudio—the one who had been so adamant that I work things out. I told him there was no working anything out. It wasn't about being with another person. I needed to be alone. I was married in name. I was miserable. And I could take no more.

He was worried about my finances. I wrote out a budget and told him how much I had already been paying over the years. And it was him who said, "Amita, yeah—if you feel this is right, then go. I think he has been stealing from you for years. If what you're telling me is true, there's no way that math adds up." It was true. It only took me twelve years to figure it out—and no way to prove it, really. But I could make it on my own and care for my daughter just fine.

I had to take Sophie and leave. We moved nearby to an apartment. Ken offered no help. No assistance with expenses. No attempt to ease the transition.

Even though we were close in proximity, he saw Sophie maybe once or twice a week—and even that felt forced. I stayed local so

Sophie would still be able to see her Ken. So she wouldn't be uprooted. It really didn't matter.

One day, I called him. Sophie was sick, and I needed to get her medicine—but I didn't have the money. Any real father I've ever known would've said, "I got it. Don't worry." Instead, he said, "If you want me to buy it, you're going to have to ask." Of course, I asked.

But wow. That moment told me everything.

***

The Exit

When I left Ken in May of 2019, I didn't ask for the house. I didn't demand half. I didn't even try to recoup what I had paid—$1,650 or more each month from my own paycheck, going into our joint account toward the mortgage and household bills.

I just wanted peace. I walked away. And I assumed—naively, maybe—that he would step up for Sophie. That even if our marriage had fallen apart, he would still show up as her father.

He didn't.

When it became clear he wasn't going to voluntarily offer a dime, I had no choice but to take him to Domestic Relations. And there he was, sitting across from me with a private attorney. A man who claimed to have no income—but had the means to retain legal counsel. He had money for a lawyer, but not for his child?

The court did their calculation, based on his claimed lack of income and my actual income. They said he could pay $99 a month. Ninety-nine dollars. For a child he helped bring into this world. His attorney said he was applying for disability. I said fine. I didn't want a fight. I told them I'd even help him—doctor's appointments, whatever he needed. He never pursued it.

And yet somehow, he always had money for his two older daughters from his first marriage. Sophie? Not so much. There was a time he even made her pay for her own movie ticket—and his—and a friend's. Who does that?

Let me be clear: Ken was not abusive, not physically. But his words? No wonder he's had two failed marriages.

He was just a man who didn't care deeply enough about anyone but himself.

A man who had a pension, a 401(k), a Harley, multiple vehicles, a house he owns, and a second house he bought in his daughter's name to hide income. He has no problem putting money into property or appearances. But child support? He plays poor and somehow, he gets away with it.

In front of Sophie, he brags about what he does spend money on. One day, he told her, "I bought a pizza and the girl handing it to me looked like she was having a bad day, so I gave her a $20 tip on a $15 pizza." Sophie notices these things. She isn't bold enough yet to call him out, but she's getting there and tells me all about it.

Now she says things like, "I'm not even calling him—he only talks to me when I call him, so let's see how long he takes." I always reinforce to her: she is welcome to her own opinions, but they have to be her own. I make sure she knows she doesn't owe loyalty to me or to him.

We may be divorced, but that doesn't mean she has to choose a side. I even tell her to call him, to stay in touch—but she usually just shrugs or makes a sarcastic comment like, "Ah, he's probably too busy with his rich daughter. I'm good."

And what really gets me? If he were a man with fewer resources—Black, brown, or working class—he could've been jailed for paying so little. I've seen that. I've worked with people who can barely survive and still get ordered to pay hundreds. Miss a payment, and they're dragged into court. But this man, with assets and access? He slides by. This isn't just about Ken. It's not even about money.

To me, presence—emotional presence—is everything.

It's about the systems that allow men like him to perform poverty while others are punished for simply being honest about it. But here's where it gets interesting.

Claudio—a man incarcerated, living on scraps, with no obligation—surprises me with a check randomly. Not because I ask. Not because I hint. Because he wants to help.

From a prison cell, he offers more—emotionally and financially—than the man I had married and built a home with. He remembers birthdays. He asks how Sophie is doing. He tries to help however he can. And he does it with dignity, not ego.

Claudio once said to me "not everything is about money Amy" as he tore up those bills. And he's right. It was about who shows up when no one's looking. Who contributes, even when they have almost nothing to give. Who values family, even from a prison payphone and a $25 account.

That's what loyalty looks like. That's what love looks like. And that's what Ken never understood.

***

Two Different Men

Claudio and Ken couldn't have been more different. Where Claudio fought to rebuild, Ken hid from life. Where Claudio offered his heart without asking for anything back, Ken kept score.

We shared a house, but lived in different worlds. He barely connected with Sebastian. He barely connected with me. Our life looked stable if you squinted hard enough—but underneath, it was nothing but silence and empty space. It was hollow.

Claudio is vibrant, emotionally present, deeply intuitive. Even locked behind bars, he finds ways to connect, to support, to show up. Our bond isn't normal. It's raw. Intense, electric, protective. It defies distance, defies the system. It survives everything. He still reaches me. He still shows me I matter. Ken, on the other hand, was just... there. Reliable at times, maybe. But detached.

Where Claudio craves closeness, Ken preferred walls. Where Claudio gives without expectation, Ken kept a ledger. Where Claudio grew, Ken drowned his lungs in marijuana, hiding from anything real.

Even as I married Ken, I knew: No one—not then, not now, not ever—would reach my heart the way Claudio had.

***

The Residue of Panic

I started having those severe anxiety episodes in November of 2007. I was supposed to be getting married in August of 2008, and we were in the middle of planning the wedding.

The panic attacks came out of nowhere—sudden, terrifying, and completely overwhelming. We tried everything to figure out what was triggering them. Was it the light? Something in the environment? Nothing made sense. And no medication seemed to help. I lived like that for years—caught in a cycle of fear, unpredictability, and shame. I left Ken in May of 2019, thinking maybe a change would bring relief. It didn't. The episodes kept coming.

Then came one of the worst medical experiences of my life. I went to see a neurologist for headaches. Not anxiety. Not panic. Just headaches. But this doctor—this woman who knew nothing about me—took one look at my long-standing Ativan prescription and decided I was a drug addict. She accused me of wanting more pills, even though I had never changed my dose in all the years I'd been on it. One milligram a day. Consistently.

She reported me to the DMV. Said I wasn't fit to drive. Told me I needed addiction treatment.

So, I called a specialist. He laughed. "You're not addicted," he said. "There's no way I'm charging you $400 a session to help you get clean from a dose that small. You don't need addiction treatment. You need a decent doctor." But because of her report, I lost my driver's license for six months. I was humiliated. I felt betrayed—not just by her, but by the medical practice I'd trusted for years. How could they continue prescribing me medication while another doctor was calling me an addict and saying I was unsafe to drive?

That's when I left. All of it. The doctor, the practice, the narrative that didn't fit.

And that's when I found Sarah.

Sarah started fresh. She listened. She didn't assume. She ordered EKGs. We ruled out seizures. We ruled out addiction. If anything, I may have needed more anti-anxiety meds. We ruled out everything that had been projected onto me for so long.

Since moving back to my home area in 2021, I haven't had a single full-blown episode like those ones before. I'm still on the same dose of Ativan—never more. And I function. I drive. I live my life. Except for one thing.

When I go near where Ken still lives, that old anxiety creeps back in. It's not about him hurting me—he never did. Not physically. He was just… a douchebag. Emotionally neglectful, indifferent, cold. But my body remembers something, and somehow, that's enough to make it panic.

***

Reflecting & Reconnecting

When Claudio and I finally connected again—really connected—it wasn't like anything we'd had before. As right as things can be when separated by barbed wire fences, steel bars, and hundreds of miles, this was our version of right.

We found a rhythm, an honesty, a place of mutual understanding. We shared everything. There were no more walls—except the ones between us physically.

We talked deeply. And when we didn't talk, we still knew.

There was a language between us that required no words. At the beginning of this book, I shared how Claudio had left me right after we sealed our relationship back in 1994. For years, I questioned that. I wondered what I had done wrong. Why did he leave in the middle of the night? Did he just get what he wanted and disappear? Was I not enough?

The truth, when it finally came out, made me both giggle and cry. Claudio didn't leave because of me. He left for me.

One day, in a quiet moment of reflection about our lives before prison, Claudio brought it up. "Why did you ask me that? Why were you afraid I wasn't going to come back?" I fired back my own question.

"Why did you leave that night? I thought I did something wrong." Then came the truth: At four in the morning, Claudio walked across town to his mother's house, woke her up, and said with no hesitation: "Mami—I found her. I found the woman for me."

That's what I meant to him. Even when I was doubting myself. Even when I forgot how to believe in love. He knew. He always knew.

***

Father and Son: The First Visit

While Claudio and I were rebuilding, Sebastian and Claudio were just beginning. They had started talking by phone regularly, but still hadn't met. There was still a gap—a silent space between them that hadn't yet been bridged.

The first visit was small. Just me, my mom, Sebastian, and Claudio. There was uncertainty in the air. Sebastian had never known much about his father. He knew Claudio was in prison. He had a rough idea of why. But I had never painted a full picture—not good or bad. Just silence.

As Sebastian matured, I could feel his anger. His confusion. A part of me feared he would go to the visit, face his father, and say,

"Why weren't you there for me?" and turn around and not want to visit again. The other part of me held hope.

And then it happened.

The bond between father and son was immediate. Undeniable.

What started as hesitation transformed into something natural and magnetic. Watching them together nearly shattered me. Claudio—a father robbed of fatherhood. Sebastian—a son robbed of his dad.

It wasn't just the system that had stolen something from them.

I had played a part, too.

I was the one who had stopped bringing Sebastian to visit.

I carried that guilt. I knew I had taken something from both of them—something they both desperately needed. I tried with everything I had to hold it together. But Claudio knows me. He read the look on my face instantly. And even though he knows not to soften his voice—he did. Even though he knows what that does to me—he did.

And that was it.

The tears came. I couldn't breathe. And of course, there were no tissues. The officer working in the visiting room had been keeping an eye on the visit. He knew how important this day was. When he saw my sobs, saw how broken I looked, he actually got annoyed—but not at me. "Man, get up and get her a napkin!" he shouted across the room. Even he was tearing up. Claudio, ever respectful, started to explain, "They're behind—"

Behind the yellow line. A boundary the incarcerated weren't allowed to cross. The officer cut him off. "I don't care! Take care of her!" It was ugly. It was embarrassing. But it was real.

And in that messy, raw, unforgettable moment—my son and his father finally connected.

***

When the System Meets the Heart

I thought I was already fighting for justice. But after that first visit between Claudio and Sebastian—watching my son meet his father in person for the first time—everything shifted.

The system had always felt wrong to me. Cruel. Dehumanizing. Cold. But now it felt personal in a whole different way. This wasn't just about my case anymore. It wasn't just about the pain I had carried or the years lost. It was about them. A father and a son, kept apart by bars, by rules, by silence—and by me.

Claudio had missed school concerts, birthdays, holidays, milestones. He had missed his son's awkward teenage years, his first heartbreak, his victories and his questions. And Sebastian had missed a father who—despite the years, the distance, the silence—still wanted to show up.

People will say, "Too bad—the victim missed all those things too." And they're not wrong. That loss is real, and it matters.

But continuing to punish an entire family long after the sentence was given—refusing to acknowledge growth, healing, or humanity—serves no one. It doesn't bring justice. It only multiplies pain. The children of the incarcerated grow up carrying a sentence they never earned. That is not justice. It's a wound we keep reopening on purpose.

I couldn't change the past. But I could change what came next.

That visit didn't just rekindle a connection. It lit a fire. A fire to make sure the world saw what the system tried to erase: humanity, redemption, relationships worth saving.

I wasn't just watching injustice anymore. I was living in its ripple effects.

I started paying closer attention. I researched more. I listened harder. I spoke louder. I began seeing every story differently—especially the ones like ours. Because I knew firsthand what it felt like to be labeled. I had been called everything. And I knew the truth.

Claudio isn't perfect. Neither am I. But we are never just our worst moments. The system doesn't want to see that. It never does. But I do. And now—I'm determined to make others see it too.

***

Chapter 13: The Fourteenth Juror

My struggles weren't unique. They were part of a national crisis—one we refuse to fix. Half the adults in this country know someone who has been incarcerated, yet we still criminalize poverty, trauma, and survival.

We don't invest in prevention. We invest in punishment. I'm not the exception to the system. I survived it because I'm white. Don't think for a minute that's not real. Don't think people just want to "play the race card." It's very real. Because my family had access to a little money. Because I was seen as redeemable. Without those privileges, I would've died in that Delaware County cell.

When lawmakers meet with me, they hear a filtered version: that I was acquitted. That I'm a survivor. They don't hear the whole story. They don't hear about the trauma, the failures of the system, or the people I've met—men and women who've grown, changed, and still have something to give the world.

Lawmakers often say, "More people need to hear your story." But what's the point if all they do is nod—and then run back to the same policies that keep people trapped in cages, stripped of hope and humanity? They want the sound bite. The pain, without the push. They want the story—just not the policy change. The struggle—without the strategy.

The truth is, I'm not separate from this system. I'm a product of it.

And part of my story—the part I carry with shame—is that once, I chose to disconnect Sebastian from Claudio. I made that choice out of pain, out of fear.

***

Beyond Rules and Reprimands

Looking back now, I realize I've survived more than I ever gave myself credit for. For years, I kept these stories to myself—stories about guns pulled on me, fights that left blood on the floor, jumping out of moving cars. I buried them, told myself they were just part of being young and reckless. But the truth? Those were traumatic things. I just didn't see them that way.

At the time, I didn't know I was walking through trauma. I didn't know I was reenacting wounds, or that I was numbing myself with danger. I just knew that I could. I could sneak out. I could disappear. I could drink, use, fight, run.

My mom worked hard. She drank too—but she's been sober now for years, longer than I have, and I give her all the credit in the world for that. She didn't deserve the blame people put on her. They'd say things like, "You've got to get that girl under control. She needs a good spanking." But I was already too far gone for that. What I needed wasn't punishment. I needed someone to see me. Someone outside the chaos. Someone who could hold a boundary when I couldn't. Someone who cared, without the exhaustion and expectation she was already carrying.

And sometimes, when a kid is spiraling, it's not about stricter parenting. It's about influence. Positive peer reinforcement. Somebody outside the family who says,

"Hey, I see you. And you're worth more than this." That's where Claudio came in. I've said he was the wind beneath my wings, but it's deeper than that. He was the one who started to show me what safety could feel like. What love, without conditions or chaos, might look like. I didn't know I was drowning until he reached for me. I didn't know how far I'd fallen until I felt someone steady beside me.

Redemption means owning your choices. It means learning. It means doing better.

And I did. Today, I stand with all of them. The incarcerated. The forgotten. The people labeled "irretrievable" by a system that never asked who they are today. I have more true friends behind prison walls than I ever found in the free world.

He can't provide financially the way he wants to, but that hasn't stopped him from sending what he can. He shows Sophie that love is presence, not just proximity.

Even from prison, he's part of her life—calling to check in, encouraging her before tests, celebrating her wins, and offering calm when the world feels too loud. She knows his voice. She knows his care. Their bond isn't defined by blood or legality—it's built on consistency, compassion, and mutual respect. He is raising her with strength, with respect, with unconditional care—even from prison. He reminds her, and all of us, what true manhood looks like.

This story started with my pain. But it cannot end there. It has to include every person who never got the chance to show the world how far they've come.

***

Why I Still Believe in Redemption

I've had people ask me, "Amy, you've lost people you love. What makes you different? How can you fight for prison reform—for people who've taken lives?"

It's simple. I believe in punishment—but I believe in redemption, too. I know firsthand that people can change. The media won't tell you that. Media is a business. They don't sell newspapers with headlines like: "Man was hungry—shot drug dealer by accident."

No. They sell: "Thug barges into home and brazenly shoots innocent victim." Because fear sells. Crime sells. And people buy it.

Lawmakers see broken communities, and rather than fix them, they profit off of them. They build prisons instead of schools. They fund punishment over prevention.

And even today, in 2025, when the Governor proposes closing prisons because crime has dropped, lawmakers fight it. Communities fight it—because closing prisons means losing jobs. And that should shame them.

Prisons are not an economic development plan. Incarcerating human beings should never be someone's bread and butter. It's sick. It's twisted. They see prisons. I see people inside them.

How can I, a woman who has lost three people she loved to violence, still stand for second chances? Because I know people change. I know a man can kill at twenty and save lives at forty. I know the courts don't always get it right. I know a woman can fall into addiction and rise into leadership. I know healing is real.

At SCI Fayette, men are imprisoned in the middle of a toxic coal waste dump. Brown water comes from the taps at SCI Mahanoy and SCI Frackville. Guards drink bottled water. Incarcerated men drink poison. We know it causes cancer. We know it costs taxpayers tens of thousands more each year as incarcerated people age and get sick. And we still allow it. At what cost?

Almost every other state offers opportunities for parole after 20 or 25 years. Not Pennsylvania.

In Pennsylvania, life means death. And we don't even track recidivism—because freedom isn't even on the table.

But sure. Pennsylvania knows best. Ignore the data. Keep sentencing people to die in prison—fueled by vibes and vengeance. We know from other states: Lifers rarely return to prison. Their recidivism rate is under 2%. And most of those are for technical parole violations—not new crimes.

Yet society still clings to the myth that "murderers" are monsters. That once you harm, you can never heal. That people are frozen in their worst moment forever.

A conviction for murder doesn't always mean a person actually committed one. Sometimes, it means they were there. Sometimes, it means they were young, scared, caught up, or used as a scapegoat. Often it was absolutely accidental.

The law may not ask why—but we should. We never cared when they were being abused. We didn't show up when they were living in chaos, when they dropped out, when they were hungry, homeless, or hurting. But the moment they make one irreversible decision—then we care. Not to help. Just to cage.

That's not justice. It's revenge. It's not public safety. It's reactive injustice.

I've met people who say, without hesitation, that all murderers should be put to death. Ironically, most of them have never experienced the kind of loss they're so quick to judge.

They'll start quoting scripture— "an eye for an eye"—as if it's the final word. But if we're going to invoke sacred texts, let's quote them accurately—and remember the context.

That phrase wasn't meant to justify lifelong suffering. It was written to limit revenge—not glorify it. It was a call for proportionality in ancient legal systems, not a green light for endless punishment. Even in traditions that allow for justice by equal measure, mercy is always lifted higher.

From the Bible to the Qur'an, from the teachings of the Buddha to Indigenous justice practices, the message is consistent across centuries and continents: True justice restores. It doesn't destroy. It makes space for truth. For grief. For accountability. But also—for healing. We can't keep freezing people in their worst moments. We need to ask: Who are they now? What led them to that moment? What's changed since then? Who have they become?

Everyone has a backstory. Everyone has a why. And no one should be judged forever by the chapter they were in when they were at their lowest, or their youngest, or their most broken.

If we truly believe in public safety, we need to ask ourselves: What's safer? Locking away every human being who made a terrible decision—or investing in their rehabilitation so they can come back and rebuild the communities they once harmed?

I believe in second chances because I needed one. So did Claudio. And so do countless others. People will say, "Sure, people can change—but the dead can't come back." And they're right. Nothing can undo the loss. But clinging to that pain forever doesn't bring healing—it just spreads it.

If someone has taken a life and spent decades rebuilding their own—if they've found purpose, accountability, and truth—how does keeping them caged serve the dead? If we want to honor life, we should invest in what restores it—not in what buries more of it behind bars. Grief deserves space. But so does redemption.

***

Rising Through the Ashes

I've never walked through life seeing myself as a victim. Not even when I probably should have. I didn't name what I went through as trauma. I didn't carry it that way. I didn't sit with it. I just moved forward—sometimes stumbling, sometimes numb, sometimes burning everything down around me—but forward.

It's only now, through reflection and healing, that I can say: yes, those were traumatic things.

Yes, there are parts of me that are beautifully broken. And yes—I've survived them all. I've survived addiction. I've survived incarceration. I've survived abuse that nearly killed me. I've survived giving birth while on house arrest.

But I've also survived grief. I've lost too many people I loved—to murder, to the streets, to overdose, and to despair. And I've lost time—time I can never get back, time that was stolen by systems that weren't built to heal.

Still, I live as a survivor now. I choose to live that way. And I want other people to know they can live that way, too. I believe the things I've been through—the danger, the chaos, the silence, the shame—are things too many people go through. And I believe we need to talk about them. But I also believe we need to stop staying stuck in the identity of victimhood.

Everyone deserves their moment to grieve, to sit in the pain, to be seen in their suffering.

But it shouldn't be a forever. It can't be a forever. Because we only get one life. And what kind of life is it, if we spend it stuck in misery, re-living pain that we've already survived?

Healing isn't about erasing the past. It's about learning to recognize how our past still shows up in our present. It's about understanding the quiet, persistent ways our minds and bodies try to protect us—long after the danger is gone.

It's about finding gentle compassion for the parts of ourselves still adjusting to safety, still relearning trust.

We can live with trauma without being defined by it. We can acknowledge how it still affects us, without surrendering to it. Because survival isn't just about getting through—it's about learning to be fully present in the life we have right now.

***

Fidgeting, Focus, and the Fight to Stay Present

Trauma rewires you in ways most people don't see. For me, it shows up in the little things—like my constant need to fidget. I can't sit still. I tap, I click, I reach for my phone even when I'm in the middle of a conversation. I thought I was just restless. But now, I know it's my nervous system trying to stay regulated.

I can't seem to pay attention unless I have some sort of distraction. Ironically, the distraction helps me stay focused. If I'm not busy tapping away at my keyboard or locked in on something, I need to be doing something else to stay grounded—especially during phone calls.

My foot might be twirling. My fingers might be clicking. Some people don't even notice. Some do. It's not about rudeness. It's how my body copes with overstimulation and internal noise. These aren't super distractions—they're survival strategies.

Don't get me wrong. I've learned healthier ways to manage it. I have a small fidget spinner—honestly, the best $10 I've ever spent. It's made of heavier metal, so it has a bit of weight. It spins freely and it clicks.

Most people wouldn't even realize I have it in my hand. I don't use it in ways that are meant to annoy anyone. Okay—maybe Claudio would disagree. He hears me click my phone and used to think I was multitasking, not paying attention.

But once I explained it—how it wasn't about distraction but regulation—he started to understand. He quickly knew it's a recovery tool. Sometimes I'm literally just scrolling to keep my brain anchored. Not checking anything. Just staying steady.

I can't sit through an entire movie without needing to move or shift my attention. Stillness has never felt like safety to me. Somewhere deep down, my brain still equates being still with being exposed. I've lived in survival mode for so long that rest feels unnatural.

I get up. I fidget. I walk around. It's like my body says, "You're not doing anything—so something must be wrong."

The same thing happens with time. I've spent my whole life fighting against lateness—and still, if something isn't life-or-death urgent, I might show up an hour late. Not because I don't care. Not because I'm careless. But because my nervous system has always equated "being on time" with high-stakes survival.

Court? Medical emergencies? Work? I'm there on time or early. But coffee dates? Casual meetups? My brain resists it. It stalls. I lose track. I freeze.

And honestly? I'm not getting better at it. If anything, I think I'm getting worse. The more I try to explain it, the more some people judge it—and when someone starts getting nasty or acting like I'm doing it on purpose, I can feel myself subconsciously rebel.

Like something in me says, "Oh, you want control? Watch me push back." It's not logical. It's not strategic. It's trauma. It's a nervous system that still confuses accountability with threat.

What makes it even harder is that it's the people I care about most who feel most let down by it. My parents. Sebastian. The ones I love deeply. They see me make it to work on time, or show up early for a prison visit, or never miss a hospital appointment—and I know what they must be thinking: "So why can't you do that for us?"

But it's not about who matters more. It's never been that. It's about what my body perceives as emergency versus emotional exposure. Those high-stakes moments—work, doctors, courtrooms—they're not personal. I can armor up for them. But family? Intimacy? Being fully present with people I love? That's where the wiring short-circuits. And I hate that. I know it hurts them. And I wish they could see that it doesn't mean they matter less. It means they matter so much that I feel vulnerable showing up late, flawed, or unprepared. It's not a reflection of my love. It's a reflection of my trauma.

Explaining trauma? That's a whole other struggle. There are still so many people who don't understand it—who hear the word and roll their eyes, like it's just a buzzword or an excuse.

They weren't taught to talk about it. They didn't grow up with language for it. So, when someone like me tries to name it—tries to explain how trauma shows up in things like lateness, fidgeting, panic during a TV show, or the inability to sit still—they shut it down. They act like I'm being dramatic or like those things are over and I should suddenly be normal.

But here's what I've learned: trauma isn't always loud. It's not always obvious. It doesn't just live in the big, violent memories. It lives in the patterns we can't break. In the things we don't talk about. In the way our nervous systems still respond like we're in danger, even when we're safe.

Honestly, I used to dismiss it too. Until I started healing. Until I started writing. Until I started paying attention to my body and realizing—it's all connected. The past doesn't just disappear. It shows up in everyday life. It hides in our habits. It surfaces when we least expect it. That's what trauma does. And that's why healing isn't about forgetting. It's about understanding.

While we're at it—no, I don't laugh at most comedies. People are always surprised by that, like it means I don't have a sense of humor. But I do. I have a lot of humor. I just don't find it in over-the-top jokes or scripted punchlines. My laughter lives in the real moments—sarcastic banter, dark truths, ironic twists, and those raw, honest exchanges where life is so messed up, it's funny.

That said, sometimes I do laugh harder than anyone at something completely ridiculous. Because when it lands, it hits deep. Absurdity becomes medicine. And sometimes the only thing left to do with the madness of life… is to laugh your ass off.

These aren't flaws. They're the traces of survival—and they're slowly becoming tools for healing. My body got smart. It found ways to protect me when no one else could. Now, it's letting go. Gently. And I'm learning that presence, not perfection, is the real goal.

If you're reading this and you've been through something too—just know this: There is no timeline for recovery. There is no deadline for pain. You might live through something horrific and feel fine, only to break down years later. Or you might crumble right away. We're all human. We all process things differently.

Some people make it through trauma seemingly untouched. Others carry it in their bones, in their breath, in the way they move through the world.

One isn't stronger than the other. One isn't braver. They're just different. And all of it is valid.

***

The Board of Pardons—Mercy by Roulette

Five people hold the power over life and death in Pennsylvania:

A psychiatrist.

A corrections expert.

A victims' advocate.

The Attorney General.

The Lieutenant Governor.

They don't meet the applicants. They don't walk the tiers. They don't hear the laughter, the leadership, the apologies. They read paperwork. They rehash trial summaries from decades ago.

They listen to prison staff who barely know the person they're evaluating. They look for reasons to say no—not reasons to say yes. And when they say no? It's final. Without explanation. Without accountability. They tell people to grow. Then they punish them for doing exactly that.

The Board isn't supposed to retry cases—but that's exactly what happens. And the people doing it? Some have no relevant experience. One of them—the "corrections expert"—was involved in a $68 million CHRIA violation settlement for approving the illegal sharing of inmate data.

And this is the person deciding who's worthy of mercy?

They allow victims' family members who weren't even alive when the crime occurred to speak, while ignoring others who have suffered unimaginable loss—but still want to see healing, release, and second chances.

There's no consistency. No transparency. No trauma-informed approach. Just bureaucracy dressed up as justice.

Where are the supports for grieving families? Where is the checklist? Where is the clarity about what the Board is actually looking for?

Applicants don't get to speak. They don't get to respond to rumors, to last-minute questions, to misrepresentations made by people who haven't seen them in years or never seen them at all. No rebuttal. No context. Just silence.

That's not justice. That's erasure.

We rely on unit managers and counselors—people who may barely interact with the applicant.

Not the COs who see them daily. Not the volunteers who teach them. Not the peers who rely on their leadership. Just staff who skim the paperwork and pass it up the chain or form their own narrative. Evaluations often focus more on the original case than the growth that's happened since.

Superintendents sometimes question a person's faith if it doesn't match the dominant culture.

In early transformation, faith is fragile. But instead of supporting it, the system treats honesty as a red flag.

Then there's the Secretary of Corrections—who decides whether the Department supports commutation. Not based on personal interaction. Not based on lived experience. Based on paperwork. And sometimes, politics.

If you're a psychologist and you don't believe people can change, why are you in that role?

If you're a corrections expert who hasn't walked the prison tiers, how can you assess rehabilitation?

That's not expertise. That's a clipboard and a superiority complex. These people are making life, death, and freedom decisions—without truly knowing the human being at the center.

And guess what Pennsylvania pays these board members to hold lives in their hands?

Less than $25,000.

In California? Six figures. In New York? Over $100,000. In Pennsylvania? We pay less, require almost nothing, offer no trauma-informed training—and expect miracles.

What do we get?

Exactly what we have now: An underinvestment in mercy.

A failure of leadership. A system that retraumatizes people instead of restoring them.

***

Pennsylvania: The Outlier

Let me be blunt:

Pennsylvania is the only state in the nation that requires a unanimous five-member vote to commute a life sentence.

Five people. One "no"—and that's it. Door closed. Hope gone.

It doesn't matter how long you've been incarcerated. It doesn't matter what you've done to grow, to give back, to heal.

If even one board member says no, you are done the process and must start over, sadly for some it will be too late.

This isn't justice.
It's bureaucracy.
It's a performance of fairness with no intention of mercy.

Meanwhile, other states? They've figured it out:

- Some require a majority vote, not unanimity—3 out of 5, or 4 out of 7.

- Others give the governor full discretion—no board, no performance for five strangers who've never met you.

- A few, like Georgia and Nebraska, allow independent parole or clemency boards to decide. The governor doesn't even get a say.

- Many states let people apply for commutation after 10, 15, or 20 years. Not 30. Not 40. Not "maybe never."

And here's the most important part:
Most of those states have lower recidivism rates than Pennsylvania. Why? Because they look at who someone *is today*—not who they were in a moment of chaos decades ago.

Pennsylvania's system isn't just harsh. It's extreme. It's political. It's outdated.
It punishes redemption.
It buries transformation.
It silences second chances.

It doesn't ask:
"Is this person safe to return home?"
It asks:
"How scared are we to say yes?"

To the lawmakers reading this:

> Fix it.
> You have the power to change the vote requirement. You have the power to make this process fair, trauma-informed, and rooted in actual public safety—not fear. There is *no logical reason* for Pennsylvania to cling to this unanimous rule while 49 other states take a more balanced approach.

To the public:

> Don't wait until it's your loved one.
> Don't wait until you meet someone who changed everything behind bars and can't get out because one board member played politics with their life.
>
> This isn't justice. It's cowardice. We are better than this.

To the Incarcerated:

> This is your life.
> And your families? They *are* the public.
> Ask them to stand up. Speak out. Organize. Vote.
>
> You've done the work.
> Now ask them to help make your freedom possible.
>
> Because silence won't save anyone.
> But truth, pressure, and persistence? They might just change everything.

To the Ones Who Would Retaliate:

> I know that just by writing this book—by telling the truth, by refusing to stay quiet—I may be putting Claudio at risk.

That should not be.

In a system that claims to value rehabilitation, transparency, and redemption, the idea that someone could face retaliation simply because the person who loves them dared to speak out… is proof of how far we still have to go.

If truth puts someone in danger while dishonesty gets a pass, then we've built a system that rewards manipulation and punishes integrity.

Let me be clear: I am not putting Claudio at more risk than his co-defendant, Jorge, who continues to lie. He bends the truth for sympathy, distorts the past to rewrite history, and thinks he can continue without consequence.
But those lies? They're not protecting anyone. They're keeping *both* of them stuck. They're delaying healing, preventing accountability, and damaging any hope for resolution.

Retaliation is not accountability. Silencing people is not justice. It's control. It's cowardice. It's fear pretending to be order.

And if this book makes someone uncomfortable enough to hurt the man I love—then you've only proven my point. Because lies don't threaten power. Truth does.

> I am done being quiet.
> I've been quiet. I've towed the line. I've followed the rules, stayed polite, focused on getting people home—and where has it gotten any of us?
>
> Nowhere. Still stuck. Still silenced. Still waiting.
>
> So, no—I won't be quiet.
> Not now.
> Not ever again

***

Stop Weaponizing Humans

I fight because the system tried to weaponize me—and I refuse to let it. I fight because the system erased people I love—and I refuse to stay quiet.

Stop weaponizing me and people like me. Stop looking at people like me—people who have been through hell and survived—and using us as some kind of political prop. I'm not a statistic. I'm not an exception.

I'm a living, breathing example of what happens when someone is given a chance. I benefit my community. I sit on boards. I mentor others. I work with incarcerated people and the people who oversee them. I provide training and support. I fight for change.

We are not the worst thing we've ever done or been accused of doing. And it's time this system—our system—starts recognizing that. We all deserve a system that sees growth, that sees humanity.

Let's stop standing for what's easy. Let's stop standing for what's white. Let's start standing for what's right.

Whether you are a lawmaker, a regular everyday citizen who has never experienced anything involving the carceral system or the broken commutations process—whether you know an incarcerated person or have never known one—you hold more power than you may know.

I have met with senators who have put such little thought into what they say. Members of the judiciary who say, "None of this is a priority. Talk to the Governor. He alone can commute any sentence without anyone else involved." Hello? How can you be leading the judiciary committee and really not understand that this is not how it works?

It is the lawmakers who ultimately decide whether we remain a nation of cages—or a nation of redemption. It is everyone who can decide whether justice is built on punishment—or transformed through truth.

What will you stand for?

***

Claudio, Me and the System That Tried to Break Us

Claudio and I both survived the system—just in different ways. We were thrown into fires neither of us started, and we carry different burns.

But even now, all these years later, I know this: Our story didn't end in that courtroom. It just changed shape.

And so did I.

There's a brutal irony to all of it. When Claudio was reviewed internally by the prison for commutation support, they focused a lot on me. My existence. My past. Our relationship.

But this process isn't about me. It's about Claudio. Yet, I could offer clarity. Not control. Not manipulation. Just truth.

They could put us in separate rooms, ask questions, and confirm that everything Claudio has said matches the truth.

They could see his honesty for themselves. But because I was acquitted—because I'm suddenly "untouchable"—they want to use their curiosity about me against him.

And they won't let me speak. What a double standard.

They could've taken just 30 minutes to read the parts of court transcripts Claudio had ready.

In a process that's already taking over three years for many, what is another 30 minutes—or an hour—to get it right? They say they want justice. But justice without truth isn't justice at all.

There were individuals hired to visit every prison, to train staff and applicants on the commutation process. Many people are asking: Where are they? Where are the people who were hired to help? Where is the transparency? Where is the guidance?

We say the system is about rehabilitation—but we hide from the people who've actually done the work. That's not oversight. That's avoidance. And if you don't want to hear from the people who know the truth, then stop pretending truth matters to you at all.

***

Chapter 14: Growth

He Was Five Years Old

Our prisons are filled with people who needed intervention, not cages. People who needed trauma-informed care, stable housing, addiction treatment, education, mental health support, and community—not cold cells and indifference. We cannot expect change while doing the same thing over and over. That is the definition of insanity. The cycle will continue until we are brave enough to break it—with policy, with humanity, with the courage to choose healing over punishment.

Claudio was born in Utuado, Puerto Rico—a mountainous region of the island. He came to the mainland as a child, caught between languages, cultures, and trauma. When he was just five years old, he and his siblings were taken from their mother. They didn't take him because she hurt them. They took him because she was the one being hurt.

He was placed in a foster home that only spoke English. He only spoke Spanish. And instead of being embraced, he was punished for it. They beat the Spanish out of him. Paddled until he bled if he mispronounced a word. Soap in his mouth if he resisted.

He. Was. Five. Years. Old. Let that sink in.

Eventually, he ran away—on a bike—and found his way back to his mother, miles away. But the system forced her to return him.

Later, he was sent to Chicago to live with the very man whose actions had torn their family apart—his father. There, he was beaten for speaking English. When they returned to Puerto Rico to live with his stepmother he was beaten again, this time for refusing to call her "mom."

By the time he returned to Pennsylvania, Claudio could barely speak either language fluently. And his own siblings teased him for it. He turned to the streets. Not because he was bad. Because he was lost. Because the very systems that were supposed to protect him only broke him further.

That search for belonging—born out of trauma and survival—put him on a path that led to a life sentence. But that sentence never told the full story.

Even now, all these years later, I know this: We came from different worlds, but the system treated us the same: as problems to contain, not people to understand.

And somehow, despite everything—despite poverty, language barriers, trauma, and cages—we're still here. Still speaking. Still growing. Still fighting. That's not the end of a story. That's the beginning of transformation.

***

Where My Accountability Begins

Everyone needs to take responsibility for their actions. If you do or say something wrong, you need to own it. You need to ask yourself what you could have done differently—what you never should have done at all.

Under the law, we were all adults. We could vote, drive, go to college, join the military, and go to jail. In 1994, we could even legally buy cigarettes. I couldn't legally drink yet, but I was considered old enough for everything else. Claudio was considered old enough to make wise decisions.

But was he?

Not when you know what he lived through. Not when you understand abandonment, instability, and what it feels like to hear the person you love say, "You'll have to leave if you don't provide."

I didn't know what that threat meant to him at the time. I didn't understand what it triggered in someone who had never truly known stability, who had already survived too much to bear. I didn't know his full story. He didn't know mine. We were young. We were still hiding the worst parts of ourselves, even from each other.

But here's the truth I cannot escape:

My words began the whole goddamned nightmare.

Claudio, I am sorry.

So fucking sorry.

***

The Humanity They Refuse to See

Some people will read this and think, well, he is where he belongs. Others will write him off without a second thought, using his conviction as a justification for dismissal.

But if they knew his story—if they truly understood it—they might pause. They might hesitate. They might even begin to see things differently.

Because the truth is this: Claudio never set out to hurt anyone. He never planned to take a life. Yes, he was part of something he should not have been, but what happened that night was never his intent.

He reached for a gun, because he was afraid. He grabbed that gun from the person who bought it and brought it, and it fired. There was no plan, no malice, no intention—just a split second of chaos that led to tragedy.

And he has lived every day since with the weight of that moment, carrying remorse in silence while the world moved on, uninterested in anything beyond the label "murderer" stamped on his name.

That's what the system so often forgets: context, complexity, humanity.

But I have seen that humanity—over and over again. I see it every time I visit him. I see it in the letters and conversations I've had with so many others still inside.

People who are mentoring one another, creating purpose, healing from the inside out. People who continue to grow despite a system that insists they are beyond saving.

And then there's Irvin Stanley Moore, who after 52 years is finally free— he continues to give back with humility and grace, working with students, supporting lawmakers, and offering hope to those still waiting for a second chance.

Yes, Claudio made a terrible decision. So did I. So do a lot of people—especially when we're young, scared, or desperate.

But we don't talk about that. We don't talk about the reasons behind the choices. We just reduce people to their worst moment and use it to justify their permanent exclusion from society.

I once chose to walk away from Claudio. I once chose to disconnect Sebastian. But I learned. I grew. And I came back. I'm still coming back. That's what growth really looks like—it's not linear, not neat or easy. It's layered, human, and sometimes painfully slow. But it's real.

That's why I created Reentry Ready.

It started with a simple idea: that people serving long or life sentences deserve real preparation—not false hope, not silence, but truth. I work with them long before the gate opens. We help them through commutation, prepare mentally and emotionally, work with their families.

We work with the incarcerated through strategic mentorship to help those who may not be quite ready, become ready. It's holistic, it's about giving back to the communities harmed, building the bridge between the incarcerated and those harmed.

These human beings should not be an afterthought. The truth is, we can't talk about redemption if we're not equipping people for release. And I refuse to let them walk that road alone.

Some of the people I work with have been incarcerated longer than I've been alive. Some were children when they were sentenced. Many were thrown into prison with no path out, no voice, and no belief that anyone still cared. But they kept growing. Kept trying. And now, some of them have a shot—if the system has the courage to look.

***

Becoming Who I Was Meant to Be

Claudio has spent thirty years incarcerated. He has spent more years in prison than he was alive before incarceration. During that time, I have grown from a scared girl into a mother, an advocate.

I worked my way through the ranks at the bank, had a career and did well. The reality is, my heart, my passion is working with the incarcerated, the broken, the disenfranchised, the marginalized.

I am no longer interested in dressing to the nines and shaking hands with corporate executives. I'd rather be in my jeans and a t-shirt or hoodie and on the beat, using my peer certification, my humanity, to stand with the incarcerated—to change the narrative. To not stand for them, but walk alongside them.

I have walked through fire and come out changed—but not alone. Every time I doubted myself, every time I wanted to give up, there was someone inside the system who reminded me what resilience looks like. Who reminded me that this fight is not just personal. It is communal.

This book began as my story. The reality is, most of my adult life story does involve Claudio, so you have read a lot about him. In fact, after doing a search, you have read his name 415 times so far, but it's not just about me or him. It is about the people who have carried unthinkable sentences with grace. The ones who fought to become more than what the system said they were. And the ones still waiting to be seen.

For years, my past was the only thing I could see. I thought it defined me, limited me, and controlled my future.

What I've learned is that the story I tell myself matters. If I only focus on the pain, I will always feel stuck.

When I began to view my story as one of survival, growth, and resilience, I saw that my past didn't limit me—it gave me the tools I needed to build a future. Now, I carry my past, not as baggage, but as proof of what I've overcome. Proof that others can and do overcome.

I didn't always realize how much my story could help others. I thought, "Who would want to hear this?" But the truth is, sharing my story has opened doors, built bridges, and given others hope.

Every time I share—whether it's with someone currently incarcerated, a family member of an incarcerated person, someone returning from incarceration, someone in recovery, or someone just struggling to believe they're worthy—I see the power of saying, "I've been there, too." It helps others feel less alone.

The greatest gift of my truth is that it reminds people that recovery is real—and that second chances matter. I'm not standing here because I did something extraordinary.

I'm standing here because I was given the space to grow. I was given another chance, and I didn't waste it. You don't have to be perfect to be worth saving. You don't have to have it all figured out. You just have to be willing to keep going—step by step, choice by choice.

For people who have made mistakes, who have hurt others or been hurt themselves, a second chance can mean the difference between being buried alive and being brought back to life.

If sharing my truth helps one person believe they are not too far gone—if it convinces one lawmaker to vote yes, one counselor to advocate harder, one warden to recommend support—then every step of my journey, even the most painful ones, has a purpose.

Because redemption doesn't begin with perfection—it begins with possibility. And every person, no matter their past, deserves the opportunity to show who they are now.

If you are a lawmaker, the Governor, the Board, someone on the edge of throwing away the key or keeping the cages locked, I hope this book shows you real people with real struggle and the real ability to overcome. We need you to change the narrative. Stop with the fear of the political career and start standing for people—all people.

**

From Innocence to Action: COVID, Clemency, and CADBI

In 2019, I began to speak vocally about actual innocence cases, bringing to light the epidemic we have in this country. But in 2020, when COVID was running rampant and prisons became breeding grounds, the question was no longer just *who is innocent*—it was *how can we allow thousands of human beings to die in confinement?*

I started searching for practical, compassionate ways to reduce the harm. I looked at who hadn't been written up in years. Who was aging. Who had serious health conditions. Who had already served half their minimum—or 25 or more years of a life sentence. Even if only for a temporary reprieve, we needed to make space. We needed to make room for mercy.

Through that work, I met some incredible people. Saleem, a former juvenile lifer, introduced me to the Coalition to Abolish Death by Incarceration (CADBI). For the first time, I found an entire family of people—some formerly incarcerated, some with incarcerated loved ones, and others who had never known anyone in prison but still believed death by incarceration was wrong.

In 2023, despite living on the eastern side of Pennsylvania, I was asked to become the organizer for CADBI Pittsburgh-West. I've remained in that role ever since. Our members come from as far away as North Carolina and as close as Pittsburgh's neighborhoods. And we're always open to more—more voices, more hearts, more people ready to believe that no one should be defined by their worst moment forever.

Change Is Real

I've met hundreds of deserving men and women. People who are my friends. My comrades.

People I trust. People who deserve a second chance because they have worked hard for it, they have taken responsibility and are living as pillars of their community. People who will never harm again.

People like Irvin Stanley Moore, who went to prison before I was even born. Irvin served 52 years inside the prison walls. When he finally came home, he carried light—not bitterness. Today, he works tirelessly through Penn State's Restorative Justice Initiative, teaching students, guiding lawmakers, and offering hope to others still trapped inside. He is beloved. He is proof that transformation isn't rare—it's real.

Jeffrey went to prison when I was just 11 years old. He had made a life for himself, serving in the Army Reserves, trying to break free of the oppression around him. When a gang member pulled a gun on him, Jeffrey defended himself. The victim didn't die from a gunshot wound but from an aneurysm more than 50 days later. The full medical truth has been kept buried—and Jeffrey has paid for it with his life. He will continue to pay until we begin seeing him.

Kenyatta grew up too fast—forced into the role of "man of the house" before he was ready. Pulled into the streets, caught in survival, a single moment defined him in the eyes of the state. But it doesn't define who he is today. He is a leader, a mentor, and a source of resilience within the prison community.

Rob, whose case is heartbreaking in ways most people will never understand, has spent decades being a voice for reform from inside the walls. Lawmakers from both sides of the aisle have attended his events—and many support his cause.

Richie, who has served over 40 years. He's been misconduct-free for over 35 of them. He earned college degrees, stayed connected to a devoted sister who visits him faithfully, and even had the support of a District Attorney for his release. Still—the Board said no.

Eli, an incredible artist and Certified Peer Specialist, who helps men battling mental health struggles every day. He too has earned college degrees. He recently adopted a three-legged kitten inside the prison—a living metaphor for resilience. Slowly, the kitten has opened up to trust—just like the men he supports.

Terry, now 77 years old, has served 47 years. Like everyone else who has gone for commutation merit review, he didn't have a chance to speak. All while the facility he lives in dealt with its own corruption scandal involving a superintendent who ultimately died by suicide after an embezzlement investigation.

Shelby had full institution support; he even had the support of some family members of the victim. Shelby has been an exemplary incarcerated person, he has a solid home plan, a great reentry plan, he is no threat to the community, yet the board denied him.

Kevin, who was held under advisement. They give no reasons for being held under advisement and when they finally returned, he did not receive the vote. Clearly, the Board had a question or concern. Who better to ask than the applicant or the Superintendent who knows the person? Yet, they sit and hold an application with some secret question and ultimately vote no.

Gail has served over 40 years. While incarcerated, she saved the life of a staff member who was choking—and was awarded a humanitarian award for it. Her story is unlike any other. After an extended wait, Gail finally received a unanimous vote—five out of five—from the Pennsylvania Board of Pardons. She sent everything home. Her family prepared to welcome her. She was ready.

But her release never came. Confused and heartbroken, her family waited for answers.

It was later revealed that an aunt of the victim wrote to the Governor, well past the 60-day window for victim input, urging him to block Gail's release. In response, the Lieutenant Governor—who also serves as Chair of the Board of Pardons—declared that the victim's family had a "right to be heard." A revote was scheduled.

Three board members stood by their original yes. But two—the so-called "corrections expert" and the psychiatrist—changed their votes. The same psychiatrist who claims to understand transformation couldn't recognize it in someone else.

What would've happened if Gail had already walked free? Would they have sent her back to prison over a late letter?

This was unprecedented. Yes, victims' families deserve a voice. But a voice should not become a veto—especially after a unanimous vote. To reverse an entire clemency process based on one delayed letter isn't justice. It's betrayal. It's justice reversed.

Justin is different. He's the youngest lifer I support as of this writing. I call him my cub. My baby bear. I won't share much—this mama bear is protective. But I'll tell you this: Justin was just 19 when he went in. He's filed appeals. I've personally been to some of his court hearings, and every time I hear the Attorney General's Office present their argument, I find myself asking, "Did they even read the case file?"

And yet society says that something he did at 19 means he can never come home. That's what we do—we define people by one moment in their youth and act like their lives are disposable.

We run with the headline instead of reading the evidence.

Commutation is real. It is a real opportunity for people who have worked hard, people who are truly remorseful, who will not harm again to have an opportunity to complete their sentence on parole.

It is not a free ticket out, if the individual has a life sentence, they are still sentenced to life except they will serve that time on parole, they will still have supervision. They will however have the opportunity to work, help family members, benefit communities.

These are individuals who are no longer a threat to society. These are individuals who have lived in one of the harshest, most adverse places and still became better people.

We have seen people come home and do great work, not reoffend. Yet, there is no rhyme or reason how the board decides to vote. How they find someone worthy, and if they have concerns, there is no indication of what those concerns are.

Sure, it would be nice for a candidate have a college education but guess what? College is not available in every prison. Some prisons are limited on the programs they run and the reality? Governor Shapiro made 92% of Pennsylvania Government jobs no longer require a degree! College degrees can be nice, but the reality is, society is truly beginning to embrace lived experience.

Not everyone communicates the same, not everyone is the best at expressing themselves and this is a reason why we need to listen to those who know and observe them on a daily basis.

These are human beings who I call family. My brothers and sisters. These are the people you're told to fear. These are the people society says are beyond redemption. But I know the truth.

They are not their charges. They are not their case numbers. They are not disposable. They are human beings. And their growth matters.

Note: I have many close connections throughout the DOC. There are far too many who I care about to name. This is a very miniscule sampling of individuals who agreed to be mentioned in this book and is in no way intended to exclude any other person I am proud to call family, individuals who I would readily support for a second chance.

***

What Pennsylvania Refuses to Admit

Pennsylvania has one of the highest rates of death-by-incarceration sentences in the nation. We are one of only two states—Pennsylvania and Louisiana—where first- and second-degree murder mean mandatory life without parole. No judicial discretion. No exceptions. No matter the circumstances.

Meanwhile, Pennsylvania continues to cling to fear. Continues to cling to vengeance. Continues to pretend it's justice. We call it "life," but it means death. Death by incarceration. Death by bureaucracy. Death by political cowardice.

We claim to believe in redemption, but we legislate like it's a fairy tale. We preach about rehabilitation while designing a system that buries the proof that people change. We tell incarcerated people to better themselves. We tell them to get an education, to earn certifications, to mentor others, to demonstrate growth.

But when they do? We punish them with silence. We refuse to listen. We refuse to see.

And that's where I draw the line.

***

The Commutation Process: A Broken Path

They say prison is for rehabilitation. They tell the public that the system is about second chances. But the truth is, most prisons aren't built to heal. They're built to contain. They contain pain. They contain potential. They contain every ounce of progress—and pretend it doesn't matter.

And when someone finally does everything they were told to do—when they change, when they grow, when they embody redemption—we make the path to freedom damn near impossible.

There is no roadmap. There is no idea given of what makes a great candidate. There's no checklist. No transparency. Just a long wait and a hollow hope.

The Board of Pardons doesn't review humanity. It reviews paperwork. It reviews case summaries written decades ago. It rehashes trial testimony that was often biased, incomplete, or flat-out wrong. It doesn't look at the living, breathing person standing in front of them now.

And too often, that review ends with a single word:

Denied.

Denied—not because someone failed to grow.

Denied because someone failed to listen.

The system isn't just broken.

It's rigged.

It's a slow-motion death sentence disguised as due process. We spend over $60,000 a year to incarcerate one adult. We spend over $200,000 a year on older, sicker incarcerated people. That's more than we spend per student in schools.

More than what a family of four gets in public assistance. More than what it would cost to educate, to heal, to restore.

Let's be real. Not everyone in prison is guilty. Our society shows us this over and over—stories of men and women wrongfully convicted, spending decades behind bars for someone else's crime.

And yet, when a person submits an application for commutation based on actual innocence? The board doesn't want to hear it. There is overwhelming evidence of actual innocence for two individuals I care deeply about.

I won't name them here, because their fight for truth and justice is still ongoing. But both were denied. Not because the evidence wasn't there—but because acknowledging it would mean admitting the system got it wrong.

District Attorneys stand by convictions like they're sacred. They refuse to test DNA— even when it's available, even when it could change everything. They'd rather spend millions housing an innocent person than risk exposing a mistake.

Worse, they let grieving families believe that the right person was held accountable—even when there's reason to doubt. They allow those families to live in pain and fear, convinced that the person who killed their loved one has never taken responsibility, terrified they might one day walk free.

One of my actually innocent friends who continues to fight for his freedom applied for commutation, and the family of the victim spoke out, heartbroken and angry, convinced of his guilt. And the District Attorney let them believe it.

They could have tested the DNA. They still could. But instead, they choose narrative over truth. They uphold a conviction not because it's right—but because it's easier. Because it protects their reputation. Because they'd rather maintain the illusion of justice than confront the fact that they got it wrong.

And the Board of Pardons allows this vile narrative to continue and simply deny. No questions. No discussion. Just denial. They choose to ignore it.

And still — we choose cages. We choose suffering. We choose silence. But it doesn't have to be this way.

Look at my own case: In the sentencing transcripts—after I was already acquitted—the judge found it appropriate to assert what he "knows" to be true—without evidence, without testimony from me. While it did not matter in the legal sense, he was overriding the jury's finding. I didn't testify.

I had no voice in the courtroom or at sentencing. And this is precisely the kind of judicial commentary that undermines due process and continues to impact my life even after acquittal.

I have the benefit of having official court transcripts. I have been readily available to discuss my case. But not everyone has that opportunity.

The Board or prisons will find what they want to find and retry a case. This in itself should be illegal—because under the Constitution, we all have the right to face our accuser.

If the Board is evaluating a case as if it is ironclad and making judgment, they are also denying due process by denying every applicant the opportunity to answer any questions, to fill in any gaps.

My trial lasted eight days. During the sentencing hearing for Claudio and Jorge, I was referred to in the transcripts as "Jaime Sortino." What else did they get wrong? What else was misspelled or mistyped through the fast-moving trial.

Oh, I know the courts got a lot wrong. The DA got a lot wrong. But how about those that transcribed the documents? Things that may have been useful to either Claudio or Jorge in the decades they worked on filing PCRAs?

The commutation process takes approximately four years—sometimes longer. Yet they seem perfectly okay with issuing a denial and forcing someone to wait another four years to try again? What is wrong with that picture?

Not all change requires legislation or constitutional amendments. Some fixes are within reach—right now—if the will exists to act. So, what could we do differently, starting today?

***

What the DOC Could Do Today—No Law Required

Not everything needs a bill. Some things just need a backbone—and a reminder of what "corrections" is supposed to mean. The Department of Corrections could do better by taking accountability.

97% of incarcerated people will return to society. Even some with Life Without Parole. Because innocence is being proven. Because some sentences were based on lies, exaggerations, or various other reasons. Because second chances are finally being fought for—and sometimes, granted.

So, the question becomes: who do you want coming home? Someone who was supported, encouraged, and treated with dignity? Or someone left to rot and dehumanized for decades?

If the DOC doesn't mandate humanity—if it ignores its own mission—it's not neutral. It's shaping people into something less than whole. And we're all worse off for it. We say this isn't about guilt anymore—it's about who they are today—but too often, the process still feels like a quiet retrial held behind closed doors. That has to change.

One of the easiest, most impactful steps would be requiring the DOC Secretary to meet with applicants—regardless of whether a prison Superintendent or staff member "approves" the visit.

There should be a simple, standardized threshold: if a person has served 20 years of a life sentence and has gone 10 years without a violent write-up, they get a visit. If they've served at least half their minimum on a non-life sentence with a certain number of years without trouble, they get a visit. No deep dive required. No packet review needed.

Just a high-level understanding of the case—because again, this isn't about guilt or innocence. DOC policy already says that. It's about who they are now. So go meet them.

The staffing process could be made more consistent and less arbitrary. One person shouldn't get denied just because the staffing happened on the wrong day or under the wrong shift. Fix the process—and follow it.

Each staffing should include the unit manager, the assigned counselor, the block psychologist, and a corrections officer who actually knows the applicant—preferably one chosen by the applicant.

If the person spent most of their time on a different housing unit, then that's the team that should be involved. Not whoever happened to be assigned most recently. This is about a person's entire arc—not the last few months they spent sitting on a bunk in limbo.

Superintendents should also be required to meet the people they're judging. I've seen decisions come down from leadership who never once looked the person in the eye, never shook their hand, never asked them a single question about their growth. Just read a summary, stamped "no," and moved on. That's not leadership. That's pretending you know someone because you glanced at their worst moment on paper and decided it was enough.

Staff should be allowed—and encouraged—to speak the truth about someone's growth. I've had corrections officers quietly pull me aside to say, "I've seen what he's done. How he mentors the young guys. How he keeps the peace. If anyone deserves a chance, it's him. But I can't say that publicly."

And I've heard others admit they've been discouraged, even threatened, for trying to support someone's release. That's not safety. That's fear-based silence.

The DOC should be proud of Certified Peer Specialists. These men and women are doing the work your own systems often fail to do—building trust, reducing violence, supporting change. They mentor, guide, and hold people accountable in ways no top-down approach ever could.

Instead of treating that as a side project or privilege, the DOC should embrace it as core to its mission.

And trauma-informed care? That shouldn't be a buzzword or a checkbox. When a person is acting out a trauma response, punishing them instead of helping them is not rehabilitation. It's re-injury.

We say we want people to grow, to prepare for the outside world, to be different than when they came in. But we don't create the environment for that to happen. We demand change but don't reward it. We tell people to rehabilitate, but we don't model what healing looks like.

This is corrections. That's the name. That's the mission. If you're working in corrections and you don't believe people can change, why are you here? The people who do live up to that mission—the ones who walk the block with integrity, who take time to know the individuals behind the uniform and the charge, who believe in transformation even when it's messy—they're the ones honoring the name.

The Department of Corrections should stand for growth, redemption, and a belief that we are all more than our worst mistake.

***

The Board Has Power – They Just Won't Use It

Pennsylvania is the only state in the country that requires a unanimous five-member Board vote for a person to be granted a second chance.

Once again, we're an outlier. That law absolutely must change. But because it would require a constitutional amendment, we know it will be an uphill battle—years of waiting and political gridlock while we continue to prioritize punishment over restoration.

Still, there are changes we can make right now. Quietly. Easily. Without legislation or amendments.

The Board could create a checklist of what they're actually looking for in an applicant. We could reverse the order of operations so that people who meet basic readiness criteria—those who've been trouble-free for a decade, completed nearly all programming (even though lifers are deprioritized for programs), have a home plan and a job offer, and have served over twenty years—go automatically to a merit review. Merit could become presumptive.

If the minimum is met, they move forward to a public hearing.

Board members could take time to talk to applicants before any merit decision is made. Immediate family members—parents, siblings, grandparents—could be notified within sixty days of the hearing and offered supportive services through the Office of Victim Advocate. Victim input could still be measured but not made final. The question we need to ask isn't whether their loss was painful—we know it was. The question is: What now? What can this person do to honor the life that was lost?

Maybe the family wants that person to give back in a tangible way—maintain a community garden, donate a small percentage of their wages to a restorative justice fund. There are creative, healing ways forward that don't involve perpetual punishment. And it's not just the victims' voices that matter.

After the merit review, corrections officers, fellow incarcerated people, and those who have been positively impacted by the applicant should be invited to speak up—truthfully, for better or worse.

Changing this process slightly would not only give more deserving people a path to freedom—it would reduce the burden on the already overworked Board of Pardons, whose members are paid just $22,608 a year. It would also alleviate pressure on exhausted prison staff.

None of this would require a constitutional amendment. It wouldn't even require a new law. It just requires the will to follow a better process.

Instead of having the governor appoint political allies to the Board, we could choose the most qualified people. We could require mandatory training, as is done in other states. We could make decisions based on transformation—not paper trails from decades ago. But we don't.

Instead, we bury that transformation beneath bureaucracy and indifference.

Even when the Department of Corrections has clear, written policies and procedures—it ignores them. Even when it preaches rehabilitation—it punishes growth. And even when it has the tools for mercy—it chooses silence.

That's not justice. That's a system that refuses to live up to its own ideals.

***

When the System Ignores Its Own Ideals

I've watched public hearings where District Attorneys—who weren't even born when the crime happened—show up just to defend the conviction.

They don't look at the human being sitting in front of them. They don't ask what's changed. They stand to protect a record. They stand for politics. Not for justice.

In Pennsylvania, first- and second-degree murder carry mandatory life without parole. Judges have no discretion. None. No matter the circumstances. No matter the age.

That's not justice. That's abandonment dressed up as law.

And inside the prisons? It gets even worse.

The prisons seem to follow their own rules. Despite having written policy, they routinely fail to complete the commutation staffing process the way it's outlined in their own documents.

Staff do not run the process the way they are supposed to. They allow some people into the staffing who do not belong while excluding others who should be present.

They focus on the case, on the conviction, not on the growth. I am not saying all prisons do this. SCI Coal Township and SCI Chester have exemplary Superintendents as of this writing but there are over 20 other prisons throughout the state that are failing at this process.

The Department of Corrections is supposed to have a process for commutation staffing. But staff routinely ignore their own procedures. They allow the wrong people into staffing meetings. They exclude the right ones. They focus on the case—not the growth.

DOC Policy 11.04.01 can be found in the appendix. This is publicly available—yet the prison isn't aware?

It states very clearly in (2)(b) that the decision is not based on the crime or an admission of guilt. It is based on mercy and evidence of change. It further states that a Corrections Officer should be present and that the Facility Manager's review should not include the incarcerated person.

When challenged, when the staff run this process wrong, they dismiss it. The superintendent will claim they are allowed to "talk" to the applicant. That the "folks in central office say there is nothing wrong with it."

Why does the DOC even have policies if they aren't followed or enforced? We expect these men and women to follow policies, to be better people, to take ownership when they do wrong—yet the leadership, those who are supposed to be correcting behavior, make excuses when they step outside the guidelines. Not just excuses—they will outright lie on replies to grievances. And the higher-ups don't correct the behavior. They allow it to continue.

Pennsylvania needs an independent oversight committee, an ombuds group to begin checking the system.

To be clear: The people in charge of rehabilitating—of seeing that people change—refuse to admit their own errors. And it gets better.

When they realize they didn't do something as expected? There is no accountability. The Board of Pardons doesn't allow them to correct their mistake.

DOC Policy 11.04.01, pages 9-9 & 9-10, specifically states the following:

C. Staffing Process

1. The Counselor will prepare a DC-46 Vote Sheet to determine whether to support the application.

a. The DC-46 should briefly summarize the crime(s), contributors to criminal conduct, compliance with the corrections plan, conduct, work performance, contributions to the prison community, public risk, and reentry plans.

b. The DC-46 shall include special program recommendations if granted commutation.

c. A recommendation can specify which indictments are supported.

2. Completion of the DC-46

a. Each voting staff's rationale must be recorded.

b. A favorable recommendation is not to be based on guilt. The issues in question are mercy and evidence of change.

3. The Unit Manager chairs the staffing team and includes a Corrections Officer. The inmate shall be informed that the Facility Manager/designee makes the final recommendation.

4. The Special Review Committee consists of DOC leadership and does not interview the inmate.

5. The Facility Manager has the final say, overriding all subordinate staff votes.

6.   Follow-up must summarize Correctional Plan info, Special Review votes, and Facility Manager rationale.

In far too many cases, those with ready access to this policy don't follow it. They make an assessment based on the case. Based on a narrative. Based on their opinion.

In Claudio's case, they moved his staffing date up by two days. They excluded any Corrections Officer—despite many wanting to be there in support. These are the individuals who see him every day. Who do know him. Union rules prohibit officers from writing letters or speaking on behalf of someone's application. So, the one time they can show support? It's taken from them. They are silenced—when their voices are needed the most.

I have permission to speak about Claudio's process. But this happens in many institutions. To many people. People who would be assets to our communities.

I've had officers—even security staff—ask me to look out for specific individuals. I've heard them name people they'd gladly welcome as neighbors. But I don't have the power to speak for prison staff. I can't just "look out" for them in an official capacity.

Not only foes this process take years, it involves psychiatric evaluations, paperwork, planning, preparation and in less than an hour, people with the power to shape someone's freedom can end it.

Some will retaliate if the applicant filed a grievance against them. Imagine standing up for yourself over something serious—and that same person now has the power to kill your only shot at freedom.

That's what thousands of men and women are facing across the DOC. Not a process. A gauntlet. Run by people who think mercy is weakness and power means silence.

***

The DOC—A Mission Worth Living Up To

DOC Motto: Creating Success, Inside and Out
Mission Statement: The Pennsylvania Department of Corrections provides those committed to our care with programming, education, and mental health services to reduce recidivism, while respecting victim rights and collaborating with stakeholders to ensure every reentrant has the opportunity to successfully reintegrate back into the community.

Those are beautiful words—if you stop at the brochure. If they were lived out—if they were more than just slogans—they would represent real hope. They would mean the difference between destruction and redemption.

But inside the walls? The reality is something else entirely. There's no uniformity. No consistency. No true accountability. What one person experiences at one facility could look nothing like what someone just a few miles away experiences.

The Department has adopted language from the Scandinavian model. They've even sent staff to Norway to observe it. But what came back wasn't the model. It was just the language.

It would be unfair to say there's been absolutely no change— Little Scandinavia at SCI Chester has brought in lawmakers, educators, and visitors. The Superintendent that runs the prison is phenomenal.

The men are well adapted. It's a positive place for continued growth and (hopefully) reentry. But when they're short staffed, or bring in people who aren't trauma-informed—who aren't familiar with how the unit runs—it becomes a setback.

Little Scandinavia has been a work in progress since 2019 and it was officially inaugurated in May 2022. There are pushes to get this model in every prison in the state--and that would be wonderful-- but it requires more than facility upgrades. It requires a mindset shift. Not just from individual staff, but from the DOC as a whole.

We still allow guards to put their hands on incarcerated people at certain prisons. It gets swept under the rug. And it's not isolated—it happens more than anyone admits. Those guards aren't terminated. They're protected by the union.

I always wonder where the integrity is. They expect honesty but fail to offer it. Recently, Claudio submitted a transfer request for family reasons. His mother and sister can no longer make the trip to see him, and he qualifies for a transfer. The prison he requested is accepting people. Still, he was denied.

He submitted the request shortly after filing a grievance against his counselor. And suddenly, the answer was no.

As an advocate, I know others are transferring—through Right to Know reports and firsthand confirmation. Some for similar reasons. Some simply for good behavior. The DOC has policies that support it. But they still said no.

Claudio's counselor held his request for three months, constantly saying it wasn't important to her and that the request was in her miscellaneous pile. (This is how they subtly retaliate).

It wasn't important to her because he had a grievance against her. It wasn't important because he was holding her accountable to do her job that we the taxpayers pay!

When she finally put it in? She didn't send the justification for the move and he was denied. When I reached out to population management, they said they were not doing inter-regional transfers. I guess I am imagining those busloads of people and their own reports showing otherwise.

I received a letter in the mail stating the same and at the end, it noted they saw he had an open grievance and would have to follow internal procedures. This may not look like anything to the layperson but the reality was, that was a hint. "Drop the grievance and you'll get your way."

No! We are done playing their games. Sadly, it is Claudio's family who suffers, but they have valid justification under Federal law so it will take time. It will take the Justice Department getting involved.

And we talk about rehabilitation? We talk about how important family visits are and allow the DOC to get away with their nonsense? And they think that the Scandinavian model can be successful with their mindset of punish, punish, punish? It's a joke.

As an advocate working closely with men and women in prisons outside of Philly, I can assure you: many staff in other facilities don't even know what the Scandinavian model is. They've never stepped foot into SCI Chester to see it. Maybe it's too logical to allow staff from across the state to see what progress actually looks like. Because the system still thrives on oppression. On control. On fear-based leadership.

The motto talks about "success." But staff are rarely trained—or expected—to foster it. Success still depends on random chance: Who your counselor is. Which facility you're sent to. Which rumor was scribbled into your file decades ago. Whether someone in power chooses to see you as human—or leaves you buried under old paperwork. And it seems that if you're a pillar—if you mentor, mediate, or help others—they don't want to let you go.

If you're someone who averts crisis, who keeps the peace, you become too valuable inside to be considered for release.

I would be remiss if I didn't say that disappointment doesn't even begin to cover what I feel—not just with DOC leadership, but in myself. My moral compass doesn't bend. I won't advocate for second chances for one group of people and ignore another.

In January 2023, when the current Secretary was appointed by Governor Shapiro, there were a few outspoken individuals who opposed the nomination for valid reasons. But as a whole?

I believed she deserved the opportunity. To stand together to block her appointment felt wrong. To judge her for things we'd "heard" or things she may have done early in her career—felt hypocritical. I wasn't fighting for her. I was fighting against assumed judgment. I saw her as human—just as I want our men and women inside to be seen.

We didn't simply stay silent. Some of us met. We drafted questions for her confirmation hearing. We did our homework. Because we've seen the pattern. Appointees to the Board of Pardons or DOC are often pushed through with little public notice. Dates get changed. Hearings get rushed. Opposition is stifled.

As a young woman working in male-dominated industries—IT and banking—I've lived what it means to be overlooked. To be seen as aggressive if you're assertive. To be seen as weak if you're accommodating. We women often have to be twice as good to get half as far.

So yes—I believed in giving the Secretary a chance. Because we preach second chances. And that includes people in power. But the person we didn't oppose strongly? She hasn't changed. Research shows she values unit management—an approach that promotes individualized attention. But when will the DOC actually train staff to follow through?

When will they be held accountable to actually make time for the people in their care?

***

Leadership Matters

During Secretary John Wetzel's tenure, there was a glimpse of humanity. He personally followed up with applicants. He knew prison recommendations weren't always fair. He knew change was real—even if it didn't fit neatly into a DOC checklist. He wasn't perfect. But he showed up. And that mattered.

Under the current leadership, that personal investment is gone. Denials come without conversation. Without a second glance. Applicants are reduced to file folders and suspicion.

I've seen officers and staff who do embody what corrections could be. Officers who recognize growth. Who see dignity. Who care. But they succeed in spite of the system. Not because of it. If the DOC wants to truly "create success, inside and out," then it needs to start living its own mission. Not just printing it on paper. Not just posting it on websites and brochures. Actually, living it.

And that starts with seeing people. Hearing them. Giving a damn.

***

Model Institutions Do Exist

I've had the privilege of meeting some truly remarkable staff—unit managers, deputies, and corrections officers—who genuinely believe in transformation.

They understand that the purpose of corrections is not to punish. The punishment is the removal from society. The role of the institution is to provide structure, safety, and the opportunity for change.

These staff members see the person behind the conviction. They uphold institutional security without losing sight of human dignity. They don't rely on excessive force or subtle retaliation. They don't need to. They lead with integrity, and their pride comes from seeing someone grow—not from exerting control.

Unfortunately, not everyone in the system follows that example. Far too many remain fixated on power and punishment. And because they work in an institution shielded from public view, there's often no accountability.

Written policy exists, but it's frequently ignored. Growth gets sidelined by paperwork. The focus shifts away from the person and back to the past.

Many staff aren't even familiar with their own Code of Ethics, which clearly states:

- "Employees shall perform their duties with integrity, impartiality, and respect for the rights and dignity of all individuals."

- "Employees are expected to treat inmates with fairness, dignity, and respect."

- "Employees shall strive to create a safe, secure, and rehabilitative environment for all individuals within the Department's custody."

Translation? DOC staff are not only allowed—they are encouraged—to support rehabilitation and fairness. That can look like speaking truthfully on behalf of someone who has changed, mentoring, offering second chances, encouraging programming, or advocating for someone's release when they've done the work.

Some Superintendents, like Thomas McGinley of SCI Coal Township, have done just that. He's spoken on behalf of individuals he knows personally to be remorseful, rehabilitated, and safe to return home. These actions aren't violations of DOC policy. They are expressions of it at its best.

There are institutions in Pennsylvania where things are handled with integrity—where leadership leads, and policy is not just a paper formality.

Superintendent McGinley is one of them. His leadership reflects fairness, consistency, and a real investment in human beings. He knows the men in his prison—not just their files, but their truth. Who they were, who they have become, where they will go. He engages with them, walks the blocks, listens. He has personally spoken on behalf of several individuals seeking commutation—men he believes in, men he's watched grow.

There is no way this man—someone who has spent nearly three decades in corrections—would risk his career to speak up for someone who posed a threat to public safety. There is no way he would ever put a community at risk. If Superintendent McGinley says a person is ready, it's because he knows them. He's seen their transformation. He understands the weight of the recommendation he's making.

And yet, even with that credibility, the Board of Pardons still often votes no. His voice—someone who actually knows these men, who sees them daily, who watches their growth in real time—is minimized. Dismissed. Ignored. And that silence? That dismissal of experienced, reform-minded leadership? It tells you everything you need to know about how deeply this system resists change.

SCI Chester is another example of what leadership can look like when vision meets action. They make intentional choices by leaders who believe correctional environments should reflect the humanity of those inside. They have programs, they connect with colleges and restorative justice advocates and while there will always be people who are employed in corrections who are not trauma informed or simply don't care or want to use their uniform as a tool for their own self-empowerment, the leadership will work to better those individuals. This is showing what is possible when leadership prioritizes transformation.

Inside these same institutions, people serving life are doing the work every day—quietly, without credit, without pay, without promises of release. They lead Lifelines. They run Triumph. They mentor, facilitate trauma groups, and model accountability. They give back because they believe in preventing harm, in helping others heal, and in transforming systems from the inside. Many of them are the very individuals being ignored in commutation reviews. But make no mistake: they are contributing to public safety and community restoration—whether the system acknowledges it or not.

These prisons aren't perfect. No institution is. But they are proof that the way we do corrections is a choice—and that some leaders in Pennsylvania are making the right one.

Some prisons took advantage of the pandemic—when it was genuinely necessary to limit movement—to pull back from meaningful interaction. That part was understandable.

But now? Now they continue to segregate the incarcerated people, to limit time out of cell, even though the health emergency has long passed. Many facilities no longer allow incarcerated individuals to eat in the chow hall. And for a lot of men, that time mattered. It wasn't just a meal—it was a chance to connect with peers, to be human, to experience some sliver of normalcy.

To them, that was part of rehabilitation.

Not every incarcerated person feels that way. Some prefer to stay in their cell to eat, to avoid conflict or triggers. And that's okay too. But really—how hard would it be to offer the option? How difficult is it to allow dignity as a choice, instead of removing it for everyone?

Unfortunately, there are still over twenty other facilities where leadership either misunderstands commutation or avoids it entirely. Where staff actively obstruct the process or allow bias and assumptions to dominate the room.

Where growth is ignored, voices are excluded, and lives are denied—not because the person isn't ready, but because the system refused to listen.

This isn't just a procedural failure. It's a leadership failure. And if every institution followed the example of SCI Chester or SCI Coal Township, we'd be far closer to justice than we are today.

***

Degrees in Denial: Call It What It Is

I have to ask—what exactly is criminal justice anymore? People go to school for it. They put it proudly on their résumés. But do they even understand what they're really studying? Because what I see in practice isn't justice. It's punishment. It's control, fear dressed up as righteousness.

Maybe the degree needs a new name:

Criminal Punishment, Mass Incarceration Studies, Systemic Oppression 101.

At least that would be honest.

Real justice requires room for truth, transformation, and humanity. What we've built doesn't leave room for any of that. It chews people up. It stamps a permanent label on their backs. It dares anyone to question it—and retaliates if they do.

***

What Justice Should Ask

Justice isn't about who someone was. It's about who they are now. I've sat across from men labeled as monsters—only to witness mentors, artists, caretakers, scholars. I've read case files that reduce people to a single act—but I've seen lives that now center around healing, service, and accountability.

We keep asking the wrong questions.

Not: What did they do back then?

But: Who have they become?

How have they changed?

What are they doing with the life they still have?

Real justice asks hard questions. But it also listens to the answers. They are not statistics. They are not monsters. They are not disposable. They are people.

***

Bias Isn't Always Loud—but It's Always There

There's a kind of racism that hides behind compliments. The kind people say with a smile, thinking it's harmless: "That's a well-dressed Black man." "She's so articulate—for a Black woman."

"I didn't expect someone like him to be so polite." "That man was so respectful—for someone who's incarcerated." You don't hear people say, "That's a well-spoken white guy," or, "She's a sharp dresser—for a white woman." Because whiteness is treated as the default. The baseline. The unspoken standard.

Everything else becomes an exception—something to be labeled, pointed out, and framed as surprising. That's bias. Whether we want to admit it or not. People love to say, "I'm not racist," or "I don't see color." But if race only shows up when you're surprised that someone is kind, intelligent, or professional—what does that really say about your expectations?

It's not just an awkward compliment. It's a window into unconscious bias. And we've built entire systems around those assumptions. We sentence longer because of them. We deny parole, deny commutation, deny mercy—because some part of us still imagines "those people" as more dangerous, less redeemable.

And yet, when white families hear these truths, some of them tense up—as if acknowledging systemic racism somehow means their incarcerated loved one doesn't matter. But this isn't about exclusion. It's about proportion. It's about truth.

In Pennsylvania, the Department of Corrections only tracks two racial categories: Black and White. If someone is Hispanic and light-skinned, they're marked as White. If they're darker-skinned, they're marked as Black. That's it. As if entire cultures, identities, and communities can be reduced to two boxes on a form. Has the DOC really not learned by now?

Not everything is Black and White. And this isn't just about race either. It's about poverty. About addiction. About trauma. About how we treat anyone who's ever struggled.

When someone outside of prison turns their life around, people applaud. "Look how far they've come." But when someone inside does the same, their progress gets erased. They're still "just an inmate." Their trauma is seen as an excuse. Their growth is called manipulation.

Their humanity is buried beneath a label.

We need to stop pretending the system is fair when it's built on foundational bias. We need to stop pretending everyone starts at the same line when entire communities are held back before the race even begins. And we need to stop reducing people to the worst word someone else ever used to describe them—criminal, junkie, thug, inmate—as if those are their names.

This isn't just about the system. It's about us. Who we forgive. Who we fear. Who we see as worthy. Who we offer second chances to. Because the truth is: Justice isn't blind. But it damn well should be.

***

A Moment I'll Never Forget

I remember a few years ago, a friend of mine was dating a police officer. I've grown since I was arrested. I don't automatically hate anyone in uniform. I believe in nuance. Some police officers are decent. Some are corrupt. Same with any profession. But after everything I've seen—after everything I've lived—I know better than to romanticize power.

One night, after hearing me talk about second chances, this officer said something that still burns in my memory: "That's never going to happen. You're wasting your time." I pushed back. I told him change had to happen.

Too many cases where police get it wrong and DAs push the wrong narrative. Too many wrongful convictions. Too much over-sentencing. Too many people are thrown away. His response? "We don't have to get it right. If we get it wrong, there's this thing called the appeals process." I never spoke to him again.

Here's the truth:

Taxpayers pay law enforcement to do their job. It means getting it right, especially when the stakes are so high. Not gamble with people's lives. The chances of a person winning an appeal? Less than 3%.

One day behind bars for an innocent person is one day too many. But that officer didn't get it. And that's the real problem. Too many people in power don't have to understand. They just get to decide. Decide your fate. Decide your worth. Decide if you'll ever breathe free air again.

Some people in these roles believe they can do wrong without consequence—like they're untouchable. They tell themselves they're just doing their job. That if they get it wrong, it'll be fixed on appeal.

But here's the truth: The appeals process rarely fixes anything and the damage is often permanent. When you help send someone to prison—especially for life—you hold a piece of their future in your hands. If that person dies behind bars, you weren't just a bystander to injustice.

You were part of the chain of failure that kept them there. And maybe the worst part? The person who actually caused the harm might still be free—because the system rushed to judgment or relied on a false narrative. That's not justice. That's complicity.

You didn't create accountability. You created a slow-motion execution. You sleep at night. You tell yourself it was protocol. But deep down, you know. You know that if someone had really looked—had really cared—That life might've been spared. Whether they are police, district attorneys, or prison staff—There should be accountability.

If you have 100 people working in any of these places and there is one corrupt person, one bad apple—And 99 people turn a blind eye? You don't have one bad person. You have an entire force of bad. These people in power make decisions insulated from the consequences. While the rest of us live them.

And yet, even after everything—after the failures, the lies, the broken appeals and the arrogance of unchecked power—I still believe people can change. I've seen it. I've lived it. I've watched people rise from the ashes of their worst mistakes and become mentors, leaders, healers. Not because the system helped them. But in spite of it. And that's what makes their transformation even more powerful.

***

What Growth Actually Looks Like

I've survived things that could've shattered me. I carry scars you can't see—scars carved deep into me by trauma, violence, and survival. I will forever miss the people taken by violence, the ones who live on in scents, in songs, in sudden memories that steal my breath mid-sentence. Their loss reminds me every single day that justice isn't perpetual punishment.

Justice isn't a prosecutor's checkbox. Justice isn't locking someone away forever while victims grieve in silence.

I've known people sentenced to die in prison, and I've also known of people who took lives and walked free with probation.

My dear friend Dan was one of the purest souls I ever met. We met in the United States Civil Air Patrol—he was a cadet; I was a lieutenant. Dan was a lifelong paramedic, a state constable, and the guy everyone loved. In 2018, he was shot in the back. Not by a stranger. By someone he trusted—a fellow EMT.

Dan's killer rendered no aid. And somehow, he got fifteen months' probation. Fifteen months. Not because Dan's life mattered less, but because of power, race, zip code, and politics. That's the truth people don't want to hear.

Do I believe in accountability? Always. But accountability doesn't mean everyone who's ever caused harm should die in a cage. Especially not when the system keeps criminalizing poverty, trauma, mental health, and addiction—instead of healing them. We're not addressing causes. We're reacting to symptoms. After the harm has already been done.

Everyone knows someone. Or knows someone who knows someone. That's how close incarceration is to all of us—families, coworkers, neighbors. No one is immune from its reach, but some people are far more likely to be impacted than others. We seem to love incarcerating the marginalized, yet they are the very people facing the worst gaps in our society: underfunded schools, over-policing, and limited access to healthcare, especially mental health care. These aren't unfortunate oversights. They are engineered fractures—built into the very structure we claim is just.

When people's basic needs go unmet, they don't break laws because they're evil. They break laws because they're desperate. And when the fallout inevitably comes, law enforcement doesn't arrive to solve the desperation. It arrives to manage the consequences.

I spent years ashamed of my past, trying to outrun it, hide it. But now, I walk straight into it. I speak truth into rooms where people like me were never meant to speak. I'm not one of the women at Muncy—but I could have been. Not just once, but twice. And I'll never forget that. Today, I walk into prisons not as an incarcerated woman, but as a witness. I could have remained invisible—but I chose to speak.

I've met survivors of violence who are imprisoned for defending themselves. I've looked into their eyes and seen a version of myself staring back. Some are still locked away. Some never made it out. I've read the research; I've seen the reports—but honestly? I don't need them. Because I've lived it. We are failing. And still, despite it all, we fight.

Growth looks like Irvin Stanley Moore walking free after half a century and choosing to serve the very communities that once forgot him. It looks like the peer specialists: men and women mentoring young people to stop the cycle of violence and make different choices. It looks like GED tutors, hospice workers, mentors, reentry guides, artists, barbers, the incarcerated leaders of the Lifers organizations and program facilitators.

These are men and women who spend their days helping others heal, grow, and break cycles. They fight every day to be better—not because someone forced them, but because it's who they are. It's who they've been. And now, they finally have the opportunity to live that truth from behind the walls. These are people who have chosen healing in one of the harshest places on earth.

We must begin investing in healing with the same urgency we've invested in punishment. Whether it's healing for the person harmed or the person who caused harm, we need to spend our resources wisely—not just cage people and throw away the key.

Growth looks like the men and women still housed within the Department of Corrections—people I've gotten to know, people who have become extended family. These are not just names to me. They are individuals I wouldn't just accept as neighbors—I would welcome them into my home. I would love to see them become part of the community where I live. I can't possibly name every person, but they know who they are, and they all matter to me.

Growth looks like me—standing in rooms I never thought I'd enter, telling the truth, even when it makes people uncomfortable. Across Pennsylvania, there are countless men and women who were once lost and are now leaders. People who should have been given help, not handcuffs. People who should have received a second chance—not a life sentence disguised as justice.

Growth isn't neat or linear. It's messy. It's painful. It's beautiful. And it's human. Growth means doing the hard thing. The honest thing. The human thing. And it's happening—every single day—behind the walls most people refuse to see.

This is what growth looks like. It is messy. It is raw. It doesn't always look like smiling selfies or inspirational quotes. Growth is crying in the shower. It's apologizing. It's breaking a cycle you didn't even know you were in. It's learning how to respond instead of react. It's fidgeting because your nervous system doesn't trust silence—but showing up anyway.

Growth is doing better even if no one claps. It's telling the truth, even when it's embarrassing. It's choosing to see yourself as more than what hurt you. It's seeing someone else for who they are now, not just who they were then.

I used to see my life as a string of mistakes—bad choices, trauma, and survival. I defined myself by what I had been through. I didn't know I was still so impacted by trauma until I began writing this book. But I found the courage to leave unsafe situations. To get sober. To raise my children. To rebuild, even when it felt like I was starting from nothing. I became the person I needed when I was younger. And then I became that person for others.

***

We Are Them, They Are Us

In August 2024, I had the privilege of not just walking into a Pennsylvania state prison—I sat with hundreds of lifers. I've said it before, and I meant it: I would rather sit for lunch with a room full of transformed people—some with the most serious convictions—than dine with a celebrity. That wish was fulfilled that day.

Alongside lawmakers and justice organizations, we shared food, conversation, and a day that was nothing short of beautiful. We sat with the very people society has chosen to throw away forever. When I met Armel, and shared part of my story, he looked at me with sincerity and said, "Miss Amy, you don't look like that." I challenged him. "What does that look like?" If I were in the state brown uniform of Pennsylvania DOC, I would look just like anyone else in that room. And if they traded their browns for the clothes we wear outside, they would look just like us. Because here's the truth: we are them, and they are us.

It's not just a phrase. It's a truth I've lived. We are not different species. We are not divided by morality. We are divided by circumstances—by access, by trauma, by who got help and who got handcuffed. Strip away the labels, the uniforms, the charges, and what you'll find are people who laugh, cry, hope, grieve, and love—just like you.

And if we can't see that… then the system isn't the only thing that's broken. We are.

***

The Exit Sign, the Rain, and What Could've Been

That prison visit was just the beginning of a long week. The very next day, I drove out to Williamsport to see my dear friend Irvin Stanley Moore for a not-quite surprise birthday party. His friends from State College had hoped to surprise him, but with people traveling from all over, he caught on. Still, I was honored to be invited—and I wouldn't have missed it for the world.

On the way there, I passed the exit for Muncy. It was raining. The drive was long. And out of nowhere, it hit me like a ton of bricks: my parents are getting older. My dad is 80. My mom just turned 79. They still live in their own home, but they need more from me now. And I can give it. I can take them to appointments, help with the house, be there for them without restriction. I can see them whenever I want.

But had I been convicted in 1995; I wouldn't be seeing them anymore. I'd be thirty years in. I'd be inside that prison I passed on the highway. My parents couldn't make that trip. They'd be fading from my life while I watched from a cage. I didn't just grieve what could've been—I grieved for every woman in that prison. The loneliness. The distance. The slow erosion of support that so many women inside endure in silence.

Yes, the men experience it too. But the women? They often have even less. Fewer visitors. Fewer pen pals. Less advocacy. There are amazing grassroots groups like Let's Get Free that fight tirelessly for them, but the reality is, the men still have more support systems— wives, sisters, more outside voices. Many of the women were abused, neglected, or completely abandoned long before prison. And they are still being abandoned today.

Claudio is my why. It was seeing him again in Michigan that brought me back to this fight with full force. But it's not just his story. It's ours. And it's theirs. Yes, I fight for him. I'll always fight for him. But those women? I could have been them. And I fight as if I hope someone would have fought for me if the roles were reversed.

After Irvin's beautiful celebration, I finally made that turn off the exit and visited my friend Nicole at Muncy. I went in as a regular visitor—not a guest. Nicole and I are the same age. She's been incarcerated for thirty years, just like I would have been. And in those hours, we spent together, I felt the weight of it all—the missed time, the humanity the world refuses to see, the life that still pulses behind those walls. I know we would've been friends for decades if my path had turned out differently. And just like Armel, if Nicole could've traded her browns for mine, we would've looked just like each other.

Because we are them. And they are us.

***

I've Walked Through Fire

I've walked through fire. I've watched others burn. And now, I speak.

I speak for the people you locked away and forgot. For the ones you buried under life sentences with no second chance. For the ones who changed—who transformed—while the world refused to look again.

To every lawmaker, every voter, every "tough on crime" voice who still has power: You are the Fourteenth Juror now. Will you keep clinging to fear and fiction? Will you keep defining us by a single page of our story? Or will you finally see us—not for our worst moment, but for everything we've survived, everything we've rebuilt, and everything we still have to offer?

Will you take the time to understand that "tough on crime" doesn't work? If it did, we wouldn't still be flooding prisons and burying people in life sentences. We wouldn't still be repeating the same cycles of harm. Tough on crime sounds strong, but all it's done is destroy families, ignore root causes, and waste lives. It punishes pain instead of preventing it—and leaves justice out of the equation entirely. But it doesn't have to stay this way.

We could change course today. We could build a system rooted in healing, prevention, and truth. We could be brave enough to do something different—something better. We could be the generation that breaks the cycle. We could be the generation that finally stops pretending people are disposable. We could choose hope. We could choose second chances. We could choose to see humanity even in the places we were taught to look away.

We could do better. Not tomorrow. Today.

That's why I titled this book *The Fourteenth Juror*.

Twelve jurors gave a verdict. But justice doesn't end in a courtroom. The Fourteenth Juror is the one who comes after. The one who sees what was missed. Who dares to demand better. Not the twelfth person in a courtroom bound by instructions and legal jargon. Not someone mandated to sit through testimony and issue a verdict dictated by law. The Fourteenth Juror is not a role that exists in the courtroom. It's a role that exists in society. In every person who reads this, sees the system for what it is, and decides to do something about it. Not to weigh guilt or innocence—not anymore. But to look at the bigger picture. To examine what mandatory life without parole really means in a system that claims to believe in change. To ask why we're still handing out death by incarceration as if growth, redemption, and decades of transformation mean nothing. You've seen the cost. You've heard the stories. You've felt the truth beneath the policies and paperwork. So now it's your turn.

Not to decide someone's fate—but to decide what kind of justice system we're willing to accept. To ask: What kind of society buries people alive and calls it safety? What kind of system demands perfect behavior from the most traumatized while offering no second chances, no off-ramp, no grace? You can hold the Pennsylvania Board of Pardons accountable. You can hold the Department of Corrections accountable. For the denials. For the indifference. For pretending a file tells a full story. For ignoring the people they've never met, never spoken to, never asked: Who are you now? We don't need another verdict. We need courage. We need change. And it starts with you.

***

This isn't just my story. It's our collective reckoning—but it can also be our collective healing, if we choose it. If you've made it this far, I hope you've been moved—not just by my personal journey, but about all those men and women behind prison walls. Because this part isn't just about me. It's about all of us. It's about the people who never got a fair chance, the ones who grew in the shadows, and the system that continues to punish progress while pretending it's about safety.

I've shared my truth. But I'm not alone. Across this country—and especially in Pennsylvania—there are thousands of men and women with stories like mine, or stories that make mine look easy. They've suffered. They've changed. They've taken accountability. They've transformed. And yet, they remain behind bars, serving sentences that were never meant to account for who they've become.

We need to talk about why. We need to confront how our sentencing laws were built. We need to look at who we choose to bury and who we choose to believe is worth saving. Because the problem isn't that people can't change. The problem is that we refuse to see them once they do.

***

A Broken Sentencing Machine

Pennsylvania has one of the highest numbers of people serving life without parole in the entire country—second only to Florida. And we are one of just two states, alongside Louisiana, that mandates life without parole for both first- and second-degree murder. That means judges here have zero discretion. No matter the context. No matter the growth. No matter who that person is today.

We elect judges and then handcuff them with laws that strip away their ability to judge. And what happens? We sentence people to die in prison—people who were addicted, traumatized, abused, manipulated, or simply too young to understand the weight of their choices. We pretend it makes us safer, but it doesn't. It just keeps the cycle going.

Let's be clear: murder is wrong. Taking a life is never acceptable. But we also have to be brave enough to ask the deeper questions: who is committing these crimes—and why? Are they wealthy? Rarely. Do they have access to therapy or mental health care? Probably not—especially not in a timely way. Can they walk away from toxic homes, violent partners, or dangerous situations without facing consequences? Not without risking everything.

Unless you've lived it, you don't know how hard survival really is. And you don't know how easily one moment—one panic, one demand, one threat—can change everything. We sentence people to die in prison—then ignore how they've grown. We forget the ones who've transformed. Who've done the work. Who've mentored others and kept peace in the yard., who've studied trauma and helped each other heal. We ignore them because their story no longer matches the label we gave them.

***

The Reasons Behind the Pain

A 2017 study in the Journal of Substance Abuse Treatment found that most people make at least five serious attempts at recovery—often more. The National Institute on Drug Abuse reports that relapse rates for substance use disorders hover between 40 and 60 percent, similar to other chronic illnesses like diabetes and hypertension.

When it comes to abuse, the National Domestic Violence Hotline tells us it takes an average of seven attempts before a survivor can leave for good. Seven.

Why? Because of trauma bonding. Because of financial control. Because of custody threats, shame, isolation, and the terrifying reality that leaving is often the most dangerous moment of all. These aren't excuses. There is no excuse for taking a life. But there are reasons. Human ones. Real ones.

So where is society before the worst happens? Where are we before someone breaks? Why do we ignore the trauma, the poverty, the mental health crisis—until the fallout lands in front of a judge? And why, when someone survives all of that and finds a way to transform behind bars, do we still treat them like they're disposable?

Hurt people hurt people. But healed people help people.

Justice isn't supposed to be about vengeance. It's supposed to be about truth. About accountability. About healing—when and where it's still possible. If someone has caused unimaginable pain but has also done the work to change—genuinely, profoundly, over time—why do we pretend that change doesn't count?

***

If Your Hold Power, Read This:

If you're serious about second chances, start with the Board of Pardons. Fund it. Reform it. Hold it accountable. We trust this board with irreversible decisions, but we don't invest in proper training, mental health education, or trauma-informed evaluation. No required visits. No mandatory qualifications in rehabilitation or restorative justice. They don't even speak to the people who have waited years for a merit review. They look at applications, what the prison or DOC has decided, and say yes or no. That yes or no will decide if they will take any time at all to even talk to them. This isn't what mercy looks like.

Require qualifications that match the weight of these decisions. Require direct contact with the people whose lives they hold. And most of all, require courage—because redemption doesn't stand a chance when fear is holding the pen.

Do you hold town halls? Have you really talked to your constituents and told them how much we spend on incarceration vs. how much we spend on their children? Have you told them that we fund the school-to-prison pipeline? Pennsylvania ranks 20th in childhood poverty.

You have the power to change this narrative. But too many of you are more afraid of your political image than you are passionate about justice. You claim to want safe communities—but how are you building them? By locking people up forever, even when they've changed? Even when they could be a resource, a mentor, a stabilizing force for youth on the edge?

There are families with empty seats at the table on both sides. One doesn't cancel the other. My grief doesn't outweigh yours—but yours doesn't justify endless punishment. Real justice means making room for both pain and possibility.

I was eighteen. No diploma. Pregnant. Bleeding as I gave birth on an ankle monitor. I've been beaten, broken, addicted. I've stood trial for murder. I've been counted out but I'm still here.

Commutation isn't about excusing crime. It's about recognizing change. We can do better. We must do better. There were individuals hired to visit every prison, to train staff and applicants on the commutation process. Many people are asking: Where are they? Where are the people who were hired to help? Where is the transparency?

Where is the guidance? We say the system is about rehabilitation—but we hide from the people who've actually done the work.

That's not oversight. That's avoidance.

If you don't want to hear from the people who know the truth, then stop pretending truth matters to you at all.

***

You Are the Fourteenth Juror

Over time, all of those inside have become my why. I see them. I fight for them.

I fight for the humans—flawed, resilient, forgotten. And no matter what laws pass or don't, I will continue to fight for them. I will continue working to stop people from ever entering the system in the first place.

I have no doubt that Claudio saved me. Just before I got clean, I bought a bag of what I thought was cocaine. I was used to it. But something was off. My body panicked. My heart raced. I later learned it was likely laced with heroin—or worse. That could've been the end. But it wasn't. He stepped in.

Our story, our truth isn't simple. It's messy. Complicated. Inconvenient. It doesn't fit neatly into society's definition of a happy ending. But it's real. It's rooted in love, in accountability, and in a refusal to give up on each other.

Sentences shouldn't outlive transformation. The system won't change until we demand it—until we stop clinging to the illusion that perpetual punishment makes us safer. Real justice is not just freedom. It's policy that reflects growth, healing, and humanity. We don't need tougher laws. We need wiser ones. Until then, people like Claudio will remain trapped in a system that only sees the past. And people like me will keep fighting.

You are the Fourteenth Juror now. Not the system. Not the state. Not the press. You. You've seen the truth. You've heard the stories. You know what justice is supposed to look like—and what it too often becomes instead. You've seen how punishment is prioritized over healing, how transformation is ignored, and how a single moment in someone's life is used to define their entire future.

The question isn't about guilt or innocence. The question is whether you'll keep pretending people are disposable—or whether you'll be brave enough to see their humanity. Will you stand by a system that buries people and calls it justice? Or will you stand with us—those who know we can do better? You don't have to run for office or change careers. But you do have power. You can speak up. You can vote differently. You can call the Board, write a legislator, challenge the narrative when someone tries to reduce a person to their worst mistake. You've seen what's broken. Now, help build what could be healed.

Because justice isn't a headline. It's a responsibility. And it belongs to all of us.

***

Afterword: Writing Through the Wreckage

I didn't realize how deep this book would take me.

I thought I was just telling my story—putting words to what happened, naming the harm, and honoring the healing. But writing *The Fourteenth Juror* became something else entirely. It asked me to revisit moments I had long tucked away, to sit with memories I'd rather forget, and to feel things I thought I had already processed.

Some days, it felt like bleeding onto the page. Other days, like finally exhaling after holding my breath for years. There were tears, pauses, and nights I had to walk away because the truth was too heavy to carry alone. But I always came back.

Because this story isn't just mine. It belongs to everyone who has been discarded, misjudged, silenced, or buried beneath a system that refuses to see them whole. Writing this book forced me to look at every version of myself—broken, healing, angry, resilient—and offer her compassion.

And through it all, there was Claudio.

Even now, across miles and years and prison walls, he's been the one to remind me who I really am. The one who sees past the wreckage. The one who still knows how to hold me—sometimes with silence, sometimes with words, always with love. He didn't guide the writing, but somehow, he held space for it. For me.

I didn't expect it to hurt this much. I didn't expect it to change me *again*. But it did. And in that pain, there was also power.

If you've made it through these pages with me, thank you. You've witnessed more than a story—you've witnessed a reckoning. A reckoning I didn't even know I still needed.

Epilogue: The Reality of Justice

This was never just a story—it was a warning label the system didn't want printed. If you thought justice was served, it wasn't. If you thought this was just a survival story, it is—but it's also an indictment. The system didn't stop with the verdict. It followed me. Branded me. Tried to bury me in silence.

Still here? Good. That means you're ready for the part most people can't stomach. The part where I stop surviving quietly and start naming names. The part where I stop trying to prove I'm "one of the good ones" and start showing you what justice actually demands. I've been quiet long enough. Long enough for false narratives to settle in. Long enough for people to believe a courtroom told the whole story.

If you're expecting a tidy bow at the end of all this, you opened the wrong book.

There's no clean ending to injustice. No perfect closure for trauma. But there is truth. And there is legacy.

Let's just say this epilogue wasn't supposed to exist. This book probably wasn't either. If the court had its way, I'd be incarcerated for life—because apparently, I wasn't "grown up" enough.

According to them, I was the naive girl. The one who "knew what she was doing." The one who just needed to grow up. Well, I did. And now I've got a few things to say—starting with a man named Cleve, and ending with a challenge for every person reading this.

Cleve was one of Claudio's closest friends—a man who never got a second chance. He passed away before the system ever saw who he had become. But Cleve believed in me. One day, without me ever asking, a package arrived in the mail. Inside were legal motions. Cleve had spent his time writing out the full paperwork I'd need to expunge my record. The kind of legal help that would've cost thousands in the free world—he just gave it to me. Freely. Thoughtfully. Because he believed I deserved it.

I still have those motions. But I've never filed them.

Not because I'm ungrateful—but because I no longer feel the need to erase that part of my life. I am living proof that people can come from the darkest places—whether mental, emotional, or physical—and still rise. I don't need a clean record to prove I changed. My story is my strength now, not my shame. Cleve saw that before I did. I share his name here because so many people like him are forgotten. Buried by time, bureaucracy, or bias. People who were doing the quiet work of redemption long before the world was willing to see it.

And that's what this book is really about. Not just injustice—but transformation. Not just survival—but the people who helped me survive.

Let me also say something to the judge who sat high on that bench, looked down at my life, and said, "Hopefully, someday, she'll grow up."

Well, I did.

And part of growing up means I no longer let people like you pretend you knew what was going through my mind. You spoke like you had access to my thoughts, like being eighteen and pregnant made me incapable of trauma, fear, or seeing through manipulation.

But let's be clear—I wasn't manipulated by the man I loved. Claudio didn't twist the story. That was the job of the detectives and the Assistant District Attorney—the ones who molded narratives to fit their theory, cherry-picked details, and ignored everything that didn't align with their version of events.

And you? You ate it up. You spoke with confidence about what I knew, what I felt, what I intended—without ever truly seeing me. Without asking the deeper questions. Without wondering how the system might've shaped the version of me that showed up in that courtroom.

You want to talk about growing up? Sure. I've grown up—and I've also woken up.

And I'm wide awake to the fact that the system you believed in—the one you thought was impartial and righteous—was built on ego, assumptions, and a whole lot of theater. You remember going to Montgomery Ward as a young man? Cute memory. I remember being told the courts were fair. That illusion didn't last long.

You told the courtroom that I "knew what I was doing." No. What I knew was fear. What I knew was love, trauma, survival, and silence. What I didn't know—because no one had ever taught me—is how often people like you already had their minds made up.

You tried to define me.

You failed.

Because I've grown, I've spoken, I've fought back—and I've helped others do the same.

So, thank you, Your Honor.

You may have sentenced Claudio that day, but your words helped sentence me to a lifetime of proving people like you wrong. And look at that—I'm still here.

***

I want to be very clear about something—because people have asked, and the speculation needs to stop. They ask why Claudio took me with him. Why he would "allow" me to get wrapped up in that night. But the truth is: Claudio cannot speak for me. And he shouldn't have to. He didn't control my mind.

He didn't know what I was thinking. And I didn't know what he was thinking either. Claudio did not plan anything that night. He wasn't in the bedroom with Jorge. He was sitting in the living room with me, watching TV.

I wasn't with Claudio when he was out on the streets, so I can't begin to speculate what he knew or didn't know about Jorge. But I know Claudio—and if he knew the Jorge I knew, he wouldn't have been around him. Not for a second.

If anyone had bothered to ask me—or actually taken me up on my offer to talk—they'd already know: Claudio didn't take me along. I chased after him. I jumped into the back seat—fast, emotional, scared. I didn't want to be left behind.

Did I have any idea what was happening? No. And Claudio—he told me to get out of the car. He told Jorge to stop the car. But people don't want to hear that part. They want a villain. And Claudio's always been the easiest one to blame.

Let's be real about what happened: Jorge bought the gun. He spent who-knows-how-long in the bedroom with Jeff, playing with that gun and saying how much he liked it. He brought the gun. He drove the car. He's the one who walked out of that motel and threw the weed in the backseat. It hit me in the stomach. And he drove us home.

Claudio reached for that gun out of fear when he saw it. The gun fired. And a man is dead. Matthew DiMaggio is gone. And nothing can ever make that right.

There were no winners. Everyone lost.

But let's be even clearer about this: The commutation process should not be about blame. It should be about truth. About accountability. About growth. Every person should own their own actions. Period.

I have owned mine. I admit that my three words— "go sell drugs"— sparked the whole goddamn nightmare. I didn't pull a trigger. I didn't plan a crime. But I know the power of what I said.

And I live with that.

Claudio has owned that he grabbed the gun from Jorge. He's said clearly, over and over again: it fired accidentally. It was a semi-automatic and two shots fired through the door. One of them hitting Matthew DiMaggio. But people twist that around. They try to turn a textbook second-degree felony murder—an accidental killing during the commission of a felony—into something colder, darker, more calculated. Because it's easier to condemn than to understand.

My case was three trials in one. And Claudio should be heard independently from Jorge—who continues to downplay his role, acting as if he was somehow peripheral, when in fact, he was central. Is that blaming Jorge? No. That's the truth. We all had a choice that night. And two of us—Claudio and I—own the truth that our choices turned out fatal. That's what accountability looks like. That's what commutation should recognize. And that's what justice should actually be asking:

Who are you today? What have you learned? And what are you doing with it?

**

Now, let me be clear: telling the truth means naming things as they are. I hadn't planned to name Jorge Fraticelli in this book. He doesn't deserve the space. He continues to minimize his role and deflect responsibility. But for the sake of truth—for those who lived through this case, for the family of Matthew DiMaggio, for anyone wanting clarity, anyone who blindly follows his version of events, anyone still taken in by his "poor me" vibe—it's important to be clear.

If Jorge won't tell the truth, I will.

That doesn't mean I hate him. It means I have boundaries. I don't walk with people who distort, minimize, or deny. I walk with those who've done the work—who've changed, who take responsibility, who seek to make things right.

If someone has stayed out of trouble for decades, shows deep remorse, and is actively giving back—I will fight for them. But I won't waste time defending those still stuck in blame and spin.

I didn't want to give him ink—he's had enough free press. But apparently, someone's gotta clean up the narrative he keeps rewriting.

This book is not about him. It's about everyone the system tried to silence, everyone who found their voice anyway, and everyone still waiting to be seen for who they are today—not who the paperwork said they were at their worst. It's about Irvin, Nicole, Kenyatta, Richie, Jeffrey, Justin, Jeffery, Benny, Shelby, Cynthia, Gail, Chandler, Abi, Kevin, Francis, Armel, Mr. Mel, Matthew, Eli, Rob, and Cleve.

It's about the thousands of others who are more free in spirit—more honest, more whole—than some of the people deciding their fates. It's about second chances, and why this state is so afraid to give them.

They told me my story was over. I told them I hadn't even started. This book is my proof.

Now the only question is:

Are you going to scroll on… or stand up? Don't worry—no motion required.

Thank You

This book would never exist without pain. But it also wouldn't exist without the people who stood by me through it.

To Claudio—thank you for surviving. For refusing to let the system strip away your soul. For reminding me what love can look like, even across prison walls. You are still becoming, and I'm proud of you. You're not just part of this story—you are woven into every chapter. You are living proof that even in the darkest places, growth is possible. You've carried pain, time, and labels that never told the truth of who you are. Still, you rise. Still, you love. Still, you lead.

This book isn't just about what happened. It's about who we became—together and apart. And you, Claudio, are part of every page.

To my parents—thank you for loving me through the worst parts of my story. We didn't always understand each other, and we still don't agree on everything, but you never gave up on me.

To my dad especially—thank you for showing up when it counted, for grounding me when I was falling apart, and for being steady even when I wasn't.

To my mom—thank you for not calling me crazy when I said I saw angels. That moment held me in a way no diagnosis ever could.

To my children—thank you for being so level, so kind, and so deeply caring.

To my son: the product of a broken mother and an incarcerated father, yet still you shine. You carry light with a strength I'll never stop admiring.

To my daughter: you see the fight, and you stand for the fight—with the eyes of a child and the wisdom of someone far beyond your years. Thank you for your leadership and your love. You both make me better.

To Dr. D, you inspire me. You were the first person who knew my story in a professional setting, you have been such a champion for my growth and through non-judgement and fierce desire to see equality, have given me more courage to speak in ways I never had thought before.

To my former manager, Ryan… You were a breath of fresh air! While you didn't know my whole story, you knew that I was a "social justice warrior" and offered opportunities to bring more to the corporate world while seeing my value as an employee doing my "real job." You were one of the best ally managers I have known and without realizing it supported me in following my burning desire to see equality everywhere.

To Melissa, you've heard me many times over the years saying "what the hell am I doing working at a bank?" We always got a laugh but it always turned to serious conversation. You, my social justice warrior comrade, always inspire me.

To Shawn—To one of the most badass legal guys I know, I love your honesty and your genuine excitement when we find something big! Not a lifer, but you deserve special thanks for the work you do for the lifers.

To all of my inside family—thank you for forcing me to practice self-care, for checking me when I push too hard, and for making sure I'm safe even when you're the ones behind the walls. Especially Abi, Bert, Jihad, Hasan, Hakeem, Eli, Richie, Kevin, Francis, Anwar, Yat, Jeffrey, Jeffery, Matthew, my cub Jay, Mr. Mel, Cynthia, Nikki, Stacey, Terry, Akmad, Chandler and countless other men and women serving life without parole. So many of you should have been free long ago. Yet you remain tied down—and still, you give hope.

To George and Smokey, my inherited grandkids, keep your head up, keep doing what's right. I see you and believe in you. Thank you for always worrying about abuela... You should be! We are not that far apart in age so thanks for the laughs!

To Pam and Woody—it was a near tragedy that brought us together. Thank you for sharing your incarcerated son, Jay, with me, and for all you have done—not just for him, but for me, for Claudio, and for our entire movement. You came into this not knowing the laws of Pennsylvania, believing the system was fair and just—but you opened your eyes. And once you did, you never looked away. You've stood with us ever since. We love you.

To Rob—you drive me crazy at times, but you are the absolute resolute lifer fighting for freedom. Even when you're calling, pushing, asking me to dig up a number, make a call, or try something no one inside has ever done—you somehow make it happen. Your honesty cuts deep, especially when you talk about why you fight. And the truth is, you're right. Every time. Keep being you. Keep inspiring. And yeah—keep pissing people off. A very wise individual once told me, "If you can piss them off, they're still listening." You make sure they're listening.

To all those who work tirelessly for second chances and commutation—Not just the cases with the most support, but even those less known. Thank you for seeing value in people others have thrown away.

Especially those I've worked with the most: Ellie, Maria, Celeste, Serge, Ms. Yvonne, Yusef, Becky, Sonja, Marcie, Belle, Cynthia, Elaine, Pam Lizz, David, Irvin—your work, your consistency, and your love never go unnoticed.

Sean, Kris, Sabirha, and Nikki—your efforts, not just in the movement but for Claudio and others you've supported like family, have meant more than words can express.

To Terrance, Michael, Joe, Liv, Ev, and everyone at The Liberation Foundation and Project Hope—I'm honored to be part of this work with you and look forward to every day we keep showing up for those inside

To the beautiful people within the Department of Corrections who embody the spirit of the mission, thank you. Thank you to the ones who believe in the men and women behind those walls, who don't just enforce policy but uplift people. There are good and honest people in the DOC, and their work matters. It's unfortunate that we still live in an era where standing for what's right can get you ostracized, where you're expected to follow the pack instead of follow your conscience. But to those who see our men and women for who they are, humans who made terrible choices, but who have worked relentlessly to grow and earn a second chance, thank you. Your belief makes a difference. We need to keep turning it around, and we need to do it in a bigger way.

To every lifer who still dreams. Every man or woman who walked out of court free but never felt free again. To the ones who weren't believed, weren't protected, weren't spared, I see you.

This book was never about proving anything. It was about telling the truth. Mine. Claudio's. And the truth so many others aren't here to tell.

Acknowledgements

There are people who show up for you in the quiet, behind the scenes, when no one is watching—those are the people who hold your life together. I could not have written this book, nor survived so many of its pages, without the following souls who have shown me unwavering support, love, guidance, or solidarity over the years:

Francis, Matthew, Abi, Kevin, Rey, Anwar, Bert, Terry, Harun, Hakeem, Stacey, Nicole, Cynthia, Ke-Ke, Uno, Justin, Mr. Mel, Eli, Richie, Matthew, Rey, Nandin, Shelby, Ev, Armel, Jeffrey, Yat, Shawn and Curt — each of you has played a unique role in helping me stay grounded, challenged, and lifted. Whether through friendship, mentorship, deep conversations, or showing up when it mattered most, your presence in my life has left an imprint that lives in every chapter.

Some of you have walked this path beside me since the beginning. Others came in at just the right time—reminding me that community isn't always built by blood but by trust, truth, and time.

To those who opened doors, who kept me sane, who never asked for the edited version of my story—thank you. You are a part of my healing, and I carry your names with pride and gratitude.

To Those Who've Lost Someone

To those who have lost loved ones—I can relate to your pain. I know what grief does to a person, how it lives in your body long after the moment has passed.

Thank you to those who've read this book with open hearts. Thank you to those who want to see the cycle of pain stop.

And thank you to those who've done the unthinkable—who've stood for the person who did the unimaginable to someone you loved. That kind of strength is sacred.

Not everyone can heal. And truthfully, the system isn't built to let you heal. It's built to keep the wound open—because pain, when weaponized, serves power.

To those who refuse to be weaponized—who refuse to let the system use your pain to justify more destruction—you are noticed. And you are deeply appreciated.

***

Call to Action

If something in this book moved you—good. Let it. Let it move you into action. The reality is, the justice system isn't so just after all and it continues to fail thousands of people every single day.

Because the truth is, none of this changes unless more people start showing up.

You don't have to be an expert. You don't have to have the perfect words. You just have to care—and be willing to act on that care. There are people behind bars right now who need your voice.

Families who need your support. Systems that need to be challenged. Don't just feel something. Do something.

If you're ready to be part of something that saves lives, here are some places to start:

- Support Commutation Reform

Advocate for fair, accessible second chances. Push your elected officials to reform outdated sentencing laws and eliminate death by incarceration.

- Connect with CADBI West – www.cadbiwest@gmail.com
- Connect with Reentry Ready – www.reentry-ready.org

Support programs that prepare people for life after prison—before their freedom begins. Visit www.reentry-ready.org to learn more, donate, or get involved.

- Talk to Lawmakers

Email your representatives. Call their offices. Demand policies rooted in restoration, not retribution. I've sat across from them—you can too.

- Listen to the Incarcerated

The people closest to the problem are also closest to the solution. Their voices matter. Let them lead.

- Break the Silence

Share this book. Start conversations. Challenge the narratives that keep people locked in cages—and in shame.

This isn't just my story. It's a mirror.

And it's your move.

In Loving Memory of Joan Sehl

To my dear friend Joan Sehl—your name isn't forgotten. You showed up, every time, for the one you loved. You fought hard, and even when it hurt, you kept showing up. You stood for Terry with a devotion that never wavered.

I remember teaching you what I knew—and then watching you take off. You learned fast, you organized harder, and you never let up. You turned pain into purpose and love into motion. You were relentless. You were fire.

You were so uplifting, supposed to marry Terry but you were taken away just a day before. Your time here ended too soon, but your impact didn't. We will carry the torch forward—for you, for Terry, and for everyone still waiting to come home.

You are part of this movement. You always will be. You are part of this book whether your name is in lights or not.

You mattered. And I'll carry your fight with mine.

In Loving Memory of John Buckalew IV ("Buck")

Buck, you weren't a lifer—but the lifers claimed you. You spent many years inside, and it was the very people your mother feared—those serving life sentences—who became your protectors, your mentors, and your chosen family. Those men still call you brother.

You died far too young. You are one more heartbreaking example of how the system breaks people down instead of building them up. You served your time, and when you came home, the help you needed wasn't there. No one stepped up the way they should have. How I wish I could've been there when things started falling apart. Not being able to save you burns deep.

Recently, another man reached out to me—struggling in the same way. And all I could think about was you. You are now my torch. I will carry your name as I keep fighting for the ones who come home in pain. For the ones who need mental health care, support, and real connection to stay alive long enough to shine.

You mattered, Buck. You still do.

In Loving Memory of Those Lost Inside

Especially Cleve, Dawud, Ezra, and Edward. For all those still waiting, those who worked for a second chance, who changed, grew, and healed well beyond what the system ever asked of them.

You should have made it home. But this system does what it does: it waits, it breaks, it buries. Still, you are carried. In memory, in purpose, in every page of this fight. You are not forgotten. You are a reason I won't stop.

Resource Appendix

How to Support Commutation:

- Write letters to the Pennsylvania Board of Pardons advocating for individual cases.

- Sign and share petitions related to commutation efforts.

- Attend public hearings and provide testimony when possible.

Language Shift Guide:

- Inmate → Incarcerated person

- Ex-convict → Returning citizen

- Prisoner → Person who is incarcerated

📖 Glossary of Terms

- Certified Peer Specialist (CPS): An individual with lived experience who is trained to support others in recovery.

- LWOP: Life Without Parole, sentence where the person is not eligible for release

- Commutation: Reduction of a sentence, such as from life to a term of years.

- Clemency: Mercy or leniency granted by a governor or president.

- DBI: Death by Incarceration / Life Without Parole

- DOC: Department of Corrections

- Felony Murder Rule: A legal doctrine that allows individuals to be charged with murder if a death occurs during the commission of a felony, even if they did not directly cause the death. Even if there was no intent to harm or kill.

- Parole: Conditional release of a prisoner before the full sentence is served.

- SCI: State Correctional Institution, referring to prisons in Pennsylvania.

Reflection & Book Club Questions

Part 1: Icebreakers & Entry Points

• What drew you to this book? Was it the title, the subject, or the author's voice?

• What chapter hit you hardest emotionally—and why?

• Did anything in the book surprise you about the justice system?

• If you could ask the author one question, what would it be?

• Have you or someone you know ever had a personal experience with the legal system, even minor? How did that shape your perspective?

• What's one word you would use to describe Amy at the beginning of the book—and what word would you use by the end?

• Have you ever believed something about "criminals" that this book made you rethink?

• Which relationship in the book resonated with you most—why? (Amy and Claudio? Amy and Ken? Amy and Sebastian?)

Part 2: For Deeper Conversations

• Amy challenges lawmakers who praise her story but ignore others still incarcerated. What's the danger of lifting up only "redeemable" voices?

• How does the system treat accountability vs. punishment? What's the difference—and why does it matter?

• Discuss the 'Fourteenth Juror' metaphor. What does it mean to you? To society today?

• Amy survived addiction, abuse, incarceration, and grief. What role did storytelling play in her survival?

• What do you think about the claim that justice should be based on who someone is now—not who they were decades ago?

• How did Claudio's childhood trauma shape your understanding of him as a man? How does childhood adversity show up in adulthood, especially in prison?

• What would a truly rehabilitative justice system look like to you? Could the Scandinavian model work here?

• Amy says, 'Justice isn't supposed to be revenge. It's supposed to be truth.' Do you agree? Why or why not?

• What role does race and privilege play in sentencing outcomes, as shown in Amy's and Claudio's different outcomes from the same trial?

• After reading this book, has your view on sentencing reform, parole, or clemency changed? Why or why not?

Language, Reform & Awareness

• How did Amy's journey challenge your perceptions of the justice system?

• What emotions did you experience while reading about Claudio's case?

• Discuss the impact of language in shaping our views on incarceration.

• What steps can individuals take to support criminal justice reform?

• How does the concept of restorative justice differ from punitive justice?

Reflection & Character Insight

• Amy repeatedly describes herself as 'not present' during some of the most critical moments in her life. What does it mean to be emotionally absent, and how does trauma create that disconnect?

• How does the relationship between Amy and Claudio evolve over time? What remains constant, and what changes?

• Amy describes Ken as present but detached, while Claudio is absent but emotionally invested. How do these opposing dynamics challenge traditional views of love and partnership

Justice System & Advocacy

• What does Amy mean when she says, 'The commutation process isn't mercy—it's roulette'? How does this reflect the broader system?

• How do the chapters challenge the concept of rehabilitation within the Pennsylvania Department of Corrections?

• Amy argues that mandatory life without parole is 'a slow-motion death sentence.' Do you agree? Why or why not?

• What role should redemption play in sentencing, parole, and commutation decisions?

Growth, Healing, and Identity

• How does Amy's understanding of faith shift over the course of the book—and how does that affect her relationship with justice, advocacy, and grief?

• What does 'growth' mean in the context of this book? How is it different from perfection or recovery?

- Amy says, 'I speak for the ones who changed—and are still waiting for you to notice.' Who in your life has transformed without recognition? How do we make space for those stories?

💔 Themes of Loss & Love

- How does Amy balance grief for the people she's lost—through violence, miscarriage, separation—with her fight for justice and reform?

- In what ways does the book confront the myth of 'closure'? Is closure possible in cases of long-term incarceration or loss?

- Claudio's childhood trauma plays a critical role in understanding his adult life. How do we better support children like him—before it's too late?

🔥 Bold Questions for the Room

- What stereotypes about incarcerated people or those accused of crimes did this book challenge for you?

- What would it take for you to truly believe someone convicted of murder could safely reenter society?

- Are there moments in the book where you disagreed with Amy's choices? What would you have done differently—and why?

- Before reading this book, did you believe that life sentences allowed for parole at some point? Did you believe that all states are equal in their meaning of Life Sentences?

- Did it surprise you that people convicted of murder in most states have opportunities for parole and have such a low recidivism rate?

- Amy writes, 'You are the Fourteenth Juror now.' What does this mean to you?

Appendix

Appendix A- Partial Trial transcript of Jeff (last name redacted).
- Testimony of plea deal
- Notation of the trial being three trials in one
- Gun testimony

```
                        IN THE COURT OF COMMON PLEAS OF DELAWARE COUNTY
 1                                      PENNSYLVANIA
 2                                    CRIMINAL DIVISION

 3      * * * * * * * * * * * * * * *   No. 174-95, 4828-94,
 4                                  *       4827-94
 5      COMMONWEALTH OF PENNSYLVANIA *
 6                                  *
 7                      VS.         *
 8                                  *
 9      AMY SORTINO, CLAUDIO        *
10      MANZANET, JORGE FRATICELLI  *
11                                  *
12      * * * * * * * * * * * * * * *

13                          Media, PA, July 12, 1995
14                                      ***
15                               Courtroom Number 4
16                                      ***

17              BEFORE:    THE HONORABLE CHARLES C. KEELER, JUDGE

18                         DANIEL MCDEVITT, ESQUIRE
19                            For the Commonwealth

20                         ROBERT DONATONI, ESQUIRE
21                            For the Defendant Sortino

22                         ANTHONY SCANLON, ESQUIRE
23                            For the Defendant Manzanet

24                         ROBERT BRODERICK, ESQUIRE
25                            For the Defendant Fraticelli

26                         ALLAN ROSENBERG, ESQUIRE
27                            For the Defendant Fraticelli


                          YORK STENOGRAPHIC SERVICES, INC.
                                 34 North George St.
                                   York, PA 17401
                                   (717) 854-0077
```

1	A.	Chester County.
2	Q.	On what charges?
3	A.	Robbery, Homicide.
4	Q.	The case that's on trial here today.
5	A.	Yeah.
6	Q.	And did you plead guilty to any charges in
7	this case?	
8	A.	Yes.
9	Q.	Do you recall what those charges are that you
10	pled guilty to?	
11	A.	There's a marijuana charge, Homicide, Robbery
12	and the Conspiracy one, I think.	
13	Q.	And did you plead guilty before Judge Keeler?
14	A.	Yeah.
15	Q.	Have you been sentenced on your guilty
16	pleas?	
17	A.	No.
18	Q.	When do you expect to be sentenced on your
19	guilty pleas?	
20	A.	After trial, I believe.
21	Q.	Jeff, I'm showing you what's been marked for
22	identification as Exhibit C-68 and ask if you can identify	
23	what that document is.	
24	A.	These are the charges I pled to.
25	Q.	These are the summary of the charges that you

1 pled to?
2   A. Yeah.
3   Q. And could you read the charges that you pled
4 to?
5   A. Third Degree Murder, Robbery, Criminal
6 Conspiracy Robbery, Criminal Conspiracy Delivery of
7 Marijuana.
8   Q. And who did you plead guilty conspiring to
9 commit robbery?
10   A. To Judge Keeler.
11   Q. I know, but who did you plead guilty to...
12   A. Oh.
13   Q. ...conspiring -- you weren't conspiring with
14 Judge Keeler, were you?
15   A. No, no.
16   Q. Who did you conspire to commit the robbery?
17   A. Manzanet, Fraticelli and Sortino.
18   Q. And who did you plead guilty to conspiring to
19 deliver marijuana?
20   A. Judge Keeler.
21   Q. And who did you conspire with to deliver
22 marijuana?
23   A. Matt DiMaggio and Paul Wayland.
24   Q. And what's the total maximum sentence that you
25 could receive from Judge Keeler for all the charges that

```
 1        you pled guilty to?
 2             A.    27-1/2 to 55 years and $90,000 fine.
 3             Q.    That's the most you're faced with, right?
 4             A.    Yeah.
 5             Q.    27-1/2 to 55?
 6             A.    Yeah.
 7             Q.    Do you know the Defendant, Claudio Manzanet?
 8             A.    Yes.
 9             Q.    How do you know him?
10             A.    I met him on the streets in West Chester.
11             Q.    And about when was it that you met him?
12             A.    Around September or so.
13             Q.    Of '94?
14             A.    Yeah.
15             Q.    And how do you know him from the streets of
16        West Chester?
17             A.    Because I had a drug habit and buying some
18        drugs from him.
19             Q.    You were buying drugs from him?
20             A.    Yes.
21             Q.    What...
22                            ***
23        MR. DONATONI:
24             I object. Can we see the Court at side-bar?
25                            ***
```

YORK STENOGRAPHIC SERVICES, INC.
34 North George St.
York, PA 17401
(717) 854-0077

1   I have no problem with that.
2   MR. DONATONI:
3   Then if need be we can give the
4   cautionary instruction.
5 [End of side-bar conference]
6   ***
7 THE COURT:
8   Ladies and gentlemen of the jury, you'll recall
9   when I had previously given you my preliminary
10   instructions I told you that although this is a
11   joint trial, it involves the prosecution of three
12   separate persons and although this case involves
13   the prosecution of three persons, Amy Sortino,
14   Claudio Manzanet, and Jorge Fraticelli, you're
15   instructed to judge each Defendant and the evidence
16   with respect to that Defendant separately.
17   Each Defendant is presumed innocent. You must
18   decide with respect to each Defendant whether or
19   not the Commonwealth has proven the charges or any
20   of them beyond a reasonable doubt as to each
21   Defendant. In other words, the evidence, if it
22   applies to one Defendant, applies only to that
23   Defendant, not to the other Defendants, so you'll
24   have to judge each one separately and listen to all
25   the testimony and determine who it applies to, who

17

1   Q. What color was it?
2   A. Silver.
3   Q. What did you do with the gun after you got it
4   from Joe [redacted]
5   A. I brought it to West Chester with me.
6   Q. Okay, for what reason?
7   A. Well, 'cause one of the times I met Claudio on
8   the street he mentioned to me that he was having a hard
9   time in the neighborhood, that people were trying to rob hm
10   and stuff and asked me if I knew where he could get a gun,
11   and I said I didn't think -- if I saw one or whatever -- I
12   really didn't think I could at the time, it was just good
13   timing that I saw it and knew that he needed it. That's
14   the only reason I picked it up.
15   Q. Did you buy the gun from Joe [redacted] or was it
16   given to you?
17   A. He gave it to me under the impression that I'd
18   pay him in a couple of weeks or something.
19   Q. Did you ever pay him anything for it?
20   A. No, I never got a chance to pay him.
21   Q. Now you had some discussions with
22   Claudio Manzanet about a gun. What happened to the gun
23   that you got from Joe [redacted]?
24   A. Well, I took it back to West Chester with me,
25   and I saw Jorge, and I told him, I said if Claudio still

YORK STENOGRAPHIC SERVICES, INC.
34 North George St.
York, PA 17401
(717) 854-0077

1 wants a gun, I got one. I wanted to trade it for some
2 drugs, and then Jorge told me to follow him, and I followed
3 him back to the Seven Oaks Apartment, and that's when
4 Claudio wasn't around. I don't know where he was, and
5 Jorge says yeah, he wanted it for sure, and Jorge got it
6 off of me and gave me like about 20 bucks or something, and
7 he said he would give me some coke for it later.
8   Q. Where did the actual exchange of the gun take
9 place from you to Fraticelli?
10   A. At Seven Oaks in the apartment.
11   Q. Whose apartment?
12   A. Amy's apartment.
13   Q. Was anyone else present other than you and
14 Fraticelli?
15   A. No, Amy was home at the time but she didn't
16 see what was going on. We were in the back room.
17   Q. Now in relationship to the incident that
18 happened at the Sentinel Motel, when was it that you gave
19 the gun to Fraticelli?
20   A. About a week or two before that. About two
21 weeks before that.
22   Q. Now from the time that you gave the gun to
23 Fraticelli until the incident of the night at the
24 Sentinel Motel, the morning at the Sentinel, did you see
25 either Fraticelli or Manzanet in possession of that gun?

YORK STENOGRAPHIC SERVICES, INC.
34 North George St.
York, PA 17401
(717) 854-0077

1   A. Yeah, the night of -- I guess you said the
2   early morning of when all that happened.
3   Q. That's the next time you saw it?
4   A. Yeah.
5   Q. And who had it then?
6   A. Jorge had it.
7   Q. Where was that at?
8   A. It was at the apartment, Seven Oaks.
9   Q. I'm showing you what's been marked for
10 identification as Exhibit C-44 and ask you if you recognize
11 what that's a picture of?
12 A. Yeah, that's a window to the apartment.
13 Q. Which apartment?
14 A. In Seven Oaks.
15 Q. The one you've been referring to in your
16 testimony?
17 A. Yes.
18 Q. Being Amy Sortino's apartment?
19 A. Yes.
20 Q. Which apartment is it in the picture?
21 A. This one.
22 Q. You're pointing to a...
23 A. It's the one at the top in the far right
24 corner.
25 Q. The one on the top floor?

YORK STENOGRAPHIC SERVICES, INC.
34 North George St.
York, PA 17401
(717) 854-0077

1   A. Yeah.
2   Q. Is there a circle around that?
3   A. Yeah, it's circled.
4   Q. And is that the apartment where you gave the
5   gun to Fraticelli?
6   A. Yes.
7   Q. I'm showing you next what has been marked for
8   identification as Exhibit C-67 and ask you if you recognize
9   what that is.
10 A. Yeah, it's the same kind of gun I sold him.
11 Q. Well, what is the Exhibit C-67?
12 A. It says a Smith and Wesson model. It has some
13 model numbers, .22 pistol.
14 Q. Is it a safety instruction manual with a
15 photograph on it?
16 A. Yes.
17 Q. And do you recognize that photograph?
18 A. Yes.
19 Q. What's it a photograph of?
20 A. It's the same gun, the same kind.
21 Q. The same kind you gave to Fraticelli?
22 A. Yes.
23 Q. Have you ever seen Jorge Fraticelli driving an
24 automobile?
25 A. Yeah.

YORK STENOGRAPHIC SERVICES, INC.
34 North George St.
York, PA 17401

1 Q. What kind?
2 A. He had a Toyota, a red one, sedan.
3 Q. Pardon me?
4 A. Sedan.
5 Q. I'm showing you what's been marked for
6 identification as Exhibit C-28. Do you recognize what
7 that's a picture of?
8 A. Yeah, that's the kind of car he had.
9 Q. Kind of car who had?
10 A. Jorge.
11 Q. I'm showing you next C-27. What's that a
12 picture of?
13 A. Yeah, that's the kind of car he had. It looks
14 just like it.
15 Q. Do you know Matt DiMaggio?
16 A. Yes.
17 Q. How do you know him?
18 A. Through a friend of mine. I can't remember
19 his name now. He was only around a little while, and he
20 moved, and I met him through him. And he would come by.
21 He had a lot of pot.
22 Q. He had what?
23 A. He had came by for a lot of pot all the time.
24 Q. Did you know him by any other name?
25 A. Yeah, I just knew him as Matt. He told me his

1   Q. Did you have a discussion or conversation with
2 either Jorge or Claudio in that room?
3   A. Yeah.
4   Q. Would you tell the Court what the conversation
5 was about?
6   A. I told them that the pot was there and I most
7 definitely knew it was there, and where it was, the hotel
8 and all, and just small talk besides that.
9   Q. Well, was there any kind of plan formulated
10 when you were there?
11   A. He -- Jorge was playing with the gun and I
12 told him we didn't need a gun, that he shouldn't bring a
13 gun, and then he kept talking about bringing it, and then
14 he was playing with bullets, and I said well, you shouldn't
15 bring a gun and bullets, and then I told him just don't
16 bring a gun at all. Before we left I was telling him just
17 don't bring a gun at all, and, you know, I was scared about
18 that. I knew nobody had a gun there and I told them that.
19   Q. Describe exactly what you saw Jorge doing with
20 the gun when you say he was playing with it?
21   A. He was holding it and, you know, putting
22 bullets in the clips and taking them out, and...
23   Q. Was he saying anything while he was doing
24 that?
25   A. He just said how much he liked it, that's all.

YORK STENOGRAPHIC SERVICES, INC.
34 North George St.
York, PA 17401
(717) 854-0077

1   He thought it was a cool gun.

2   Q. How much he liked the gun.

3   A. Yeah.

4   Q. Did you recognize the gun you saw him with?

5   A. Yeah, it was the same one.

6   Q.. What do you mean it was the same one?

7   A. The same one that I traded to him a couple

8   weeks ago.

9   Q. The same .22 Smith and Wesson semi-automatic?

10   A. Yes.

11   Q. Now about how long were you in this room

12 having this discussion or conversation with either Claudio

13 and/or Jorge Fraticelli?

14   A. At least a half an hour. A lot of the time it

15 was just Jorge and myself.

16   Q. Well, on the occasions when it was just Jorge

17 and yourself, where was Claudio?

18   A. He was outside the room.

19   Q. Okay, could you see where he was going?

20   A. Yeah, he would go like watch TV and hang out

21 by there.

22   Q. And approximately -- about how many times did

23 he leave the room leaving you and Jorge in the room alone?

24   A. Several times. He would just come in and say,

25 you know, what's up and go out.

YORK STENOGRAPHIC SERVICES, INC.
34 North George St.
York, PA 17401
(717) 854-0077

1   Q. At any point while you were in the room with

2   just Jorge alone, did anyone other than Claudio come back

3   into the room?

4   A. No, I don't remember anyone else coming in

5   besides Claudio.

6   Q. And tell us what happened when you left the

7   bedroom.

8   A. When it was time to leave?

9   Q. Yes.

10 A. Just talked about -- one of them -- Jorge said

11 what about my face, should I put a mask on and I said yeah,

12 you should probably put a mask on or something, and he said

13 he didn't have anything, and I told him I'd buy him a hat

14 or something.

15 Q. Who was worried about their face?

16 A. Jorge.

Appendix B - Jeff's sentencing sheet.

249-19(b-4442

DELAWARE COUNTY COURT OF COMMON PLEAS
CERTIFICATE OF IMPOSITION OF JUDGMENT OF SENTENCE

DOB ✓ 9-30-68

COMMONWEALTH OF PENNSYLVANIA V. Jeffrey ~~[redacted]~~

Case Record No. 4826-94   OTN No. E678174-0

Info	Charges	Info	Charges
A	Murder (3rd Degree)	(F1)	
B	Robbery	(F1)	
Ict 1	Criminal Conspiracy (Robbery)		
Ict 2	Criminal Conspiracy (Delivery of marijuana)		

Sentence was imposed on (date) 11/13/95 as follows:

A. TOTAL CONFINEMENT is imposed with regard to the following charges:

Info	Minimum	Maximum	DCP	SCI	FINE
A	30 months less 1 day	60 months less 1 day		✓	$500.00
B					
Ict 1					
Ict 2					

B. PROBATION is imposed with regard to the following charges:

Info	Term of Probation	STATE	CTY	FINE
B	10 years	✓		
Ict 1	10 years	✓		

C. List SPECIFIC CONDITION of CONFINEMENT or PROBATION (i.e., ( )Pre-release/Work Release Status   ( )Partial Confinement)

recommend drugs & alcohol treatment
Credit for time served

D. Defendant is ordered to pay RESTITUTION to the following persons:

Name	Address	Sum

E. ( ) DETERMINATION OF GUILT WITHOUT FURTHER PENALTY or
( ) NO SENTENCE IS IMPOSED BECAUSE OF THE MERGER PRINCIPLE with respect to the following charges:

Ict 2

F. FINE ONLY (list amount and charges applicable):

G. The defendant shall receive such credit for time served as he is entitled by the laws of the Commonwealth of Pennsylvania. The sentences, confinement, and/or probation imposed shall be consecutive or concurrent as follows:

Info B runs consecutive w/ Info A; Info Ict 1 runs concurrent w/ Info B

The aggregate term of confinement is a period of not less than 30 months less 1 day nor more than 60 months less 1 day

The aggregate term of probation is _____

Costs of prosecution are imposed on the ( ) defendant ( ) Delaware Cty
( ) NOLLE PROSSE REMAINING CHARGES (check if applicable)

Date: 11/13/95   NOV 27 1995

Sentencing Judge

Name ADA Dan McDevitt   Name Def Atty: Yessenor M.

Appendix C - Sentencing transcript

- Misnaming me
- Once again putting the gun in Jorge's hands

- **Note:** The following are official court transcripts. I have redacted the last name of the mastermind. While this information is public record, I have made the conscious decision to not sling his name through the mud, as he did to me. It has been thirty years and I have no desire to uproot his life. Further, these are not complete transcripts. The following has been inserted to offer transparency and truth. Something the Board, the prisons and Jorge Fraticelli should all be seeking.

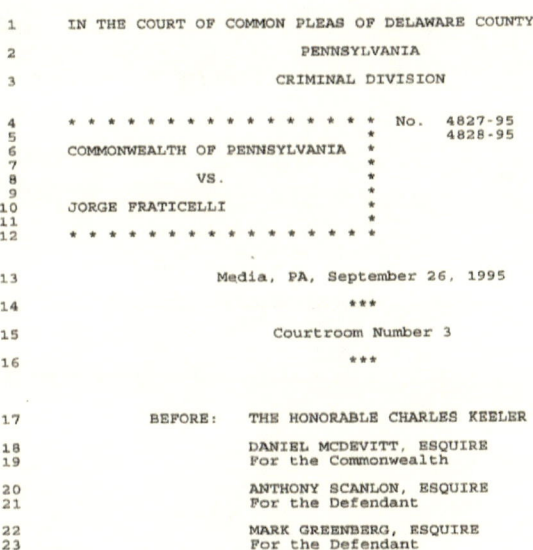

4

1   from Robert Donatoni (ph), Esquire, representing
2   Jamie Sortino (ph). She is one of the two
3   Respondents on the forfeiture petition, the other
4   being Claudio Manzanet. Mr. Donatoni and I have
5   agreed to split the money that was seized from the
6   apartment, with $538 being returned to Jamie
7   Sortino, and the balance of $538 being forfeited
8   and applied to the fines and costs in the Manzanet
9   case.
10   THE COURT:
11   Okay.

21

1   least, depreciate the value of his human life.
2   Claudio Manzanet and Jorge Fraticelli, as his
3   accomplice, took the only child from Diane DiMaggio
4   that she had in this world. That is the reason why
5   the Court should consider giving both Defendants
6   consecutive time for their role in this Robbery
7   Homicide. The gun that was introduced into this
8   case by Jeff ▓▓▓ first was in the hands of
9   Fraticelli. The gun goes from the hands of
10   Fraticelli to Manzanet at some time before he
11   enters that room. That gun has not been recovered.

that room. Claudio Manzanet does have a prior criminal record dating back to 1983. He has eight prior arrests, five convictions, two adjudications, and one dismissal. Defendant Fraticelli had no prior convictions before the commission of this offense, but had two incidents where he sold drugs to the police in the summer preceding this offense. The Commonwealth would ask the Court to consider the verdict of the jury, and consider sentencing Claudio Manzanet to consecutive time for the Second Degree Murder. And we'd also ask the Court to consider giving Jorge Fraticelli, since he was the one who was so fascinated with his gun that he had, that he brought along to this robbery, if he wasn't so fascinated with that gun, then maybe a gun was never used in this robbery. It was. Matthew DiMaggio is dead. And we would ask the Court to impose a consecutive sentence on both Defendants.

THE COURT:

Anything else you want to present?

MR. MCDEVITT:

No, sir.

THE COURT:

In sentencing, as we always say, we're directed to review the alternatives under the sentencing code, be mindful of the guidelines. I take into consideration all other matters that have been brought to the Court's attention. And, of course, where there is a mandatory sentence, which there is for Murder of the Second Degree, life imprisonment, we must and in this case, without reluctance, will impose that sentence. With respect to Defendant Fraticelli, as I indicated, being eighteen, he didn't have the opportunity, I guess, time-wise, to catch up with the record of Co-Defendant Manzanet, but he was on his way.

However, in light of the fact that he was not the individual, apparently, who pulled the trigger, responsibility, insofar as sentencing is concerned, is the protection of society. And since you've been able, you have been threatening society continuously. You are a threat to society. I've read some articles based upon interviews with Ms. Sortino. Hopefully, some day, she'll grow up. But she's got a long ways to go. Because you involved her, who was expecting your child, as the driver of a car in a drug heist. You knew what you were doing, and she knew what you were doing. And if the jury felt that they had an alternative but to impose a verdict that would have imposed a sentence of life imprisonment upon her, I think they would have found her guilty of Conspiracy to Rob, because they, I think, knew, and I surely know that she knew what she was doing.

Appendix D

Note: The following is Jorge's Non-Precedential Decision. You will note that he admitted to driving the car.

NON-PRECEDENTIAL DECISION - SEE SUPERIOR COURT I.O.P. 65.37

COMMONWEALTH OF PENNSYLVANIA,	IN THE SUPERIOR COURT OF PENNSYLVANIA
Appellee	
v.	
JORGE GEORGE FRATICELLI,	
Appellant	No. 316 EDA 2012

Appeal from the PCRA Order entered January 3, 2012
In the Court of Common Pleas of Delaware County
Criminal Division at No(s): CP-23-CR-0004827-1994

BEFORE: GANTMAN, OLSON and FITZGERALD,* JJ.

MEMORANDUM BY OLSON, J.:   Filed: January 11, 2013

Appellant, Jorge George Fraticelli, appeals from the order, entered January 3, 2012,[1] denying his fourth petition filed under the Post-Conviction Relief Act (PCRA), 42 Pa.C.S.A. §§ 9541-9546. We affirm.

We have previously explained the facts underlying Appellant's convictions for second-degree murder, robbery, criminal conspiracy, and possession of a firearm without a license[2]:

terms of imprisonment for Appellant's criminal conspiracy and firearm convictions.[3] N.T. Sentencing, 9/26/95, at 25. We later affirmed Appellant's judgment of sentence and, on July 30, 1998, the Pennsylvania Supreme Court denied Appellant's petition for allowance of appeal. **Commonwealth v. Fraticelli**, 707 A.2d 548 (Pa. Super. 1997) (unpublished memorandum), *appeal denied*, 725 A.2d 179 (Pa. 1998).

Appellant filed his first PCRA petition on July 30, 1999 and, within this petition, Appellant raised a number of ineffective assistance of counsel claims. An evidentiary hearing on Appellant's petition was held on March 7 and 14, 2000. Appellant testified during this evidentiary hearing and admitted that he was involved in the conspiracy to rob the victims of marijuana. Indeed, Appellant testified that: on the night of the murder, after Appellant's work shift ended, Appellant drove to Manzanet's West Chester, Pennsylvania apartment and met with Manzanet and Burger; Appellant agreed with Manzanet and Burger to rob the victims of their marijuana; when Appellant left Manzanet's apartment on the night of the murder, he had "the fully formed intent of robbing the individuals in the [motel] of the marijuana [and Appellant] inten[ded] to rob them by physical menace or force [although] not necessarily [by] using a weapon;" Appellant drove the vehicle to the motel and, prior to arriving at the motel, Appellant

The prison wants to claim that Matthew DiMaggio was shot in cold blood, if they simply read, they will see the courts determined that DiMaggio was struck during one of the two initial gunshots through the door.

> J-A07043-23
>
> Appellant was in possession of the gun that he had previously purchased from Burger.
>
> A short time later, the group left Manzanet's apartment; Burger drove his car, followed by Sortino, who was driving Appellant's car with Appellant and Manzanet as passengers. Appellant was concerned about his identity, so the two cars stopped at a WaWa convenience store where Burger purchased a hat and pantyhose [as a disguise] for Appellant.
>
> The four then proceeded to the Sentinel Motel. [In accordance with the plan,] Burger re-entered the room where DiMaggio and Wayland were weighing [the marijuana]. About ten minutes later[,] there was a rattling at the door of the motel room. Burger looked out [of] the window and saw Appellant wearing the knit cap that [Burger] had just purchased [from the convenience store. Burger also saw] Manzanet in possession of the gun that [Burger] had provided. . . . [Burger] then opened the door[,] looked out[,] and saw [Appellant and Manzanet move] away [from the door]. Burger reconsidered the situation[,] stepped back [into] the [motel] room[,] and shut the door. The banging [on the door] resumed and the door began to open, then two shots were discharged through the door. At this point[,] Wayland jumped into a closet in the motel room and Burger backed away from the door. The door was then kicked open completely[. DiMaggio] fell down to the floor behind [the door, with blood streaming from his face]. Manzanet entered the room with a gun [in hand] and told Burger to give him the bag of marijuana. A third shot was also discharged. . . . [Unfortunately, as the participants later learned, one of the two initial gunshots struck DiMaggio in the left eye].
>
> [After] the assailants departed, . . . Burger, Wayland, and [a mortally wounded, but alive,] DiMaggio quickly mustered their

Appendix E - Pennsylvania DOC Procedures Manual on Commutation

11.4.1, Case Summary Procedures Manual
Section 9 – Commutation Summary

Section 9 – Commutation Summary[1]

A. Commutation Process

1. The Integrated Case Summary (ICSA) – Classification Summary Update will be utilized with some content modifications for the Commutation Summary in accordance with **Section 5** of this procedures manual. Content modifications are specified in the following procedures and in the ICSA Help Sections, which are ***provided via email when Commutation Packets are requested and are*** available within the ICSA application. The Commutation Summary process promotes efficiency by utilizing existing computer applications and electronic reports that populate data in ICSA and provide the Board of Pardons with a comprehensive report.

2. *Questions regarding commutation are answered in the Clemency Application Packet, which is available for free in each institution's library. The packet also includes a copy of the current application. Department of Corrections (DOC) staff can contact the Bureau of Standards, Audits, Assessments, and Compliance (BSAAC) with questions about clemency applications using the resource account PM, Pardon Board. Inmates who have questions that aren't answered by the application packet can write to BSAAC, 1920 Technology Parkway, Mechanicsburg, PA 17050.*

B. Directions for Preparing the Commutation Summary Packet

1. BSAAC staff will notify the facility's contact person, via email, of the inmate's commutation application filing date and the date that the Commutation Summaries are due. The email notification will include the inmate's clemency application and the Commutation Summary Process Checklist (Attachment 9-A).[2]

2. The Corrections Classification Program Manager (CCPM) or Deputy Superintendent for Centralized Services (DSCS) will coordinate scheduling and report gathering for completion of the Commutation Summary.

3. Records Office staff shall provide the following information, with noted exceptions*, on the **DC-11B, Commutation/Arbitration Summary (Attachment 9-B)** and send the **DC-11B** electronically to the assigned Corrections Counselor for placement in the Commutation Summary Packet.

    a. The Identification Summary Section shall be completed as follows:

    (1) filing date (the official Board of Pardons filing date, month/day/year);

---

[1] 2-1011
[2] 2-1010

Issued: 3/21/2022
Effective: 3/28/2022

11.4.1, Case Summary Procedures Manual
Section 9 – Commutation Summary

(2) filing number (total number of applications the inmate has filed), (withdrawn applications are not included in the total);

(3) inmate's true name;

(4) state identification (SID) number (standard identification digits);

(5) Department number;

(6) Pennsylvania Parole Board (PB) number;

(7) birth date (month/day/year);

(8) current age (age as of filing date);

(9) marital status (current status: single, married, divorced, separated, or widowed);

(10) aliases (every known alias on record, no nicknames);

(11) *education; and

(12) *intelligence rating (Superior, Above Average, Average, Below Average, Borderline, or **Intellectually Disabled**).

b. The Case Data Section shall be completed as follows:

(1) offense(s) that the inmate listed on the current application and indictment number(s) for which commutation is presently being sought;

(2) county or counties in which the inmate was convicted for the specific convictions listed on the present application;

(3) name(s) of Judge(s) on present application sentence(s);

(4) sentence imposed, in years and months, relative to the present application;

(5) minimum sentence expiration date;

(6) maximum sentence expiration date;

(7) reception date (date inmate was received initially into the Department);

(8) total time served, present sentence (years, months, and days from effective date to filing date);

11.4.1, Case Summary Procedures Manual
Section 9 – Commutation Summary

(9) total continuous time served; if the inmate was paroled from a previous sentence(s) to the present sentence, record continuous time served to filing date. If inmate is released on parole, bail, or escapes, the sentence is calculated from the date he/she is returned to the Department; and

(10) facility placements for this offense. A copy of the inmate's Move Report, which lists in chronological order all Department transfers from initial reception to the present location, with transfer dates and reasons.

c. Accomplices and Disposition

   (1) The Accomplices and Disposition Section shall be completed, if the information is available, as follows:

   (a) name(s) of co-defendants;

   (b) Department number(s);

   (c) SID number(s);

   (d) sentence – charge(s) and sentence(s);

   (e) present status (serving sentence, paroled, commuted, etc.); and

   (f) where confined (name of facility).

   (2) If no information about accomplices is needed or available, then "None" should be typed next to the Accomplices and Disposition.

d. Detainers

   (1) The Detainers Section shall be completed as follows (if there are more than two detainers, a copy of the electronic version of the detainers may be attached):

   (a) identification of issuing authority as city, county, state, or federal;

   (b) date when charge was lodged;

   (c) detaining authority;

   (d) charge;

   (e) incident/warrant number; and

   (f) detainer sentence (in years and months).

11.4.1, Case Summary Procedures Manual
Section 9 – Commutation Summary

(2) If no information is needed or available, then type "None" next to "Detainers."

e. Offense History

The Offense History Section shall be completed as follows:

(1) probation violations (total number);

(2) adult arrests (total number of criminal arrests);

(3) adult convictions (total number of criminal convictions), each criminal charge is counted as a conviction;

(4) adult confinements (total amount of criminal confinements);

(5) parole violations (total number); and

(6) locations and dates of prior confinements (facility names and locations, and dates for all known confinements for past offenses).

f. The Narrative Summary of Previous Offense History shall include the following:

(1) summary of type and pattern of offense (juvenile and adult, past and present); and

(2) author's name and job title.

g. Miscellaneous Data

If no information is needed or available, then type "None" next to the "Miscellaneous Data" heading. Otherwise, this section should be completed in the following manner:

(1) all previous public hearing dates should be listed by month and year, this may be found in Section 5 of the **DC-16E, Sentence Status Summary**. Do not include Board of Pardons merit reviews (where filings were denied public hearings), filings withdrawn, hearings continued, or hearing decisions reconsidered;

(2) sentences previously commuted and dates;

(3) dates for previous parole (sentences from which previously paroled and dates);

(4) record dates of any previous parole violations and sentence(s) violated;

(5) amount of time in the community before parole violation, record total served on previous parole(s) before violation(s) occurred;

11.4.1, Case Summary Procedures Manual
Section 9 – Commutation Summary

      (6) if the inmate is presently a Convicted Parole Violator (CPV), record back time the inmate has served; and

      (7) additional data that may be pertinent.

   h. File the **Notice Commutation Applicant Form (Attachment 9-C)** on top of the left side of the **DC-15, Inmate Record Jacket**.

4. Inmate Needs Assessment

   a. An inmate applying for commutation or pardon shall be assessed using the *most current, Department-approved risk and need assessment tools/instruments*.

   b. This assessment data will populate the Classification Summary Update.

   c. *Any assessment results that do not populate into the Classification Summary Update will require a copy of the completed assessment to be included in the Commutation Packet.*

5. Existing documentation of pre-incarceration information shall be combined with facility reports that encompass the record from the inmate's reception to present. This information shall be compiled in a narrative format as described below and documented in the Classification Summary Update by the Counselor.

   a. Enter the statement "Commutation Summary" in the Other Problem Areas text field of the Additional Information Section of the Classification Summary Update so it displays on the Face Sheet.

   b. Conduct Report

      (1) The report is a narrative summary of the total number of the inmate's class one and two misconducts in the Classification Summary Update Section 6.1 Overall Adjustment. Highlight misconducts violating the crimes code of leading to an arrest (must be specific) and misconducts resulting in Disciplinary Custody. Describe patterns of misconducts such as assault, sexual misconduct, abuse of drugs or alcohol, possession of contraband (specify), theft, escape, and participation in major or minor inmate disturbances or violation of work or housing rules. Emphasize extended years without misconducts.

      (2) The Classification Summary Update Section 6.3 Misconducts provides an accurate report of the misconduct history from August 1997 to the present in the Commutation Summary.

      (3) Misconducts that occurred prior to August 1997 are not available electronically and must be summarized in the Classification Summary Update Section 6.1

Issued: 3/21/2022
Effective: 3/28/2022

11.4.1, Case Summary Procedures Manual
Section 9 – Commutation Summary

Overall Adjustment. When applicable, this information is found on the **DC-17, Conduct Record** in the **DC-14, Counselor File**, and must be attached to the Classification Summary Update as a supplemental document.

c. Educational Records

   (1) The Academic and Vocational Educational Report data must be included in Section 5.3 of the Classification Summary Update document.

   (2) Information can be obtained from the Academic and Vocational Education Report, by electronic copy of the **DC-47C, Electronic Inmate Academic/Vocational Education Report** and existing documentation of pre-incarceration information.

   (3) The School Principal is responsible for providing the electronic Academic and Vocational Education Report to the Corrections Counselor. This report is a chronological list of the classes (course title) attended and the progress made or completion. Include the names of certificates received.

d. Work Report

   (1) The Work Report is included in narrative format in the Employment History Section 5.4 of the Classification Summary Update and includes the summary of facility and community employment.

   (2) The Inmate's Employment history up to time of arrest is available from existing documentation of pre-incarceration information and self-report for documentation in this section. The inmate's pattern of stable employment or frequent job changes must be documented to reflect the inmate's work history.

   (3) The facility Work Report is available on DOCInfo under Inmate Employment, Previous Work tab; however, the inmate may have had work assignments that predate the computer application. Therefore, a complete facility Work Report can be obtained by electronic copy from the Corrections Employment and Vocational Coordinator (CEVC).

   (4) Emphasize the inmate's receipt of a license or certification for a skilled or a trusted position while in the Department.

e. Medical Report

   The Medical Report information must be entered in the Medical History Section 5.10 of the Classification Summary Update and includes the following:

   (1) medical information can be accessed from a review of existing documentation of pre-incarceration information and data in the Inmate Status System (Medical

9-6

Issued: 3/21/2022
Effective: 3/28/2022

11.4.1, Case Summary Procedures Manual
Section 9 – Commutation Summary

Status Summary, Employment Restrictions, Activity Restrictions, Assistive Devices, Functional Limitations, and Medical Housing Recommendations);

(2) the **Commutation Physical Examination Summary** (refer to Department policy **13.2.1, "Access to Health Care," Section 3**) will only be completed if requested by the Facility Manger based on the need for additional medical information or at the Facility Manager's discretion;

(3) the Corrections Health Care Administrator (CHCA) shall ensure:

(a) the completion of the **Commutation Physical Examination Summary** if requested by the Facility Manager, in accordance with Department policy **13.2.1, Section 3**; and

(b) placement of the **Notice Commutation Applicant Form** in the medical record.

(4) the physical screening will be completed at the time of each application if requested by the Facility Manager. The summary will report the date of the most recent physical exam and a description of the inmate's present health. It will list all abnormal findings and report a brief history of the dental and medical treatment the inmate received. The summary will describe any long-term physical disabilities and any treatment that may continue after release. It will *include* a list of all outside consultants required for current medical report and *will* conclude with the Physician/Certified Registered Nurse Practitioner/Physician Assistant's signature.

f. Inmate Accounting Report

(1) The Inmate Accounting Report is entered in the Financial Section 5.5 of the Classification Summary Update; information can be obtained by electronic report from the Business Office, Inmate Accounts, and existing documentation of pre-incarceration information.

(2) Focus on the inmate's spendable funds, savings, and outstanding debts (total balance owed concerning the Crime Victims Compensation Fund (CVCF), Act 143, and Act 84 at the time of the report.

(3) Summarize other factors regarding the inmate's significant assets or debts in the community. Explain if the inmate has received Public Assistance or Supplemental Security Income (SSI) and for what reason.

(4) Review the inmate's personal property, savings/checking, fines, costs, restitution, bills, loans, credit cards to assess his/her financial status regarding his/her release plans and community reintegration if commutation is granted.

11.4.1, Case Summary Procedures Manual
Section 9 – Commutation Summary

g. Chaplain's Report

   (1) The Chaplain shall briefly report the inmate's spiritual program involvement, if he/she held leadership/offices in religious organizations, and how active he/she practiced his/her faith at the facility's organized religious services.

   (2) The Chaplain's Report shall be emailed to the Counselor. The Counselor shall briefly summarize the Chaplain's Report in the Counselor Summary Section 9 of the Classification Summary Update.

h. Counselor Evaluation

   (1) The Counselor Evaluation is entered in the Counselor Summary Section 9 of the Classification Summary Update.

   (2) The Counselor will summarize the issues which are appropriate to the inmate's individual plea for executive clemency in the commutation application. Positive or negative behavioral change shall be the central theme of the Counselor Evaluation, with emphasis on clinical findings and observations with supporting documentation.

   (3) Specific areas to be addressed include time served on sentence, programming status, assessment testing analysis, level of remorse and responsibility, criminal history, potential for relapse and recidivism, public safety risk, release planning, and facility support/endorsement.

   (4) The issue of justification for Commutation processing versus availability of Court Appeals and/or Parole must be addressed regarding the category of Clemency.

i. Psychological Report

   (1) The Psychological Report is included in the Mental Health History Section 7.9 of the Classification Summary Update. This information is populated from the most recent closed Psychological Report.

   (2) The existing psychological evaluation will be utilized *if it is less than two years old*.

   (3) An updated psychological report shall only be completed for a commutation applicant if requested by the Facility Manager in accordance with Department policy **13.8.1, "Access to Mental Health Care," Section 1**.

j. The Commutation Summary will include additional sections that are not specified in these procedures but are contained in the Classification Summary Update format.

11.4.1, Case Summary Procedures Manual
Section 9 – Commutation Summary

    k. Psychiatric Examination

    When requested by the Clemency Case Specialist Supervisor, the psychiatric provider (psychiatrist or Certified Registered Nurse Practitioner, Psychiatric Services [PCRNP]) will conduct a new psychiatric examination for commutation. Psychiatric examinations will be requested for inmates listed on the Mental Health B, C, or D Roster who have been granted a public hearing by the Board of Pardons.

6. A Commutation Summary Packet is to be filed only in the **DC-15**. A copy of the summary and the original vote sheet are placed under the "facility" tab.

C. Staffing Process[3]

1. The Counselor will prepare a **DC-46, Vote Sheet** to determine whether to support the application.

    a. The **DC-46** should briefly summarize the crime(s) the inmate is requesting be commuted, contributors to his/her criminal conduct, compliance with his/her corrections plan, conduct, work performance and contributions to the inmate/prison community, his/her public risk, and reentry plans including employment and housing plans, and merits of the application. Add key factors and reasons for the recommendation.

    b. The **DC-46** shall make recommendations for special programs should the inmate be granted commutation and he/she is returned to the community.

    c. A recommendation regarding commutation of multiple indictments can specify those supported and not supported.

2. Completion of the **DC-46**

    a. Each voting staff's rationale for or against commutation must be recorded on the **DC-46**.

    b. A favorable recommendation **is not to be based on the inmate's admission of guilt**, as the issues in question are mercy and evidence of change. The recommendation is based on an evaluation of the application and commutation issues.

3. The Unit Manager chairs the staffing team that interviews the inmate to review his/her application and review the conclusions of the Commutation Summary. The staffing team should be an odd number and include a Corrections Officer. The inmate shall be

---

[3] 5-ACI-5B-03

Issued: 3/21/2022
Effective: 3/28/2022

11.4.1, Case Summary Procedures Manual
Section 9 – Commutation Summary

informed that the Facility Manager/designee makes the final recommendation after consideration by the Special Review Committee.

4. The Special Review Committee consists of the Major for Unit Management, CCPM, Deputy Superintendent for Facilities Management (DSFM) and DSCS. Each member votes independently **and must provide rationale for his/her vote**. The committee does not interview the inmate.

5. The Facility Manager/designee has the ultimate vote to recommend commutation and his/her vote overrides all subordinate staff votes. A Facility Manager/designee's vote is the facility's final recommendation. Rationale for the recommendation is mandatory.

6. Follow-Up by Facility Manager – Staff Recommendations

   a. The completed **DC-46** is routed back to the Unit Manager. Using the **Staff Recommendation (Attachment 9-D)**, the Unit Manager will summarize the following:

      (1) information on the **DC-43, Correctional Plan** by the Unit Management Team;

      (2) Special Review Committee's unanimity, majority/minority, or split opinion, with a brief rationale for each; and

      (3) Facility Manager/designee's recommendation with the rationale.

   b. The staff recommendation, with the Facility Manager's signature, will be appended to the Commutation Packet immediately under the Commutation Summary.

D. **Inmate Refusal to Participate in the Commutation Assessment**

   If an inmate refuses to participate in the Commutation Assessment, the inmate shall sign the **Refusal to Undergo Commutation Assessment Procedures (Attachment 9-E)**. *Notification should be made to the Clemency Case Specialist Supervisor and the commutation staffing should cease. The Clemency Case Specialist Supervisor will notify the Board of Pardons of the inmate's refusal and will recommend denial at the Merit Review.*

E. **Final Assembly of the Commutation Summary**

   1. The Commutation Summary and packet are assembled in accordance with the **Commutation Summary Process Checklist**.

   2. A maximum of two Commutation Summaries (representing the current and most recent previous application) are contained in a Commutation Packet.

11.4.1, Case Summary Procedures Manual
Section 9 – Commutation Summary

F. Commutation Executive Summary

1. The Facility Manager/designee shall ensure that an Executive Summary is completed for each inmate commutation application.

2. An Executive Summary consists of the factors related to the crime and the inmate's overall criminal record, his/her participation in programs, community support system, and an assessment of the public safety risk should commutation be granted. The summary shall have four brief sections and should include narrative information under each section as follows:

    a. Factors Related to the Crime and Overall Criminal Record

    This section should cover areas of concern such as substance abuse, assaultive behavior, domestic violence, deviate sexual behavior, mental health issues, and/or other factors that were related to the commission of the crime, and the inmate's prior criminal history.

    b. Program Participation

    This section should cover facility program participation that deals with the factors previously identified as being related to the crime (treatment for substance abuse, violence prevention, batterer's intervention, sex offender, mental health, etc.) and the need to complete recommended educational and vocational goals/objectives.

    c. Community Support System

    This section should contain a narrative that deals with available community resources (treatment, support by significant others, and supervision that is needed by the inmate). The treatment, support, and structure should address the needs specified in the above sections. Include reference to release plans and the inmate's reentry needs concerning reintegration back into the community with viable home and job plans.

    d. Public Safety Risk

    This section should contain a discussion of the inmate's potential for relapse and recidivism regarding community risk and safety issues. Describe what may be the likely consequences if a specific community support system breaks down. For example, if the inmate terminates treatment, experiences relationship or marriage problems, or he/she starts to abuse substances, what is the likelihood of further criminal acts, and what form are they likely to take?

3. The Executive Committee consists of the Secretary and the **Director** of the Psychology **Office**. They will review all commutation applications and reports submitted to the Board of Pardons *and will provide comments and a recommendation on each application as well*.

Issued: 3/21/2022
Effective: 3/28/2022

Resources for Healing and Help

**Mental Health &
Suicide Prevention**
➤ 988 Suicide & Crisis Lifeline
Call or Text: 988
https://988lifeline.org

➤ **NAMI
(National Alliance
on Mental Illness)**
Call: 1-800-950-NAMI(6264)
Text: 'HELPLINE' to 62640
https://nami.org

Substance Use & Addiction
➤ **SAMSHA National Helpline**
Call:1-800-662-HELP(4357)
https://www.samhsa.gov/find-help

**Domestic &
Intimate Partner Violence**
➤ National Domestic Violence Hotline
Call: 1-800-799-SAFE (7233)
Text: 'START' to 88788
https://thehotline.org

➤ **RAINN**
(Rape, Abuse & Incest National Network)
Call: 1-800-656-HOPE (4673)
https://rainn.org

**Youth &
Teen Support**
Teen Line
Text: 'TEEN' to 839863
https://www.teenline.org/

**The Trevor Project
(LGBTQ+ Youth)**
Call: 866-488-7386
Text: 'START' to 678678
https://thetrevorproject.org

Trauma & PTSD Support
National Center for PTSD
https://www.ptsd.va.gov
Sidran Institute
https://sidran.org
Give an Hour
Free Mental Health Support
https://www.giveanhour.org

Firearms Support For those in Crisis
Hold My Guns
https://www.holdmyguns.org

Pennsylvania Specific Resources
PA Support & Referral Helpline
Call: 855-284-2494
TTY: 724-631-5600

PA 211
Dial: 2-1-1
https://www.pa211.org

**DDAP (PA Dept. of Drug &
Alcohol Programs)**
https://www.ddap.pa.gov

**Pro-A (PA Pro-A Recovery
Organizations Alliance)**
https://pro-a.org

About the Author

Amy Sortino was charged under the felony murder rule at the age of 18 and later acquitted. Her lived experience with incarceration, addiction, violence, motherhood, and survival now fuels her fight for justice, dignity, and second chances.

Amy is the founder of Reentry Ready, a nonprofit preparing incarcerated individuals—especially those serving life sentences—for meaningful reentry. As a Peer Specialist, she facilitates healing-centered workshops for incarcerated individuals and works directly with lawmakers to promote fairer, more humane policies.

She serves on the board of a nonprofit focused on restorative justice for juveniles, and leads statewide advocacy efforts to end death by incarceration. Amy believes we must not only clear broken systems—but also prevent people from ever entering them.

She lives in Pennsylvania with her youngest child and, a dog and three cats (including a tortie who talks back). She believes that no one is beyond redemption—not even the system itself.

www.ingramcontent.com/pod-product-compliance
Lightning Source LLC
Chambersburg PA
CBHW020246010526
44107CB00002B/127